THE COMPLETE IDIOT'S GUIDE® TO

Understanding Iraq

Second Edition

by Joseph Tragert

ALPHA

A member of Penguin Group (USA) Inc.

To Bernadine and little Joe.

ALPHA BOOKS

Published by the Penguin Group

Penguin Group (USA) Inc., 375 Hudson Street, New York, New York 10014, U.S.A.

Penguin Group (Canada), 10 Alcorn Avenue, Toronto, Ontario, Canada M4V 3B2 (a division of Pearson Penguin Canada Inc.)

Penguin Books Ltd, 80 Strand, London WC2R 0RL, England

Penguin Ireland, 25 St Stephen's Green, Dublin 2, Ireland (a division of Penguin Books Ltd)

Penguin Group (Australia), 250 Camberwell Road, Camberwell, Victoria 3124, Australia (a division of Pearson Australia Group Pty Ltd)

Penguin Books India Pvt Ltd, 11 Community Centre, Panchsheel Park, New Delhi—110 017, India

Penguin Group (NZ), cnr Airborne and Rosedale Roads, Albany, Auckland 1310, New Zealand (a division of Pearson New Zealand Ltd)

Penguin Books (South Africa) (Pty) Ltd, 24 Sturdee Avenue, Rosebank, Johannesburg 2196, South Africa

Penguin Books Ltd, Registered Offices: 80 Strand, London WC2R 0RL, England

Copyright © 2004 by Joseph Tragert

International Standard Book Number: 1-59257-357-6
Library of Congress Catalog Card Number: 2004113223

06 05 04   8 7 6 5 4 3 2 1

Interpretation of the printing code: The rightmost number of the first series of numbers is the year of the book's printing; the rightmost number of the second series of numbers is the number of the book's printing. For example, a printing code of 04-1 shows that the first printing occurred in 2004.

Printed in the United States of America

Note: This publication contains the opinions and ideas of its author. It is intended to provide helpful and informative material on the subject matter covered. It is sold with the understanding that the author and publisher are not engaged in rendering professional services in the book. If the reader requires personal assistance or advice, a competent professional should be consulted.

The author and publisher specifically disclaim any responsibility for any liability, loss, or risk, personal or otherwise, which is incurred as a consequence, directly or indirectly, of the use and application of any of the contents of this book.

Most Alpha books are available at special quantity discounts for bulk purchases for sales promotions, premiums, fundraising, or educational use. Special books, or book excerpts, can also be created to fit specific needs.

For details, write: Special Markets, Alpha Books, 375 Hudson Street, New York, NY 10014.

Publisher: *Marie Butler-Knight*
Product Manager: *Phil Kitchel*
Senior Managing Editor: *Jennifer Chisholm*
Senior Acquisitions Editor: *Paul Dinas*
Development Editor: *Jennifer Moore*
Senior Production Editor: *Billy Fields*

Copy Editor: *Cari Luna*
Illustrator: *Chris Eliopoulos*
Cover/Book Designer: *Trina Wurst*
Indexer: *Tonya Heard*
Layout: *Angela Calvert*
Proofreading: *Mary Hunt*

Contents at a Glance

Contents

Foreword

In the wee hours of August 2, 1990, Iraqi tanks and infantry swept across the country's southeastern border into neighboring Kuwait and quickly seized Kuwait City.

Disregarding Kuwaiti sovereignty, Iraqi President Saddam Hussein's argued that Kuwait was an historical province of the Iraqi state, and that the government in Baghdad was simply exerting its authority over what was by tradition Iraqi territory.

Since then, no nation on Earth has commanded the attention of the American public more so than Iraq. In the years following, American military forces have fought two successful, one-sided offensive campaigns in that country: The first extricated Iraq from Kuwait and essentially destroyed Hussein's *offensive* military capability. The second overthrew Hussein, destroyed his armed forces, and for the most part liberated the Iraqi people.

As an unstable, strategically vital Middle Eastern country (bordered by Turkey, Iran, Saudi Arabia, Jordan, Syria, Kuwait, and a tiny strip of Persian Gulf coastline) sitting atop the second-largest petroleum reserves on the planet, Iraq continues to make headlines—or at least the top-of-the-fold—of every major daily newspaper in the English speaking world.

Yet few Americans have an adequate understanding of Iraq; its colorful history, culture, multi-ethnic and religious diversity, its wars and uprisings, and its enormous impact on global markets, strategic military planning, and the ideological conflict between Islam and the West. That's what makes *The Complete Idiot's Guide to Understanding Iraq, Second Edition*, an indispensable guide for anyone interested in grasping the particulars of this storied nation.

Author Joseph Tragert carries the reader on a fascinating journey through thousands of years of Iraqi history.

The first edition of *The Complete Idiot's Guide to Understanding Iraq* has been referred to as "essential." The new, updated second edition will prove to be an equally important, equally thought-provoking guidebook to Iraq. Within these pages, Tragert covers everything from ancient Mesopotamia, to the current war-ravaged country where the United States and her allies are involved in establishing a hopeful democracy while fighting street battles for factional control of cities, and all things in between.

Whether a high school or college student, a member of the armed forces, a Ph.D. historian searching for elusive facts and figures, a print or broadcast reporter, or anyone else interested in broadening their knowledge of the Middle East, Tragert's

The Complete Idiot's Guide to Understanding Iraq, Second Edition, will no doubt become the reference of choice.

—**W. Thomas Smith Jr.,** author of the *Alpha Bravo Delta Guide to the Korean Conflict* and other books, has written for a variety of national and international publications including *USA Today, George, U.S. News & World Report*, and *BusinessWeek*. He is a frequent contributor to National Review Online.

Introduction

Over the past few years, Iraq has been a persistent theme in U.S. foreign policy. U.S. policies, alliances, and security strategies have collided over this country and its erstwhile dictator, Saddam Hussein. One would think that once Saddam was gone, Iraq would fade into the background of the American view. However, Saddam *is* gone, and Iraq is more in the foreground than ever. Unfortunately, most of us are confronted with too much information on this subject, a lot of which is biased by personal philosophies and agendas. This book is intended to remedy that situation. It offers a painless introduction to a country that has been a recurrent "hot spot" in world history for many centuries. Iraq retains that status today, of course, but its story would remain darkly fascinating even if this were not the case.

What You'll Learn in This Book

This book is divided into six parts that will help you learn more about the modern nation of Iraq and its ancient precursor states. Iraqis are deeply conscious of their long past, just as most Westerners are unaware of it.

Part 1, "The Basics," gives you the fundamentals about modern Iraq. You'll find out why it has become such an important player in world affairs, get a sense of Iraq's ancient roots, and get a snapshot of the modern nation.

Part 2, "From Babylon to Baghdad," lets you in on Iraq's early history … which happens to coincide with that of human civilization. You'll also find out about the remarkable series of empires that have risen and fallen in this region and all the stuff that happened before Saddam Hussein came to power.

Part 3, "Saddam Hussein," offers an answer to the questions, "What made Saddam Hussein's reign possible?" The answer involves at least a century of global conflict, superpower diplomacy, ancient rivalry, and modern geopolitics. (There are some disagreements about oil along the way, too.)

Part 4, "The Gulf War, Part 1," tells you all about the origins, the key events, and the aftermath of Iraq's invasion of Kuwait, and the ensuing 1990–1991 conflict with the U.S.-led Coalition. Here you'll find out how and why the Coalition formed, how the war unfolded, and how Saddam lost the war … but won the peace.

Part 5, "The Gulf War, Part 2," explains how in the aftermath of the first Gulf War, the seeds of the second war were planted. The ground was already fertile for conflict, and the September 11, 2001, terror attacks and the Bush administration's reaction provided the water needed to grow a new conflict.

Part 6, "Aftermath and Prelude," looks at post-Saddam Iraq and answers the questions of what the current violence is all about, and what might be next for this troubled land.

At the end of the book, you'll find a number of helpful appendixes.

Extras

As you make your way through the book, you'll notice little nuggets of information distributed throughout the text. They are meant to help you gain an immediate understanding of some aspect of the topic under discussion. Here's how you can recognize them:

> **Oil Spill Ahead**
> These boxes will alert you to common misconceptions and potential problem areas.

> **Iraq Fact**
> These boxes answer important questions about Iraq.

> **Increase Your Iraq IQ**
> Quotes, background details, or supporting information that can accelerate and streamline the learning process. Breeze in and out of these boxes—we think you'll be fascinated by what you find.

> **Desert Diction**
> Here you'll find concise summaries of key terms that may not be familiar to you.

Acknowledgments

Grateful thanks go out to my wife, Bernadine Tragert; my father, Henry Tragert (builder of Baghdad power plants); my development editor, Jennifer Moore; my agent, Gene Brissie; and my senior acquisitions editor, Paul Dinas.

Special Thanks to the Technical Reviewer

The Complete Idiot's Guide to Iraq, Second Edition, was reviewed by an expert who double-checked the accuracy of what you'll learn here, to help us ensure that this book gives you everything you need to know about Iraq. Special thanks are extended to W. Thomas Smith, Jr.

Trademarks

All terms mentioned in this book that are known to be or are suspected of being trademarks or service marks have been appropriately capitalized. Alpha Books and Penguin Group (USA) Inc. cannot attest to the accuracy of this information. Use of a term in this book should not be regarded as affecting the validity of any trademark or service mark.

Part 1

The Basics

Sure, you know that Iraq is located smack-dab in the middle of the Middle East and that the United States has hundreds of thousands of troops there, but do you know how many people call Iraq home, how much oil they have, and how long Iraq has been, well, Iraq?

"Just the facts, Ma'am," could be the motto for the chapters in this part of the book—you'll find out everything you need to make sense of this most complicated of countries.

Why Iraq Matters

In This Chapter

- ◆ The United States invades, wins and loses, and wonders
- ◆ Saddam Hussein's bitter legacy
- ◆ The Bush doctrine's big test
- ◆ Can it work?

It is the summer of 2004. Victorious U.S. troops pass out candy and rebuild elementary schools in cities across Iraq. That same summer, U.S. troops come under fire and flatten buildings in cities across Iraq. Electric power is restored by civilian contractors, then those contractors are kidnapped and killed on their way back from the power plant. And, in a disturbing reminder of the Iranian Revolution in 1979, glowering clerics call for death to Americans, and their followers appear willing to die carrying out those calls. How did it come to this?

As important ... *why* did it come to this? And more important, *when* will it end?

For the past 15 years, Iraq and its former dictator, Saddam Hussein, have been a focal point for three U.S. presidential administrations. One president stood up to Saddam but let him stay in power. One tried to ignore

Saddam and downplayed his threat. And one went after Saddam and, in removing him from power, opened a whole new can of worms.

The Iraqi Threat

Since 1980, Iraq has started two wars (concluding the first—against Iran—in a bloody standoff, and being soundly trounced in the other—the first Gulf War). It also has been invaded, and its tyrant toppled, in yet a third war—a war started by the United States and its allies.

Why did the United States invade Iraq?

The threat from Saddam Hussein centered initially around oil. When Iraq invaded Kuwait in the months preceding the first Gulf War, it threatened to control a vast amount of the world's oil, which in turn threatened the economic viability of the U.S. economy.

After Iraq was expelled from Kuwait, weapons of mass destruction were found, and many were destroyed. However, the job didn't appear completed, but the inspection program had broken down. Once George W. Bush took office in 2000, his administration became increasing preoccupied with Iraq and Saddam Hussein. Government officials were convinced that Hussein still possessed weapons of mass destruction, and they were determined to remove that threat to U.S. vital interests.

The rest of the world, with the exception of Great Britain, tended not to agree with the U.S. view, and rather than support the U.S. position, they criticized the United States for maintaining crippling sanctions on the Hussein regime, and therefore, the Iraqi people.

These sanctions, ordered by the UN in the wake of the first Gulf War, denied the Saddam Hussein regime access to restricted military items, and regulated the flow of revenues used to purchase food and medicine. Over time, only the United States and the United Kingdom were willing to enforce the sanctions, which were not as effective as had been hoped, and came at a high cost of Iraqi lives.

This brings us to one of the big questions we will examine in this book: *Why did the United States invade Iraq, when much of the rest of the world basically did not agree with the invasion?*

That act of invasion and occupation will affect U.S. foreign and domestic policy for years to come.

Who Was Saddam?

Today, it's impossible to understand the U.S. focus on Iraq without understanding Saddam Hussein and the society he created. And that, unfortunately, is a very tricky business. Here's a brief timeline that will help put his rule in context:

Saddam Hussein was born in Auja, near the city of Tikrit in the vicinity of Baghdad, in 1937, to a middle-class Iraqi family. He joined the Ba'th (Arab Socialist Resurrection) Party in 1956. He participated in the two Ba'thist coups of July 17 and July 30, 1968. After the second coup (which resulted in the Ba'thists taking power in Iraq), Saddam was responsible for internal security. In that role, he became very well-known inside Iraq.

Hussein took power on July 16, 1979, when he forced out Ahmed Hassan al-Bakr, who was a relative and mentor, and purged the former leader's inner circle.

Shortly after Saddam formally assumed control of state and party structures, he claimed that an attempted coup took place; several members of the Ba'th leadership were executed for their alleged role in the plot. Whether there actually was a plot or not is still not clear, but the allegations that there was one provided Saddam with a good excuse for clearing out other factions—and bringing in his own supporters.

Saddam then tightened his grip on power in Iraq by murdering potential rivals (including his own sons-in-law), and by ordering lethal attacks on possible insurgent groups within Iraq, such as the Shiites and the Kurds. Saddam also tried to assume the mantle of leader of the Arab world and the elusive *Pan-Arab movement*. The result: wars, invasions, and sanctions.

Desert Diction

The **Pan-Arab movement** advocates Arab unity. Pan-Arabism states that all Arabs should be unified into one state (like the early days of Islam), and that all Arabs have a duty to support the freedom of Arab peoples (notably, Palestinians).

The modern Pan-Arab movement was promoted by Gamel Abdel Nasser, President of Egypt in the 1950s and 1960s, but Iraq and Egypt vied for control of the movement during that time. The movement achieved its zenith when Egypt, Syria, and Yemen formed the United Arab Republic, and Iraq and Jordan formed a rival Arab Union. Both political experiments failed after just a few years, and no formal political union has been achieved since. The Arab League of 21 Arab-majority states and Palestine continues the Pan-Arab concept, though in watered-down form, and attempts at unification were all but abandoned.

Iraq Yesterday, Iraq Today

The story of Iraq under Saddam became one of violence, chaos, and uncertainty. Today, Iraq matters because Saddam's actions caused concern, fear, and outrage among his neighbors and became an obsession of the George W. Bush White House.

Saddam and the West: A Timeline

There's a lot to say about what happened in Iraq before 1981 (and I'll say them later on in the book). For the purposes of this chapter, though, I want you to have an overview of recent events, so you can see how these events have shaped the current bloody relationship between Iraq and the United States.

Prelude: The Iran-Iraq War

In the early 1980s, Iraq was considered an ally of the United States against Iran. The United States had just gotten out from under the Iranian hostage crisis and had no diplomatic relations with Iran. Iraq had recently begun a war against Iran (the Iran-Iraq War from 1980 to 1988), in an apparent dispute over territory along the *Shatt-al-Arab* waterway.

Desert Diction

The **Shatt-al-Arab** is a name for the waterway at the confluence of the Tigris and Euphrates Rivers, where they join to flow into the Persian Gulf. The region is marshy, with several islands dotting the mouth of the waterway.

The Shatt-al-Arab is the main shipping channel for food and supplies from the Gulf to the city of Basra. Until the start of the war, the two countries bordered a portion of the main shipping channel. Controlling the islands on *both* sides of the channel would provide more security in shipping to the country in charge of those islands.

The islands originally belonged to Iraq, but they were seized by Iran in 1971. At this time, Iraq protested but did nothing. Finally, in 1981, Saddam used the Iranian occupation of the islands as a pretext for picking a fight with Iran.

The United States provided tentative support for Iraq in this dispute, on the theory that Iraq was the lesser of the two evils, and in the hope that Iraq could topple the Ayatollah.

The war, however, didn't go well for Iraq. The Iranians put up a strong fight, and the war settled into a grinding battle of attrition, where neither side was gaining much of an advantage. The battles were costly, and eventually both sides were ready to quit. Finally, after years of indescribably bloody conflict, the fighting ended in a standoff in 1988, with no change in the borders or shared control of the Shatt-al-Arab. Both sides rested and reloaded.

1987 to 1990: Iraq Turns Its Attention to Kuwait

Saddam soon began planning a new conflict with Iraq's tiny, oil-rich neighbor Kuwait. From Saddam's perspective, a new and provocative campaign had certain advantages:

- Invasion offered the potential to enrich Iraq and improve its strategic position in the Middle East.

- Military victories would help legitimize Saddam's authority within Iraq, which was diminished after the Iranian stalemate.

- New military conflicts would provide an excuse for shortages of consumer goods within Iraq.

- New military conflicts would provide cover for counter-insurgency work inside Iraq.

Thus, during this period, Iraq became increasingly belligerent against its (militarily weak) neighbor, Kuwait, and even began to behave in a way that alienated other members of OPEC.

Desert Diction

OPEC stands for the Organization of Petroleum Exporting Countries. The 11 member countries are Algeria, Libya, Nigeria, Indonesia, Iran, Iraq, Kuwait, Qatar, Saudi Arabia, the United Arab Emirates, and Venezuela. OPEC countries exert a measure of control over world oil prices by producing more or less oil.

1990: Iraq Invades Kuwait

The other shoe finally dropped on August 2, 1990, when Iraq invaded Kuwait. The United Nations (UN) Security Council Resolution 660 demanded complete withdrawal, but Saddam refused to leave. The United States led a diplomatic initiative at the United Nations to get international support for a coalition to get Iraq out of Kuwait. This initiative resulted in UN Security Council Resolution 661, passed on August 6, 1990, which imposed economic sanctions on Iraq.

Saddam responded by formally annexing Kuwait on August 8.

1991: Operation Desert Storm

By January of the next year, President George H.W. Bush's administration had completed the task of assembling a coalition of Western and Arab states to get Saddam out of Kuwait. Military action started when the coalition forces began bombing Iraq on January 16, 1991. The ground attack began on February 24 and ended three days later, with a total Iraqi military collapse and Kuwait liberated.

However, UN forces did not invade Baghdad, and didn't remove Saddam from power. The only goal of the coalition had been the liberation of Kuwait. To many policy makers' disapproval, the removal of Saddam was not on the agenda.

1991: Cease-Fire and Sanctions

The United Nations and Iraq negotiated a cease-fire that took effect on March 3, 1991. The Bush administration fully expected Saddam's government to collapse due to the spectacular failure of his military, but he managed to hang on. In fact, by April of that same year, Iraqi forces were up to their old tricks, brutally suppressing Shiite insurgents in southern Iraq and Kurdish rebels in the North. In response, the United Nations established no-fly zones in northern and southern Iraq to provide havens for the Kurds in the north, and the Shiites in the south. At the time of the cease-fire, the United Nations placed stiff sanctions on Iraq, forbidding them to export oil without UN approval. Oil is the only major export product of Iraq, and thus selling it is the only way the country could make money and buy arms. The sanctions were seen as a good way to control how much money Iraq could bring in. The cease-fire also included measures for UN weapons inspectors to monitor Iraqi facilities that may make biological, chemical, or nuclear weapons.

According to the agreements of the cease-fire, UN weapons inspectors were supposed to be able to see any facility, anywhere in Iraq, that they suspected could be used for weapons production. However, as history has taught us again and again, agreements seem to be made to be broken.

1995 to 2000: Conflicts over Sanctions and Inspections

Enforcing the sanctions turned into a public relations and logistical nightmare for the United States and its allies. First, it has been reported that hundreds of thousands, and possibly as many as 1 million, Iraqi citizens (mostly children) died due to UN-imposed and U.S.-enforced sanctions. Whatever the number, and whatever the direct cause, the Iraqi people didn't get needed medicine and died in large numbers as a result.

The sanctions became difficult for U.S. allies in Europe and the Gulf to support. Iraq counted on increasing international discomfort with the effects of the sanctions on Iraqi civilians to bring about an easing of the restrictions. On April 14, 1996, UN Security Council Resolution 986 allowed for the partial resumption of Iraq's oil exports to buy food and medicine. Iraq argued over the conditions of the program and didn't accept the terms until May 1996. The first shipments started in December 1996. The Oil for Food Program was plagued by corruption, both by Saddam and by UN officials responsible for overseeing the payments.

Inspections

The weapons inspection program also became a notable foreign-policy failure for the United States and its allies.

The initial goal of the program was to take away Iraq's ability to make weapons of mass destruction, but no one can prove the inspections worked (or didn't). The George W. Bush administration believed there were weapons of mass destruction in Iraq. Iraq has taken advantage of loopholes in the inspections agreement that stipulated that the weapons inspectors could not inspect any "Presidential Palaces." Saddam simply designated hundreds of facilities as "Presidential Palaces," and refused to allow the inspectors in to see them.

The only real enforcement mechanism available to the United Nations when Saddam didn't comply was more bombing. Over time, this drastic military response became increasingly difficult for the Arab states, and many of the Western allies, to support. Bombing seemed an unreasonable response to Iraqi stubbornness. Also, it was difficult to determine if the bombings had done the job.

Iraq Fact

The difficulty of maintaining the international coalition against Iraq was underscored by international distaste for the continued bombing campaigns, and even some support for Saddam as the "victim" of U.S. aggression.

On October 31, 1998, Iraq ended all forms of cooperation with the UN Special Commission to Oversee the Destruction of Iraq's Weapons of Mass Destruction (UNSCOM) and threw out the weapons inspectors. The United Nations did virtually nothing in response.

The United Nations replaced UNSCOM with the United Nations Monitoring, Verification and Inspection Commission (UNMOVIC). Saddam rejected this commission as well. The Bush administration was all the more ready to knock Saddam off his perch.

2002 and Beyond: The United States Goes It Alone

During the Cold War, the big question was what to do about the Soviets, but in the post–Cold War era, it is what to do about *rogue states*. The George W. Bush administration has singled out three countries in particular as the so-called "Axis of Evil": Iran, Iraq, and North Korea. The United States and the West in general have had a very tough time dealing with these rogue countries. In fact, the Bush administration has alienated its European allies with the "Axis" analogy, and by lumping the three nations together.

> **Desert Diction**
>
> **Rogue states** are states that don't work with the rest of the world and are probable exporters of terrorism. Isolation from the rest of the community of nations, imposed from outside or self-created, is a hallmark of a rogue state. Rogue states typically also threaten their neighbors with destruction.

The need for diplomacy never seemed greater than in years just prior to the U.S.-led invasion of Iraq. However, diplomacy at that time took a new track in the post–September 11 era. Bush made it clear that the United States would act unilaterally and peremptorily if its security was threatened. Rather then respond to an attack, the U.S. would attack first. This logic, and the claim of weapons of mass destruction in Iraq, was the justification used by the George W. Bush administration to invade Iraq.

The second Bush administration finally invaded Iraq in 2003. The invasion ended quickly, and Saddam's regime was toppled like a house of cards. A few months later, Saddam, as the Ace of Spades in a widely distributed most-wanted-Iraqis card deck, was pulled out of a hole in the ground, and one would think the United States would leave Iraq triumphant, with a democracy blooming in its wake. Instead, the United States finds itself with relatively few allies, ensnarled in a morass of violence, with no end in sight, and the only progress appears to be the growing body count on both sides, punctuated with the shocking realization that the U.S. mission in Iraq is losing any moral authority it may have once claimed.

Will It Work?

Today, Iraq is a focal point of an ongoing and escalating global controversy. This controversy has three main elements:

- **The Ability of Iraq to Govern Itself or to Even Exist in a Democratic State.** Being a member of the new Iraqi government is about the same as putting a big bull's-eye on one's chest. Too many leaders in the post-Saddam Iraq have been assassinated, and the threat to their lives persists. The underlying question is *who is in charge?* Is it the Sunni minority? The Shiite majority?

What about the tribal leaders who control their particular pieces of turf? Will the Kurds play ball? Will neighbors get involved, to forward their own interests. With Saddam gone, the lid is off the box, and the frustrations of 25 years of Saddam's domination are being played out.

- **The Wide Gulf Between U.S. and Arab Interests, in Boardrooms and on the Street.** Despite the ongoing "hearts and minds" campaign to win popular support from Iraqis, and the efforts to restore living standards to the average Iraqi that didn't exist even before the Iran-Iraq War, Iraqis dance when Westerners are blown up in car bombs, and they drag dismembered bodies through the streets. Meanwhile, the terrible truth of U.S. torture of Iraqi detainees enrages the Arabs and haunts the Americans. The unilateral U.S. invasion isolated the United States from its traditional Western allies, and its more tentative Arab allies. As the occupation wears on, the United States is forced to ask for help from the UN, and in so doing, finds itself in the perverse position of losing control despite having thousands of troops on the ground.

- **The Undeniable Importance of Iraqi Oil.** Iraq sits on one of the largest pools of oil in the world. Its potential production capacity, particularly if controlled by U.S. interests, could seriously diminish the pricing power of OPEC and help ensure the continued predictable flow of oil to the West. The unrest in Iraq is spilling over into neighboring oil states, and rather than a more stable situation, the picture is even more clouded.

The Big Question

One big question looms for U.S. policy-makers: "When do we get out of Iraq?"

The answer to *when* to get out will come only after the U.S. administration determines *how* to get out. As we will see in the rest of this book, that is a very difficult question indeed.

The Least You Need to Know

- Iraq is vital to U.S. interests due to its strategic location in the oil-rich Persian Gulf region.

- Iraq is an ongoing focal point for U.S. policy-makers, and an ongoing PR headache for the U.S. administration as the occupation drags on.

- Rather than solving the Iraq problem, the U.S.-led invasion and occupation has created an even greater problem for U.S. policy makers.

- The future of Iraq remains uncertain.

Just the FAQs: Common Questions About Iraq

In This Chapter

- Where is Iraq?
- Is oil important to the Iraqi economy?
- The Kurds
- Shiites vs. Sunnis
- Common misperceptions

Now that you know why Iraq matters so much to stability in the Middle East and, consequently, the world more generally, you probably have a lot of other questions about this troubled state. In this chapter, we'll tackle some frequently asked questions about Iraq's geography, religion, its leadership, and its role in the world economy.

Let's start with a very basic question.

Where Is Iraq?

Iraq is smack dab in the middle of the Middle East, a perpetual "hot spot" in world affairs. The country sits astride the Tigris and Euphrates Rivers, in the ancient region of Mesopotamia. Iraq borders Kuwait, Saudi Arabia, Iran, Turkey, Jordan, and Syria, and has a narrow outlet to the Persian Gulf. Most of the world's oil (including more than 40 percent of U.S. daily consumption) comes from this region. The United States and the West need this oil to keep flowing in a predictable and safe manner.

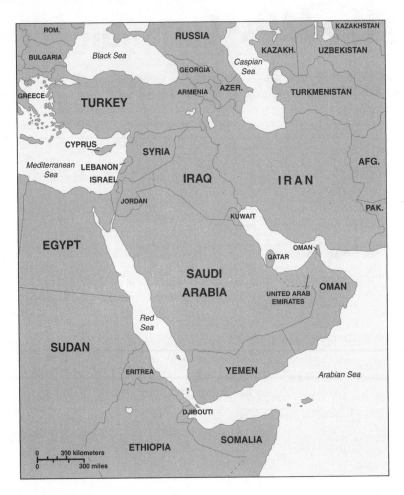

The Middle East.

Iraq.

Oil Spill Ahead

The Middle East is fraught with instability that seems to constantly threaten to blossom into full-fledged war. Continued Iraqi internal instability could result in full-fledged civil war that would draw in neighboring countries, or foreign fighters, who would use the situation to further their own goals. A constant state of turmoil would also require a large contingent of U.S. troops stationed either in Iraq or in nearby countries.

Is Oil Important to the Iraqi Economy?

Absolutely. Oil basically *is* the Iraqi economy. Even the non-oil sectors of the economy are supported by subsidies funded by oil dollars. Iraq sits on top of one of the largest pools of oil in the world. It has about 115 billion barrels of *proven reserves* of oil, which is about 10 percent of the world's total known supply. Iraq is third only behind Saudi Arabia and Iran in the world in this category. (In comparison, the United States has about 2 percent of the world's proven reserves of oil). There are roughly 1 trillion barrels of proven reserves worldwide.

Iraq's economic recovery and political stability rest on the rejuvenation of the oil sector. The Iraqi economy has suffered over the past 20 years, due to wars that heavily damaged oil production, shipment, and refining infrastructure. In addition, UN sanctions limited imports of critically needed goods and materials required for oil production (as well as for human consumption). More recently, internal acts of sabotage have inflicted more damage on the oil infrastructure and have discouraged foreign expertise and investment across the economy.

In the 1990s, Iraq exported about 2 million *barrels per day*, under the United Nations control, in a program set up after the first Gulf War. Almost all of this oil found its way to the United States. In fact, just prior to the second Gulf War, Iraqi oil accounted for 5 percent of U.S. oil imports. This number fell off dramatically in the aftermath of Operation Iraqi Freedom, as internal attacks on Iraqi and Western oil workers has slowed the work in country as well as potential investment in future oil projects. Still, given the huge amounts of reserves, and the relatively large production capacity of 735 million barrels per year (once the infrastructure is repaired), oil will no doubt continue to play a central role in Iraqi life. What's more, that same oil will force the United States to maintain a strong physical and political presence in the region.

Desert Diction

Oil that has been discovered but not yet pumped to the surface is called **proven reserves**. Since they cannot actually see the oil in the ground, geologists use a variety of techniques, including seismology and flow pressure through a well head to estimate the size of the reservoirs that hold these reserves.

Barrels per day is the standard international measure for oil. A "barrel" equals 55 gallons of oil. Barrels per day is a measure of volume of oil that is produced, or consumed in a single day.

Who Are the Kurds?

The Kurdish people occupy a region known as Kurdistan. Kurdistan is divided between Turkey, Iraq, Iran, Syria, and Armenia. The Kurds are a minority in each of those countries and have controls placed upon them that are not placed on the majority populations in those countries. The Kurdish people aren't Arab; rather, they are of Indo-European descent. Most Kurds are Sunni Muslims.

The name of the Kurds is attributed to a name for Babylonian palace guards in 600 B.C.E., the "Kardakas." These guards came from the ethnic group that later become known as the Kurds. The high point for the Kurd people came around 1150 C.E., and paralleled the rise of King Saladin. Saladin was himself a Kurd, and gained fame in the West during the Third Crusade.

Saladin's armies defeated England's King Richard the Lion-Hearted and reinstated Muslim control over Jerusalem. Saladin was credited with showing extraordinary mercy toward the defeated Crusaders in Jerusalem. Rather then slaughter them (as earlier Crusaders had done to the Muslim inhabitants of Jerusalem when they took power), Saladin spared their lives. Saladin's Ayyubid Empire also defeated the Shiite (Fatimid) rule in Egypt and Syria in 1171. The Ayyubids continued to rule these regions until 1250, when they gave way to the Mamluks. As the Ayyubid Empire receded, the relative power of the Kurds receded with it. Over the next centuries, the Kurds were not an integral part of the ruling groups that controlled the region where Kurdistan is located. As a result, the Kurds did not gain political independence.

Kurdish lands.

By the end of World War II, Kurdistan (the region where the Kurds live) was divided among Turkey, Iraq, Syria, and Iran, and no provisions were made to accommodate Kurd autonomy. The Kurds have rebelled against these governments to varying degrees of violence ever since.

The Iraqi regime under Saddam Hussein consistently suppressed the Kurds and waged conventional and even chemical war against them. The Kurds have been a relatively friendly partner to the United States since the end of Saddam's regime, and they are included in the new Iraqi government structure. It is doubtful they will ever be given autonomy, due to the fact Turkey (a NATO member) and Iran would not tolerate an independent Kurd state on their borders, for fear that the Kurds in their own countries would want to break away and join them.

The best the Kurds can hope for is more rights and autonomy under the new Iraqi government. The Kurds enjoyed greater de facto autonomy under the protection of the United Nations and the no-fly zone over their territory in latter half of the 1990s. In a way, the Kurds could find themselves in a less secure position under the new Iraqi government, since they probably won't have U.S. fighters or troops around to protect them. The theory, of course, is that in the new, post-Saddam, Iraq, the Kurds will have nothing to fear from their own government. Whether this theory will hold true for long remains to be seen. If history is any indicator, the Kurds are still in a very delicate position.

Who Are the Shiites and the Sunni?

The two dominant Islamic groups in Iraq are the Shiite Muslims and the Sunni Muslims. About 90 percent of all Muslims in the world today are Sunni, whereas fewer than 10 percent of all Muslims in the world are Shiites. However, the Sunnis are the minority within Iraq (about 32 percent), where Shiites make up over 60 percent of the population.

The Shiite-Sunni split is the result of early political controversies over who was going to be *caliph*, or spiritual leader, in Islam.

The split occurred over the appointment of a nondescendant of Mohammad as caliph in the ninth and tenth centuries. Up to that point, the caliphs had been linearly related to Mohammad. For a variety of political and social reasons, the powers that were selected a nondescendant to assume the role of caliph, but a minority of Muslims objected. This minority eventually became known as the Shiites, and they insisted that the Prophet's authority as imam (spiritual and political leader) of the community was transmitted in his lineage through Ali, Mohammad's cousin and son-in-law, and thus to Ali's descendants. According to the Shia view, only Ali's descendants could lead the faithful.

Iraq Fact

The Shiites are a majority within Iraq (about 60 percent) and are the vast majority in Iran. Iraq and Iran are the only two Muslim countries in which the Shiites constitute the majority of the population.

Those Muslims who became the Sunnis in the ninth and tenth centuries held that preservation of the unity of the Muslim community and avoidance of difference, even at the expense of acquiescing to the less-than-morally-pure rule of a given caliph, was of primary importance. They tolerated a wider range of difference of opinion. In the Sunni view, the Ulama, men of religion, became the authorities on proper practice and considered the tradition of the caliph being descended from Mohammad to be less important.

There remain two major branches of Shiism: the Twelvers in Iran, Iraq, and elsewhere, who await the return of the twelfth imam who occulted (that is, disappeared from human view in the "great occultation") around 939 C.E.; and the Ismailis, who have a living imam (the Agha Khan). The Twelvers believe that the twelfth imam will reappear as the Messiah when Allah commands.

Desert Diction

The **caliph** was the spiritual leader in Islam who claimed succession and authority from Mohammed. Over time, the power of the caliphs was diminished, and they were relegated to a purely spiritual role by the end of eleventh century. The word "caliph" comes from the Arabic word khalafa, meaning "he succeeded", in the sense of succeeding the Prophet.

Over the centuries, several groups have splintered off the main Sunni body of Islam, but most have not survived the death of their first leader. The Shiite sect, or Shia, is the only major Islamic sect that has persisted in the face of overwhelming Sunni predominance. This persistence and minority position is also a major element in the Shiite view of itself and the world.

Increase Your Iraq IQ

Despite their minority status in Iraq, the Sunnis have always held the real power. Under the Ottomans, British, and then the Ba'th Party, Sunnis ran the powerful government ministries, the army, and the state-controlled economy. Sunnis were empowered to discourage the emergence of a Shiite-dominated state, which would be anathema to the Sunni majority in most of the countries surrounding Iraq. A Shiite dominated Iraq would be unusual in the Arab world. The only other Shiite dominated state is Iran.

The Saddam Hussein regime systematically waged a counter-insurgency campaign against any resistance groups in the Shiite-dominated southern part of Iraq. This program ranged from military and possibly chemical weapons attacks on Shiite rebels, to more long-term methods of disrupting the Shiite livelihood and social fabric. For example, the Hussein regime launched a canal building program in the Shatt-al-Arab region that has drawn off much of the back water that formed the marshes in southern Iraq. These marshes have nurtured a significant portion of the Shiites, known as the "Marsh Arabs," in Iraq and their way of life. This canal project disrupted a traditional Shiite power base. As the marshes have drained, the Shiites have been forced to leave the area due to the increased salt content of the water, which makes it useless for agriculture and drinking. The program has stopped with the fall of Saddam Hussein, but ecological and social recovery is a long way off.

As we will see later in this book, the Shiites are finding their voice and struggling to assert their place in the new Iraqi social and political order. This process has been marked by factional battles, and attacks on U.S. and non-Shiite Iraqis.

What Else Do I Need to Know?

It's easy to assume that the Iraqi people are all carbon copies of their leaders, particularly since most people in the West know very little about the country and its culture, and most of the time the media only focused on Saddam's supporters, who stubbornly resist the establishment of a post-Saddam state, and the various moderate and radical clerics and their followers. But don't make the mistake of thinking all Iraqis think alike! In the following sections, I present some common misconceptions.

Saddam Followers Don't Represent All the Iraqi People

Saddam Hussein was the leader of the Ba'th Socialist Revolutionary Party, but most Iraqis were not party members. Saddam was not freely elected, and in fact, oversaw a brutal dictatorship within Iraq.

The Iraqi people never had a democratic state, and they certainly didn't pick Saddam as their leader. He was picked for them by the Ba'th Party leadership. That party came to power against a monarchy that was picked for them by the British, and the British supplanted the Ottomans, who invaded like countless others before. All that history will be reviewed in the scope of this book, but the key point here is that Saddam Hussein was not a popularly elected leader, governing by the will of the Iraqi people. His followers resist the new government because they have nothing to gain if a stable, non-Ba'th government perseveres in Iraq. However, most Iraqis did not enjoy privileges under Saddam, and so they are not aligned with this group.

The Shiites Supporting Certain Clerics Do Not Represent All Iraqi Shiites

The news is full of militias that support specific "radical" or "moderate" clerics fighting each other, or U.S. troops, in and around Shiite holy cities and in Shiite neighborhoods in Baghdad. These militias do not, by any means, represent every Shiite in Iraq. These fighters are just the ones the TV cameras show. Most Shiites are not taking up arms to fight for a specific cleric or to shoot at occupying troops.

Arab Islam Doesn't Represent All Islam

Islam is a widespread religion, just like Judaism or Christianity or Buddhism. It is practiced by more than 1 billion people across the world. Iraqi Islam does not represent all of Islam, any more than the Arabs represent all of Islam. There are vast numbers of non-Arab Muslims, in places like western China, Central Asia, Indonesia, Iran, and Turkey. These people are not Arab, yet they are Muslim.

Oil Spill Ahead

Any statements about the Iraqis should not be extended to include all Arabs or Muslims.

Iraqi Arabs Don't Represent All Arabs

The Arab world is vast, complex, and culturally rich. About 250 million Arabs live in an area stretching from Northern Africa, across Egypt into the Persian Gulf region. The history of the Arab world, and its relationship to the West—from the Crusades to its relationship with Israel—goes far beyond the story of Iraq.

Increase Your Iraq IQ

Arabs are people living in North Africa and the Middle East, from western Morocco to Oman, and from Turkey in the north to Yemen and Sudan in the south. Two hundred-fifty million Arabs live in this area, about four million live in Europe, and two million in the Americas. The Arabic heartland is a region called "Hijaz" (now western Saudi Arabia).

Ethnically, Arabs are mostly dark haired with brown eyes, and medium light skin. But some Arabs are black, and others are blond. These differences are regional, and a result of the intermixing and absorption of populations. The number of ethnically pure Arabs is down to a single digit percentage. More than 95 percent of all Arabs are Muslims, while fewer than 5 percent are Christians. An estimated 55 percent live in urban areas and 45 percent live in rural areas. Today, less than 1 percent live as nomads, and of these many are nomads only in the dry season.

Not all Iraqis are Arab or Kurd. Iraq includes a number of other minorities, including Turkmans, Nestorian Christians, and Persian-speaking groups, none of whom are Arabs.

Terrorists Come from Many Cultures

The escalating conflict between terrorist movements and the civilized nations is taking a new shape. This book will examine Iraq's role as an arena for terrorist groups to attack U.S. troops and the new Iraqi government. However, this is not to say that all Iraqis, Muslims, or Arabs are terrorists … far from it. This book will examine terrorism that is being inflicted in Iraq, by terrorists, who happen to be Arab and Muslim. Before assuming that all terrorists are Arab Muslim fanatics, one should consider that some of the most persistent terrorists are Irish and Catholic, and work their trade in Belfast, not Baghdad.

The Least You Need to Know

- Iraq is located in the heart of the Middle East and is bordered by six countries.

- Oil is a major factor in Iraq's economy, and a main reason for U.S. interest in the region.

- The Sunni-Shiite conflict will continue to influence Iraqi social and political life for years to come.

- Not all Iraqis are alike, and they differ culturally, ethnically, and religiously from many of their neighbors.

Chapter 3

By the Numbers: Iraq Today

In This Chapter

- ◆ Iraq's size and population
- ◆ How Iraq is governed
- ◆ About the Iraqi people
- ◆ What Iraq produces

Remember those old social studies textbooks that were chock-full of information like the population of Bangladesh, the size of Mexico, and the climate of Australia—all of which you had to memorize for a test? Without proper context, such statistics are quite meaningless. However, now that you know why Iraq is important to world affairs, where it is located, and a little bit about its people and culture, Iraq by the numbers should help to round out your understanding of this most important of countries.

I promise: There *won't* be a quiz at the end of the chapter.

The Lay of the Land

Size: Iraq is 169,235 square miles (437,072 square kilometers). It's smaller than Iran, and slightly larger than Syria. Iraq is much larger than Kuwait.

Climate: Iraq temperatures swing substantially between summer and winter. The mountain region in the north has cold winters with occasional heavy snows. It would be tough to play hockey in Iraq, but it does get cold. The mean January temperature in Mosul, the chief city in the north, is 44°F; the mean July temperature there is 90°F. Farther south, away from the mountains, it gets much hotter. The mean January temperature in Baghdad, which lies in the central lowland part of the country, is 50°F; for July it is 95°F.

CAUTION

Oil Spill Ahead

Dress light and bring along a fan if you find yourself summering in Iraq. Temperatures as high as 123°F have been recorded.

Increase Your Iraq IQ

Iraq's coastline along the gulf is only 19 miles long. Its only port on the gulf, Umm Qasr, is small and located on shallow water, so big tankers cannot use it. Iraq's other port is further inland at Basra, on the Shatt-al-Arab waterway. There are also larger offshore oil loading facilities for tankers..

From October to May, 12 to 22 inches of precipitation fall in the mountainous north, but in the central region, in the south and near the Persian Gulf there is only 6 inches for the whole year. The desert in the west gets little or no rain. Seasonal sandstorms and dense fog can also occur across the middle and lower parts of the country.

Terrain: The desert lands are mostly plains, with marshes along its border with Iran in the south, and mountains along the Iran and Turkey borders in the north. The highest point in Iraq is Haji Ibrahim at 11,834 feet, or 3,600 meters, near the border with Iran. The vast majority of the landscape is a grayish sandy plain that eventually merges into the Syrian Desert. The Tigris and Euphrates Rivers have created a broad plain, with a fertile area between and on both sides of the rivers, and in the irrigated areas that are fed by canals drawing from the two rivers. The extreme southeastern portion of Iraq is a low-lying, marshy area adjacent to the Persian Gulf, and along the Shatt-al-Arab.

Natural resources: Iraq's biggest natural resource by far is oil, then natural gas and sulfur. The country has large concentrations of phosphates, too. Otherwise, there isn't much else there in terms of natural resources. There are small deposits of salt, coal, gypsum, and sulfur.

Land use: About 12 percent of Iraqi territory is farmable. A series of flood control and irrigation dams on the Tigris and Euphrates Rivers feed an irrigation system and maintain a more even flow of water through the seasons. The rest of the land (79 percent) is mostly desert, and is not well suited for agriculture or other human activity. The land is mainly used as pasture.

People and Places

Principal cities: Baghdad is the capital and largest city of Iraq. Other major cities include Basra, Iraq's port on the Shatt-al-Arab, and Mosul, a primary oil nexus in the northern part of the country. Most of the people are concentrated in the urban centers. The Shiite holy cities of Karbala and Najaf are located in the central part of the country.

Population: Iraq has approximately 24 million people. By comparison, the United States has about 280 million people. In 2001, Iraq had a population growth rate of 2.84 percent.

Life expectancy: Males: 66 years, Females: 68 years. Forty percent of the population is younger than 14, showing the high birth rate in the country. Health standards have declined significantly after the end of the Gulf War as a consequence of the imposition of UN sanctions that have limited imports of food and medicine to Iraq and, more recently, because of the internal fighting and sabotage of the critical infrastructure in the period of U.S. occupation.

Ethnic groups: Most of the population is Arab. Arabs are 80 percent of the total in Iraq. The Kurds are 17 percent of the population; and other ethnic groups, including Turkoman and Assyrian peoples, make up the remaining 3 percent.

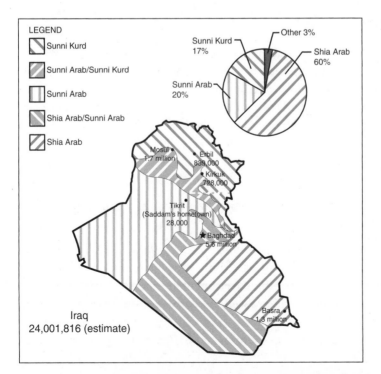

Ethnic distribution in Iraq.

The Word on the Street (and in the Mosque)

Language: Arabic is the official language of Iraq and is spoken by the majority of the population. The Kurds speak Kurdish. Armenian and Assyrian are spoken in some rural areas in the north and west.

Iraq Fact

Iraq dates its independence from October 3, 1932, when the League of Nations mandate freeing it from British administration was issued. Prior to the British administration, Iraq didn't exist as a political entity called "Iraq," but was a part of the Ottoman Empire, and several empires before that.

Religions: The official religion of Iraq is Islam. Muslims make up 97 percent of the population. (Shiites are 65 percent and Sunnis are 32 percent of the total.) The remaining 3 percent of the population represents a scattering of other religions. These include a few Christian Nestorians, Jacobite Christians, and offshoots of these two sects, respectively known as Chaldean and Syrian Catholics. In addition, smaller religious groups include the Yazidis, who live in the hill country north of Mosul, and a Gnostic sect known as the Mandaean Baptists living in Baghdad. The Yazidis are a syncretic sect, which combines the beliefs of different religions. A small community of Jews lives in Baghdad.

Politics: The Lowdown

Government: Iraq is nominally a republic, with 18 provinces. Baghdad is the capital. The Iraqi government consists of executive, legislative, and judicial branches, in a parliamentary structure. There is a president with some power (it is not a figurehead role). There is a prime minister with several ministers reporting to him. There is a popularly elected legislature, and an independent judiciary. The judiciary is not an Islamic court, though consideration is given to Islamic law. On paper, Iraq's government, like Turkey, is secular. However, like Turkey, the fact that Iraq is an Islamic country influences the laws and regulations that are enacted.

The ministries are allocated to the major groups in the country. The Sunni, Shiites, and Kurds each hold some of the posts.

Leadership: Saddam Hussein wielded absolute power for more than 20 years. He was president, prime minister, and chairman of the Revolutionary Command Council that used to control Iraq. The rest of the governmental leadership were Sunnis who were part of Saddam's inner circle. There were no Kurds or Shiites in Saddam's inner circle. That has changed in the post-Saddam era, as the United States created an interim authority that included Shiites, Sunnis, and Kurds. During Saddam's time, the leadership of the Kurds and the Shiites was split among several factions. There is no clear single leader among the Kurds or Shiites who can rally the full support of either group in a consistent way. The stability of the new Iraqi government depends on the Kurds and the Shiites being able to work through their factional differences.

The other key pieces of the leadership puzzle in Iraq are the tribal leaders. Several tribes in Iraq have existed for centuries, and they predate the creation of Iraq as a state. Saddam Hussein was able to play the tribes off one another, rewarding those who supported him, and punishing those who did not. The U.S.-created provisional authority put in place immediately following Operation Iraqi Freedom did not acknowledge the true power of the tribes, and many experts believe that omission has resulted in much of the strife now plaguing the country. These experts argue that the tribal leadership allows the acts of sabotage and attacks that occur in their territories. Those same experts believe that the tribal leaders could *not* prevent those attacks from happening, if they wanted. The new Iraqi government is creating a place at the table for the tribes. If this can be done in a way that accommodates most of the tribal demands, the acts of domestic resistance could be significantly reduced, if not eliminated entirely.

Increase Your Iraq IQ

Political parties: In the 1980s and 1990s, the only legal political organization in Iraq was the Arab Ba'th Socialist Party, which in theory based its policies on pan-Arab and socialist principles. In reality, it was the instrument of Saddam Hussein's totalitarian rule. Other (then illegal) parties in Iraq included the Iraqi Communist Party (ICP), the Kurdistan Democratic Party (KDP), and the Patriotic Union of Kurdistan (PUK). The two main Shiite opposition parties were the Da'wa Islamic Party and the Supreme Assembly of the Islamic Revolution in Iraq (SAIRI). There was no single alternative party that represented a majority of the Iraqi people. As of the writing of this book, those parties were finding their voice in the government, and new parties were starting to emerge to take a role in the first meaningful elections in decades, if not forever, in Iraq.

Money, Money

Economy: Iraq's economy is dominated by the oil sector, and the country is a member of OPEC. Iraq has about 10 percent of the world's proven reserves of petroleum, and oil provides about 95 percent of Iraqi foreign exchange earnings. Other Iraqi products include dates, wool, and hides and skins.

Currency: The official currency is called the "dinar" (ID). One dinar equals 20 "dirham" or 1,000 "fil," the Iraqi coins. As of the time of writing of this book, the dinar was not convertible, though a convertible dinar will be created as the economic situation stabilizes.

GDP: Iraq's Gross Domestic Product (GDP) was approximately $57 billion in 2000. The GDP of the United States, by comparison, was greater than $8 trillion in 2000. Iraqi economic activity dropped significantly in the immediate aftermath of the U.S.-led invasion, but as basic services (water, electricity, sewerage, roads, and so on) are restored, the GDP is slowly recovering. The longer those services take to be restored, the longer the GDP and standard of living for the average Iraqi will stagnate.

Industries: Most Iraqi industry revolves around petroleum and its peripheral industries. Iraq also has chemicals, textiles, construction materials, cigarettes, and food processing operations, based upon imports of raw materials for those industries. Under Saddam, most major national enterprises were governed by specific ministries that managed all the enterprises in their respective sectors. This tight government oversight has so far continued in the post-Saddam Iraq.

Military: The Iraqi army is being reconstituted as of the writing of this book. The army has played a crucial role in uniting this divided country throughout its history. In Saddam's time, the army also was used to prop up his totalitarian regime and suppress resistance in Kurd and Shiite areas. In the post-Saddam Iraq, domestic security will be handled by a police force, though it will be a heavily armed police force. Early performances by these police in 2004 were not good. In fact, the police often refused to do anything, or collapsed almost immediately upon being pressured. Along with creating an army that can provide national defense, an effective police force will be vital. The tribal leaders can play a pivotal role in establishing this police force, if allowed a place at the negotiating table. The Interim Iraqi government, with U.S. military training and support, has begun to create an effective counter-insurgency and domestic security force.

The Least You Need to Know

- Iraq is a major oil-producing country, in the middle of the major oil-producing region of the world.

- Iraq is a fledgling democracy, with no tradition of democracy.

- Iraq is a complex combination of peoples (Arabs and Kurds) and religious sects (Sunni and Shiite).

- Iraq's military is being reconstituted, along with a more traditional police force for internal security and stability, but this is proving to be a very difficult process.

Part 2

From Babylon to Baghdad

The area comprising modern-day Iraq has been continuously populated since the dawn of human civilization. But like its desert sands, the region's population and rulers have undergone a remarkable number of shifts.

In the following chapters, we'll trace the series of empires that have risen and fallen in this region and find out about a few of their major contributions—if you call the wheel and writing major, that is—to the world. We'll take a look at the lasting impact of one of the empires—the Arabs—and how Western powers, lured by empire and oil, were responsible for the creation of the modern state of Iraq.

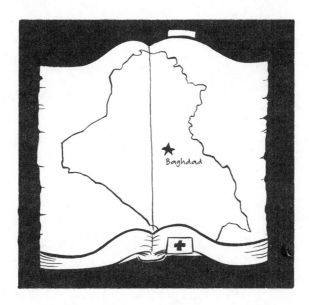

4

All the Stuff That Happened Before World War I

In This Chapter

- ◆ Ancient urban civilization in the area we now know as Iraq
- ◆ The empires that rose and fell, and rose and fell ...
- ◆ The Arabs and the coming of Islam
- ◆ On the border between the Ottomans and the Persians

The story of Iraq begins with two rivers—the Tigris and Euphrates. From the bounty of these two rivers we can attribute the earliest writing, the development of the wheel, and many other features of modern civilization that we still rely on. And it all took place where Iraq is today.

Who Was First?

Urban civilization emerged in *Mesopotamia* over 7,000 years ago. Some of the earliest known cities, including Ur, Lagash, and Uruk, emerged in what is now Iraq.

Archaeologists and other scholars continue to debate exactly where the earliest urban civilization emerged. Most scholars believe urban life appeared at Jericho, hundreds of miles to the west, even earlier than in Mesopotamia. Nonetheless, it is impossible to deny that the civilization that came out of what is now Iraq is among the oldest, and was certainly more influential, than any that came before.

What happened in Mesopotamia had a huge influence on Western culture, science, and history.

Settle Down!

Indications of permanent settlements in Mesopotamia appear around 5000 B.C.E. Before that, the people of the region tended to be more *nomadic*, or lived in less permanent structures.

The first permanent settlement in the region that can be confirmed appears at a place called Jarmo. At Jarmo, there is evidence of domesticated animals and plants, as well as permanent structures. It's estimated that as many as 150 people lived in the village of Jarmo. Residents lived in permanent mud-walled houses; grew wheat, barley, and lentils; and had domesticated animals.

Stuff to Drink, Stuff to Eat

What led ancient nomads to settle down and build Jarmo and settlements like it? The struggle for water and food. Simply put, the region between the Tigris and Euphrates Rivers was a good place to find both.

Remember that this region is basically desert. And yet these two rivers, and the silt that they deposited along their banks, made it possible for people to survive and grow food year after year in this otherwise forbidding environment. The two rivers flow almost parallel from mountains in the northern

Desert Diction

Mesopotamia, in Greek, means "the land between the rivers." The area between and Tigris and Euphrates Rivers was known as Mesopotamia. This region stretches from the Persian Gulf through modern Iraq, into the northwest portion of modern Syria. Mesopotamia was a perfect spot for civilization to emerge. It had abundant water, fertile land, and an agreeable climate.

Desert Diction

Nomads are people who don't live permanently in one place. They tend to move from place to place, generally in a specific pattern. That pattern could be governed by the seasons or by the availability of food. Nomads typically have herds of animals that travel with them, providing food on the hoof.

Iraq Fact

The Tigris is east of the Euphrates, closer to Iran. The rivers join before they reached the Gulf, into a single river called the Shatt-al-Arab.

parts of Mesopotamia to their mouth, at the head of the Persian Gulf, and the region between them is a great place to grow food.

These early settlements set in motion a series of cultural advances that leaves us face-to-face with some enterprising, expansionist folks known as the Sumerians.

Increase Your Iraq IQ

Before they were tamed by irrigation and flood control dams, the Tigris and Euphrates meandered across the Mesopotamian plains. They would sometimes flood and sometimes run very low; the water level fluctuated because rainfall is scarce in the region. A heavy rain (or winter snow) would mean flood. An extended dry spell would mean the river levels would drop.

In ancient times, canals were dug from the Tigris over to the Euphrates, which is lower than the Tigris. These small waterways provided irrigation in the plain between the rivers. (Today, a series of dams and irrigation canals control the rivers' flow and maximize water for irrigation.)

The Sumerians Get the Ball Rolling

The ancient Sumerians are credited with inventing, among other things, the wheel, the plow, and cuneiform writing. These three inventions enabled transportation, increased agricultural yields, and commerce—cornerstones to the success of ancient urban centers.

Getting Acquainted

While little is known about the Sumerian origins, a great deal is known about their accomplishments. Among other things, the Sumerians invented cuneiform writing, and wrote their words on clay tablets.

Archaeologists have found hundreds of clay tablets in the region bearing cuneiform writing. The presence of these tablets indicates that knowledge was being transferred to other people and being saved in writing. This allowed the early inhabitants to build (literally) on the

---

Increase Your Iraq IQ

Little is known about the Sumerians' origins and where they came from. They spoke a language that's not related to the Semitic languages (like Arabic or Hebrew), Indo-European languages, or really any other language spoken by peoples in the region at that time. So what might have been a valuable clue—tracing common linguistic roots—is useless when tracing the Sumerians' origins.

intellects and memories of other people, to codify laws, and to establish a permanent record of their oral traditions.

Many of the oldest surviving cuneiform tablets detail commercial transactions and property listings among the ancient Sumerians. These transactions seem mundane, but they are invaluable to showing us daily life in Mesopotamia.

Like the Greeks who followed them, the Sumerian religions were *polytheistic* and their gods were *anthropomorphic*. The Sumerians developed unique cults and religious beliefs in their various city-states, but they shared the polytheistic and anthropomorphic characteristics.

Desert Diction

Polytheism refers to belief in a group of gods where each represents a specific human action, or emotion, or a physical element, such as one for the sun, one for the moon. **Anthropomorphism** is the belief that gods take human form, have human emotions, and act in many ways like humans.

Settlement and permanence promoted the cultural and economic growth of the region, and attracted the attention of other cultures and traders. The rivers themselves were natural trade routes, enabling the cities that sprouted beside them to trade their surplus commodities with other regions. Even the predecessors to the Silk Road passed though Mesopotamia, opening the riches of the Orient to these urban populations. The central position of Mesopotamian cities resulted in trade with other emerging civilizations in the Mediterranean and North Africa, as well as the Far East. This trade brought further riches to the region, and prompted further innovations in technology.

Increase Your Iraq IQ

People have been trading across the world for centuries. Overland trade routes from ancient China and India to ancient Mesopotamia and on to ancient Egypt and Phoenicia were established almost as early as the first cities emerged. The earliest people were mostly nomads, so it's easy to see how they would wander into one another and compare goodies. Over time, this developed into more sophisticated trade. Along with trade came trade routes. The more modern Silk Road was simply the descendent of a series of ancient routes that wound their way from various parts of China and India, across various parts of Central Asia, through various cities in Mesopotamia, and on to the Mediterranean. Marco Polo certainly wasn't the first to go to China from the West, but he was the first to get lasting credit for it.

Lawyers, Guns, and Money: The Early Ruling Class

Along with the new wealth came spare time for those who didn't have to work every waking hour for their survival. As a result, these cities were able to further improve their situation through the development of new technologies, and even leisure pursuits. Temples and city walls were among the results of this surplus, the temples indicating the ability to devote some of those riches to feeding the spirit, and the walls indicating the need to protect those riches.

The food surpluses meant that a ruling class and its bureaucracy and army could be supported by the work of other people. These institutions, and the power elites who ran them, gradually solidified their authority by making themselves kings and establishing administrators in the place of the tribal elders of the nomads. The kings further entrenched themselves by claiming that they were divine relations of the gods of the day.

Iraq Fact _____

The oldest wheel yet discovered by archaeologists was found in Mesopotamia (present-day Iraq). It is thought to be more than 5,500 years old.

The evolution of the divinely justified king, supported by a bureaucracy and propped up by an army, who ruled over an increasingly complex social and economic structure, accompanies the development of the pre-Sumerian city-states in Mesopotamia. The king enriched a priest-class bureaucracy and military class, so that they would support him and remain loyal to him. They benefited by not having to work every day in the dirt to survive.

A Question with Modern Implications Arises

Why would people allow themselves to be ruled by a king in that way? In other words— why did people collectivize and submit to central power? And for that matter, why do they still do so?

The simple answer was, and is, survival.

In the case of the ancient region of Mesopotamia, it was a tough and dangerous place. Water and food were often hard to come by if you decided to go it alone, but there was some guarantee of access to both within the storehouses and

Iraq Fact _____

The city-states that rose in Mesopotamia in the 4000 to 2500 B.C.E period weren't a cohesive empire. It wasn't until 2750 B.C.E that the first Sumerian dynasty of Ur was able to consolidate political hold on the major cities in southern Mesopotamia. This was the first empire in the region, where the central authority (based in Ur) was able to control the surrounding city-states.

reservoirs of the cities. Then, too, there was the ever-present problem of marauding bandits and tribal warfare.

Much like in feudal Europe, people accepted the king because the king promised protection during dangerous times. Along with their king, people in one city-state would regard people in another city-state as potential enemies, to be conquered and plundered, before the other city-states decided to conquer and plunder first.

While not exactly patriotism or tribal fealty, the individual's association of membership to a state (instead of a tribe) marked the beginnings of more modern concepts of citizenship. This notion eventually took hold during the Sumerian era, and enabled the Sumerians to come together and create a unified identity that paralleled—or even surpassed—one's immediate family circle.

This is the occasionally bloody, not always graceful dance of civilization. And as far as we can tell, it first played out in the place we now call Iraq.

Iraq Fact

Some highlights in Mesopotamian pre-history.

◆ 5000 B.C.E.: First settlements at Jarmo.

◆ 4700 B.C.E.: Hassunah period—pottery-making emerges. The ability to make pottery is considered a requirement for urban living.

◆ 4400 B.C.E.: Halaf period—metal-working emerges. Like pottery, a requirement for urbanization.

◆ 3900 B.C.E.: Ubaid period—first temple and complex buildings appear. The ability to build temples means surplus materials, food, and time, all by-products of increasing efficiencies and urbanization.

◆ 3600 B.C.E.: Warka period—first written characters appear. The ability to record information, to pass along, and add to it, is a foundation of modern civilization.

◆ 2900 B.C.E.: Sumerians appear. These people use all the innovations that came before them, and create a sophisticated urban civilization.

Biblicalities and Mesopotamia

Believe it or not, when you walk into a church or synagogue, you are, in a way, walking into a Sumerian temple (or at least *through* one to get to your pew or bench). That's because historical Mesopotamia (the precursor to the modern Iraq) greatly contributed to Western Judeo-Christian beliefs. In this and subsequent sections, you will learn how ancient Sumerian legends found their way into contemporary Hebrew culture, and thus into the Bible we know today.

In the Book of Genesis, the first humans emerged in Mesopotamia. The Garden of Eden, some scholars believe, was located near modern Mughair in the southern part of ancient Mesopotamia, in the ancient Tigris and Euphrates delta region, though the actual site hasn't been confirmed. To the ancient Hebrews, humanity itself was regarded as having arisen in Mesopotamia.

Why Mesopotamia?

Why did the Hebrews designate Mesopotamia as the starting point for everything? And why does this region figure so prominently in the stories of the Hebrew struggles throughout the ages?

The importance of Mesopotamia in the Bible really isn't surprising when we take two things into account:

♦ The Hebrews were held captive in Mesopotamia (that is, in Babylon), and so it is no surprise that their scriptures would include stories that came from there.

♦ The Mesopotamians invented writing, and recorded many ancient legends and lessons on their clay tablets. The Hebrews came into contact with this trove of surviving writing, and certainly read some of what they saw.

> **Increase Your Iraq IQ**
>
> Nineveh, a major center in Mesopotamia, and home to a great library of ancient writings, is mentioned some 20 times in the Hebrew Scriptures, and there are more than 130 references to Assyria, the empire that ruled Mesopotamia during the time of the Hebrew captivity in Babylon.

Overlapping Stories

Some key stories of the Hebrew Scriptures may have been copied from ancient Mesopotamian legends. Many of these legends are found in a Sumerian legend called the "Epic of Gilgamesh."

The Epic of Gilgamesh (in Brief)

The "Epic of Gilgamesh" is a collection of legends of the ancient Sumerian king, Gilgamesh. Around 2600 B.C.E., Gilgamesh was king of Uruk (known as Erech in the Hebrew Scriptures). The story recounts the exploits of Gilgamesh, who was semi-divine—part god, part human—but a brutal ruler. The people under Gilgamesh's rule ask Anu, chief deity of Uruk, to help them deal with Gilgamesh. Anu creates Enkidu, a subhuman wild man to counter the super human Gilgamesh. Enkidu is gradually humanized by shepherds, and then enters the city, where Gilgamesh is presiding over a wedding. Gilgamesh, the lout, is about to claim the right to sleep with the bride on her wedding night. Enkidu is outraged, and bars the way to the wedding chamber. In the manner of many epics and legends, Gilgamesh and Enkidu fight for days.

Enkidu finally concedes to Gilgamesh, and the two become friends. They go out to cut down all the cedars in the forest in what we would now identify as southern Iran to make a gate for Uruk, but before doing so they must defeat Humbaba, the monster who guards the forest. With a god's help, they are able to succeed against Humbaba and proceed to make the gate.

When they get back to Uruk, Gilgamesh and Enkidu battle and kill the Bull of Heaven, and ultimately the gods take revenge by causing Enkidu to die. Upon his friend's death, Gilgamesh goes out from Uruk, and meets Utnapishtim, who is immortal. Utnapishtim tells Gilgamesh of how he survived a great flood by making a boat, riding out the storm, and coming to rest on a mountain. After Utnapishtim shares the secret to immortality, a sly and devious serpent steals Gilgamesh's immortality from him. Finally, Gilgamesh returns to Uruk, where the epic ends.

Any of that sound familiar?

Many scholars believe the "Epic of Gilgamesh" precedes the composition of the Hebrew Scriptures, and the fact that both the "Epic of Gilgamesh," and the Hebrew Scriptures share many of the same story elements indicates the influence Mesopotamian culture had on the Hebrews and their culture.

References to Mesopotamia in the Hebrew Scriptures

The Hebrew Scriptures repeatedly mention Mesopotamian people and places. However, most of the Mesopotamian cities referenced in the Old Testament are not given high marks by the Hebrew authors. This isn't surprising, given that the Hebrews were taken as captives to Babylon in 586 B.C.E.

Thus Spake Zarathustra

Zoroaster (Zarathustra) is credited with creating the briefly powerful religion that bore his name: Zoroastrianism. The Persians introduced the religion of Zoroastrianism to Mesopotamia. Rather than an examination of man's struggle with himself, Zoroastrians saw the world as a fundamental struggle between good and evil. Zoroastrians believed in the final victory of the ultimate good god, Ahurah Mazdah. The Zoroastrian Persians, who conquered Babylon while the Hebrews were captive there, were more tolerant of other religions and other gods. When they met the Hebrews, and learned about their God, they included Yahweh, the Hebrew God, into their constellation. The Zoroastrians believed that Yahweh was a "good" god, whose power would only further their goal of battling evil and would support Ahurah Mazdah in the struggle. The Persians eventually allowed the Hebrews to return to Jerusalem and rebuild the Temple of Solomon. The Books of Ezra and Nehemiah narrate this portion of Hebrew history.

While the Hebrews didn't embrace the fundamental good versus evil philosophies of the Zoroastrians, they probably brought these ideas with them in some form when they came back to Jerusalem.

Increase Your Iraq IQ

Look how much of the Bible takes place in (what we would now call) Iraq:

- Adam and Eve live in the Garden of Eden, now connected with southern Mesopotamia.
- Noah is from Fara.
- Job is from the area around Uz.
- Abram is from Ur. He becomes Abraham, father of the Hebrew nation; God commands him to lead his people from Mesopotamia to Canaan.
- Assyrians, from Nineveh, conquer the northern Hebrew kingdom of Israel.
- The Chaldeans, from Babylon, conquer the southern Hebrew kingdom of Judah and exile the Hebrews to Babylon.
- The Tower of Babel is built by Nebuchadnezzar near Babylon.
- Jonah is commanded by God to preach in Nineveh.

It's possible that the first Christians may have taken the fundamentals of both Judaism and Zoroastrianism with them when they launched Christianity. (This is, however, an extremely controversial point—one where scholars have not yet reached agreement.) If this were true, ancient Mesopotamia's role in the development of both Judaism *and* Christianity would be critically important.

The moral: Whether you realized it at the time or not, you were reading about the region we today identify as Iraq when you read or heard some of the most famous stories from the ancient Hebrew Scriptures.

The Cultural Chain: Empires in Iraq

Viewed from the distance of history, it seems as though the ancient world consisted of successive waves of invasions and counter-invasions. And the wealthier the region—in terms of agricultural resources, storehouses of food, and/or a thriving trade economy—the more likely jealous neighbors and vandals were to invade.

The emerging Sumerian city-states' great wealth became the prized target of one invader after another. As we shall see, in most cases, the prize captured them. The invaders often abandoned their own culture in favor of the one they found there. Ultimately, the larger movements of world events eventually led to the decline of Mesopotamia as the central prize.

Loosely Connected

The city-states that rose in Mesopotamia in the period from 4000 to 2500 B.C.E. were not a cohesive empire. These states generally worshipped different gods, and maneuvered with alliances to maintain their own independence, or to exert dominance over their neighbors.

It wasn't until 2750 B.C.E. that the first Sumerian dynasty of Ur was able to consolidate political hold on the major cities in southern Mesopotamia. This was the first empire in the region, where the central authority (based in Ur) was able to control the surrounding city-states.

Sumerian Technical Innovations

Sumerian civilization is credited with many inventions. Many people even claim the Sumerians invented time!

Inventing time may be a stretch, but it is true that the Sumerians developed a mathematical system based upon 60, which is still the basis for hours and minutes and seconds. They came up with new irrigation methods and architectural techniques. They used double-entry accounting methods and even had early forms of banks. Deposits of grain, cattle, metals, and tools were accepted at palaces and temples that emerged in the ancient cities. The priests who ran these temples would meticulously record the deposits and make the appropriate payments on behalf of the account holder. We know this because of the durability of their writing.

The Sumerians also developed a calendar system of 12 lunar months. Over time, they realized that the lunar year was significantly shorter than the solar year, so they added a "leap month" every third year to get things back on target.

The Sumerians were almost constantly at war with each other and outside groups. The struggles for control of water and arable land were almost ceaseless, and the Sumerian city-states under the Ur dynasty slowly succumbed to outside invaders.

Meet the New Boss ...

Around 2340 B.C.E., the Akkadians swept up from the Arabian penninsula and subdued the Ur dynasty. The Akkadians were a Semitic people and spoke a language that is related to Hebrew and Arabic. They founded a capital city at Akkad, later called Babylon.

The Akkadians adopted the best of what the Sumerians had to offer in the ways of government, societal structures, religion, and law, and abandoned much of their own culture when they gained control of the Sumerian territories around Ur.

Sargon I started the era of Akkadian rule that lasted for about two centuries. The Akkadians were the first to unite the region of Mesopotamia under one ruling system. The Sumerian city-states had operated as a loose confederation, but the Akkadians centralized their control.

Rather than destroy the Sumerian cities, the Akkadians instead occupied them as a prize of conquest. In this spirit, the Akkadians allowed the various Sumerian city-states to recover from the conquest. The Akkadians eventually succumbed when the Sumerians in the city of Ur revolted in 2125 B.C.E., and the other Sumerian city-states followed suit.

Iraq Fact

This method of copying the best of what the Mesopotamian city-states had to offer became a common practice for most of the conquerors of the region over then next few thousand years.

The Sumerians Come Back, But Not for Long

The demise of the Akkadians led to the reemergence of a Sumerian dynasty of Ur founded by Ur-Nammu. But this reemergence of Sumerian dominance was short-lived. The Sumerians were again overwhelmed by another migration of Semitic peoples, known as the Amorites, who consolidated their hold on southern Mesopotamia around 1900 B.C.E. They founded a capital at Akkad, in the center of Mesopotamia.

An Eye for an Eye

The Amorites centralized their empire on the city of Babylon, which was founded near the old city of Akkad. The Amorite capital is known as Old Babylon, and the

Amorite Empire (1900–1600 B.C.E.) is known as the Old Babylon period. The Amorites claimed their rulers were descended from gods, and that the central state had more power over people's lives than their own city-states did.

Iraq Fact

The Amorites instituted far-reaching taxation and involuntary conscription to finance and maintain their new empire. This increasing centralization of power led to a new set of laws that defined crimes against the state, rather than against other individuals. The state also took a more active role in punishing criminals.

The Amorites enacted a body of law, now called *lex talionis*, or law of retribution. Punishments matched the nature of the infraction, creating the principle of "an eye for an eye, a tooth for a tooth, an arm for an arm, a life for a life." About this time, an Old Babylonian king, Hammurabi, set these laws down in writing. This written body of law is known as the Code of Hammurabi; it reflects the key tenets of Amorite and Sumerian law.

The Code is made up of some 282 individual laws, including one that even decrees death for "bad behavior in a bar." Basically, the Amorites took the Sumerian law, and made it more severe, and more state-oriented, to serve their needs.

The main concepts of the Code are:

- **Administration:** Law is retribution that is administered by a centralized authority, not by individuals acting on their own or their clan's behalf.

- **Writing:** Law is written and has a higher authority than individuals. Oral or cultural traditions are not written and are subject to individual interpretation. The written law is permanent and supercedes the life of any one individual.

- **Retribution:** Law is basically a method of exacting revenge. By using law to exact revenge, society avoids personal vendettas and an increasing cycle of retribution for a given crime.

The Hittites Spread the Word

Despite their centralization of power and authority, and conscript armies, the Amorites were unable to withstand the constant pressures of the Hittites, who swept away the Amorites around 1600 B.C.E. Like the conquerors before them, the Hittites adopted much of the cultural and societal elements of the region. The Hittite Empire eventually stretched from Mesopotamia to Syria and Palestine. The Hittites spent a great deal of energy and resources battling with the Egyptians, who regarded them as savages.

The Hittites own empire covered a huge region, and they traded and fought with the Greeks, Egyptians, and other Mediterranean cultures. The Hittites never had the same grip on their territories that the Amorites had, and their legal system was much less punitive than Hammurabi's. The death penalty only applied to a relatively small number of crimes.

The Hittites also freely accepted the gods they encountered and even included them in their own religion. The other side of this looser authority was the increasingly loose grip that was maintained over the Mesopotamian city-states. Hittite control over these cities fluctuated, and eventually the Hittites gave way to an invasion of the Kassites, around 1100 B.C.E.

Iraq Fact

The Hittites are responsible for exporting Sumerian customs and innovations (that they encountered when they got to Mesopotamia) to other parts of the Ancient World.

Enter the Kassites

The Kassites came into Mesopotamia from Asia. Like the Hittites, they were fleeing from invaders who displaced them from their original lands. The Kassites stormed into the central part of Mesopotamia, around Babylon (the city founded by the Amorites). They renamed Babylon Karanduniash, and built a new capitol city called Durkurigalzu. The Kassites never controlled more than the central area around Babylon, and after a few centuries, they were swept away by a new wave of invaders, the Assyrians, who seized Babylon in 1200 B.C.E.

The Military Men Step In

The Assyrians pushed both the Kassites and Hittites aside, starting in 1200 B.C.E. and finally subdued the last Hittite strongholds around 700 B.C.E. The Assyrians gradually built an empire that included Syria, Armenia, Palestine, and Mesopotamia.

Unlike the conquerors before them, the Assyrians adopted a policy of forcible migration of the peoples they conquered. This included the peoples of the city-states in Mesopotamia,

Desert Diction

Diaspora is a term that means a scattering of people from a central place. As we see here, the Assyrians used the dispersal technique to eliminate organized resistance from conquered peoples. Many cultural groups have suffered diaspora, some never to survive it. The ancient Hebrews suffered a number of diaspora, including ones forced by the Assyrians, the Chaldeans, and the Romans.

including Babylon. The Assyrian king Sargon II also forced the migration of the Hebrews from their northern kingdom of Israel, marking the first Jewish *diaspora*.

However, the Assyrians also tolerated the religious beliefs of the peoples they conquered. (The Assyrians allowed the Hebrews to maintain their religion, even when their lands were taken.) And in the case of the Babylonians, even feared the native gods. True story: The Assyrians razed Babylon and then, fearing the wrath of Babylonian god, Marduk, started rebuilding it again.

The Assyrians set up their capital at a new city, called Nineveh. Rather than destroy the Sumerian culture they conquered, they attempted to preserve it. The last great Assyrian king, Ashurbanipal, assembled a huge library of Sumerian writings at Nineveh. The 30,000 tablets that survive are thus both an invaluable record of Sumerian culture and a testament to that culture's ability to win the respect of incoming conquerors like the Assyrians.

The Assyrians were a highly militaristic society, with the largest army in the region at the time. They developed a number of innovative weapons, and their technological advancements were significant. Despite their military and technical achievements, the Assyrians eventually succumbed to a revolt led by the city-state of Babylon, which culminated in the fall of Nineveh in 612 B.C.E.

Babylon on the Ascent

The emergence of the Babylonian city-state heralded the start of the Neo-Babylonian, or Chaldean, period. King Nebuchadnezzar II expanded and improved Babylon (remember, the Assyrians had wrecked the place, then started to rebuild it), and conquered the southern Hebrew kingdom of Judah. They destroyed the Temple of Solomon, and deported the Jews to Babylon.

Babylon itself flourished under the Chaldean period. Nebuchadnezzar built the famous Hanging Gardens of Babylon (one of the Wonders of the Ancient World). He also built the Tower of Babel as a temple to the Babylonian god, Marduk. However, the Chaldean empire collapsed in less than a century.

The constant attacks from the recently displaced Assyrians drained the empire. Finally, the Chaldeans succumbed to the Persians rather than yield to the ceaseless Assyrians, who had again conquered their city. The Chaldeans decided that the Persians would make a better master than the Assyrians—and they supported the Persians against the Assyrians as the Persians crossed into Mesopotamia from the East.

Oil Spill Ahead _____

The location of the Hanging Gardens isn't certain. In fact, their existence at all is uncertain. The Babylonian records of the time do not mention the Gardens, though later Greek writings describe them in great detail. Many scholars suspect that these latter day Greek tourists made the whole thing up. If they did exist, the Gardens didn't actually "hang" but were supported on huge terraces. Supposedly, Nebuchadnezzar built the Gardens for his wife.

The Persians—and Alexander the Great—Pass Through

In 539 B.C.E., the Persians conquered Babylon. The conquest of Mesopotamia by the Persians signaled the end of Mesopotamia as a central focus of world cultural evolution. The Persians were bent on world domination, not just control of Mesopotamia; the Greeks who in turn conquered the Persians were, in essence, marching through Mesopotamia on their way to Persia and beyond. The great Sumerian city-states became a sideshow, from that point forward, on the stage of world history.

Cyrus the Great, from Persia, took control of the whole region by 500 B.C.E. Cyrus extended the Persian Empire from India to Macedon and Mesopotamia.

Cyrus was a devotee of the new religion of Zoroastrianism which, as you'll recall, saw the world as an epic struggle between good and evil, light and dark. When Cyrus conquered Babylon, he freed the Jews, and encouraged them to rebuild the Temple of Solomon and worship Yahweh. (Cyrus saw the Hebrew god, Yahweh, as a "good" god.)

The Persians set up *satrapies*, or administrative regions, to rule their lands, including the territories of Mesopotamia. Thus the region became just another department in their empire. Several of the city-states led revolts against the Persian satrapy during this time, and Persian grip on the city-states fluctuated from tight control, to loose control, to no control. Eventually, Persian authority over Mesopotamian city-states was reconsolidated by Darius the Great, in his push to extend the Persian Empire.

Desert Diction _____

Satrapies are administrative regions within ancient Persian Empire. A satrap was the title of the ruler of that regional division. The Persians were able to maintain control of their far-flung empire by giving the satrap relative autonomy in his region (or "satrapy").

The Persians pushed on to Greece, were stopped there, and then came under attack themselves by the Macedonians under Alexander the Great. Steadily, Alexander pushed the Persians out of Asia Minor and Mesopotamia. Alexander crossed the Euphrates in 331 B.C.E. and entered Babylon in 330 B.C.E. Alexander continued on through Persia, Central Asia, and even into India before turning back. On his way back through Mesopotamia, when heading home, Alexander stopped off in Babylon. He fell ill, and eventually died in Babylon in 323 B.C.E.

After Alexander's death, his followers divided the empire. One of Alexander's military commanders, Seleucus, was given control of Mesopotamia, Syria, and Persia, creating the Seleucid dynasty. This empire was governed from Antioch in Syria and a new city, called Seleucia, in Mesopotamia. Seleucia and the other new power-center cities in Mesopotamia were founded by Greek and Macedonian colonists and soldiers. These colonists chose to create new cultural centers, rather than move into the Mesopotamian cities like Babylon or Nineveh.

The Seleucid Empire eventually lost control of Mesopotamia to the Parthians, who invaded from what is now Iran, around 170 B.C.E. The Parthians ruled Mesopotamia from a new city that they founded and called Ctesiphon. Ctesiphon was across the Tigris from Seleucia. This marked a physical as well as symbolic shift of power from Greek to Persian (the people who came from what is now Iran) control.

The Parthians and Sassanians Pass Through, Too

The Parthians were able to withstand Roman attacks, including a bold defeat of Crassus in 53 B.C.E. at Haran in northern Mesopotamia. The Parthians eventually gave way to the Sassanians—who, like the Parthians, also emerged from within the region we would identify as modern Iran.

The Sassanians ruled Mesopotamia from 224 C.E. to 637 C.E. Like the Parthians before them, the Sassanians resisted Roman and later Byzantine attacks on their territories, and maintained their own control over Mesopotamia. But the region still wallowed in relative obscurity during this time, as the great movements of history took place outside its borders.

The End of Ancient Mesopotamia

The Sassanid period is a fitting place to mark the end of ancient Mesopotamian history.

After the Sassanians came the Arabs, and with them a new religion called Islam. The dual impact of Arab culture and Islamic theology ultimately would redefine the region's culture in a way that no previous invader could.

The Least You Need to Know

♦ The Sumerians started it all, and laid the groundwork for civilizations that came after, including those whose influence extended into the Jewish, Christian, and Muslim traditions.

♦ The region was subjected to repeated waves of invasion, though it gradually fell into a secondary role under the Persian and Greeks.

♦ The Arab invasion brought with it Islam, and the establishment of Baghdad as the central seat of a vast new empire.

Chapter 5

The Arabs, Islam, and the Ottomans

In This Chapter

- ◆ The Arab conquest and the Golden Age of Baghdad
- ◆ The Mongol invasions and decline of the region
- ◆ A series of petty dictatorships give way to Ottoman control

As you learned in the previous chapter, Mesopotamia was peopled by many different groups, including Sumerians, Assyrians, and Sassanians, all of whom came and went, swept away by the ones before. It was only in the seventh century C.E.—thousands of years after Mesopotamian civilization first began—that the Arabs began to dominate the area and introduced Islam. Unlike their precedessors, these late arrivals managed to hang on to their land and bring about dramatic changes to the area. Even the subsequent shocks of two Mongol invasions and a Turkic imperial overseer didn't displace the Arab-Islam foundations.

The Beginning of an Era

In 638 C.E., the Sassanians fell before an Arab Muslim invasion, marking the beginning of Arab dominance of Mesopotamia and the introduction of Islam to the region. This invasion, while it seemed like so many of the others that came before, was different in that it brought two elements to Mesopotamia that have survived to become dominant elements in modern Iraq:

Oil Spill Ahead

Don't confuse the words "Arab" and "Muslim." The first refers to a culture; the second refers to a religion. There are many Muslims who are not Arabs. The Muslims in Iran, Malaysia, the Philippines, Central Asia, Pakistan, China, and Turkey are not Arab. Also, there are Arabs, such as Lebanese Christians, who are not Muslims.

- **The invaders were Arabs,** who gradually came to dominate the region and remain the vast majority in Iraq to this day.

- **The invaders were Muslims,** bringing Islam to the region and eventually wiping out the pantheistic (many-gods) and anthropomorphic (imposing human qualities on divine beings) religions that they found there. Islam is still the dominant religion in Iraq.

Increase Your Iraq IQ

The word "Arab" describes the people whose culture and language derive from the Arabian peninsula, an area that borders present-day Iraq. The word "Muslim" describes an adherent of the global religion known as Islam, which traces its origin to the prophet Mohammed (570?–632). Arab groups have predominated for centuries in the region we know today as the Middle East, but not all Middle Eastern Muslims are Arabs.

Mohammed's New Faith

To understand the Arab conquest of Mesopotamia, you have to understand a little bit about Islam, one of the world's great faiths and the youngest of the three global monotheistic (single-God) religious movements, the others being Judaism and Christianity.

"Islam" translates as "submission." "Muslim" translates as "one who submits." The emphasis in Islam is on submission to the will of a single God. The "five pillars" of this great and enduring religious tradition are the following:

- ◆ Confession of faith in God and in his prophet Mohammed ("There is no God but God; Mohammed is the Prophet of God.")

- ◆ Ritual worship

- ◆ Almsgiving

- ◆ Fasting

- ◆ Pilgrimage (See the notes on Mecca below.)

What You Should Know About Mohammed

Here are 10 key points to keep in mind about Mohammed, one of the most important figures in all of human history.

- ◆ Mohammed was born in Mecca (in present-day Saudi Arabia) around the year 570.

- ◆ Prior to the rise of Mohammed in the early seventh century, Arabia had no prophetic tradition.

- ◆ Mohammed is believed to have experienced the first of a series of intense religious visions around the year 610 in a cave near Mecca.

- ◆ The Qur'an, Islam's central religious text, is held to record Mohammed's encounter with God plus the later revelations of Mohammed, and is regarded as the final and authoritative word of Allah (God).

- ◆ After more than a decade of preaching, Mohammed had been unsuccessful in converting Mecca to the new faith; in 622 he and his followers moved to Yathrib (later known as Medina, the "City of the Prophet"). This year is celebrated as the first year of the Muslim era.

- ◆ Mohammed was an extremely charismatic teacher and military leader who emphasized absolute reliance on a single God and a ban on idolatry.

- ◆ Mohammed continued to encounter resistance in spreading the new doctrine, but eventually mounted a military and religious campaign that succeeded in unifying Arabia behind a single faith.

- ◆ By the time he died in 632, Mohammed had set in motion both a great religious movement and an awe-inspiring military machine.

- ◆ Mohammed is regarded by Muslims as Allah's final prophet, and Islam is seen as the fulfillment of all previous human religious experience.

♦ Mohammed's birthplace, Mecca, is now regarded as the great Holy City of Islam and is the destination of annual pilgrimages by millions of Muslims.

The Arab Conquest

In 634 C.E., an army of 18,000 Arab Muslims, under the leadership of Khalid ibn al Walied, defeated the Persians in a conflict known as the Battle of the Chains (so called because the Persian troops were supposedly chained together so they wouldn't run). The Persians outnumbered the Arabs, but they were routinely defeated by the Arab forces in several battles. Finally, in 636, the Arabs defeated the Persians at Qadisiyah, near Baghdad, killing their leader in the process. With their leader dead, the Persians were unable to maintain effective resistance and collapsed. From there, the Arabs took the Persian-built city of Ctesiphon, effectively ending Persian influence in the region.

> **Desert Diction**
>
> The **Council of Ephesus** was a major council of the Christian church that took place in 431 C.E. The council condemned as heretical Nestorian Christianity, which viewed Jesus as two distinct but united individuals, one human and one divine. The council also deposed Nestorius, the leader of this sect.

At the time of the Arab conquest, the native people in Iraq were Christians and other non-Muslims. Most people were Nestorian Christians, a sect of Christianity that diverged from the Byzantine church after the *Council of Ephesus* in 431 C.E. The Nestorians had established a large cultural base in Mesopotamia by the time the Arabs moved in.

Baghdad and the Golden Age

Arabs came to dominate the region, and the Arab Empire centered itself on the new city of Baghdad, in central Iraq. In 750 C.E., Abu al Abbas al-Mansur became the first caliph of the Abbasid dynasty. He created his capital city in Baghdad in 762.

Baghdad represented the physical and intellectual intersection of Arab, Hellenic, and Persian culture. It was located near old Babylon, but was still a new city, founded by the Arabs.

The city became a powerhouse of learning, religion, and culture. By 1000 C.E., Baghdad was regarded as the intellectual center of the world. As the seat of power for the caliphs, Baghdad was also to become the cultural capital of the Islamic world. In fact, by 800 C.E., Baghdad was second only to Constantinople in size with almost one million people living in its environs.

Due to its position astride major trade routes between Asia and Europe, Baghdad became a commercial center as well. Silk Road routes passed through it, and the city reflected the impact of these Far Eastern products, philosophies, and innovations. For example, the Arabs introduced "Arabic numbers" to the Western world. In actuality, those numbers came from Indian mathematicians.

You Do the Math

The story of a prominent Arab mathematician is a good representative case of the Arabs' role in taking the best of East and West and adding the best of their own to it. These scholars and scientists worked out of great schools that were founded in Baghdad. The leading Arab mathematician of the Golden Age who lived in Baghdad was Abu Ja'far Muhammed ibn Musa al-Khawarizmi. Al-Khawarizmi discovered some of the key concepts of what would eventually be known as algebra, and he presented the new invention of the zero to the West.

Al-Khawarizmi wrote several math texts, 10 of which survive. In one of them, he introduces the Hindu number system (including the zero) to his readers. Even al-Khawarizmi's name and book titles have been forever ensconced in modern mathematics. When western Europeans received translations of one of his math texts and saw the author's name, they called him "Algorismus" as a Latinized version of his given name. Modern mathematicians and computer programmers have retained the term "algorithm" to describe a step-by-step process for carrying out computations.

At its pinnacle, Baghdad had a teaching hospital, a university, palaces, and civil engineering projects that were the equal of any in the world at that time. In fact, many of the medical treatises written in Baghdad during this time were standard reference texts for European doctors for the next 600 years.

Iraq Fact

Al-Khawarizmi's major text is called "Kitab al-jabr w'al muqabalah" which translates to "Restoration and Balancing." The text outlines several of the key elements of algebra. The name "algebra" is derived from the book's title (a-jabr) itself.

Increase Your Iraq IQ

Another famous figure of the time, Abu Hamid al-Ghazzi was a professor at Baghdad's great religious school, the Madrasa al-Nizamiya. Al-Ghazzi wrote several religious treatises that blended orthodox and mystic Muslim religious opinions, and he is considered one of the greatest reformers in Islam.

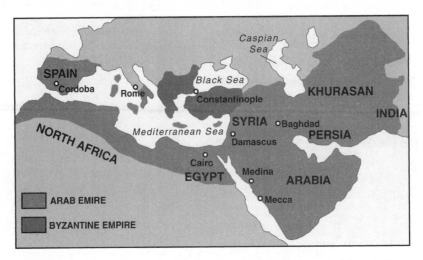

The Arab Empire, at its greatest extent, around 850 C.E. It reached from India in the east to Spain in the west. Baghdad was its heart, and at the time the city was unparalleled in its science, art, and literature.

Turn Out the Lights, the Party's Over

Despite a remarkable flowering of culture and thought in a very short period of time, Baghdad gradually saw its central role diminished in the face of new centers of Islamic thought and commerce in places like Egypt, Persia, and Central Asia. On the religious front, a schism staggered the Abbasid Empire.

The schism started in 661 C.E., when Ali ibn Abi Talib, Mohammed's cousin, son-in-law, and the last of a group known as the Rightly Guided Caliphs, was assassinated, and a nonfamily member was made caliph. Ali's death triggered political and religious dissension among the Muslim faithful.

Debates regarding succession led to the development of the Shiites, a sect of Islam that recognizes Mohammed's descendants through Ali as the only legitimate leaders of the faithful.

> **Increase Your Iraq IQ**
>
> The Fatimid dynasty wrested North Africa away from the Abbasids by 969 C.E. The Fatimids founded Cairo as their new capital. Cairo became a major center for learning and culture. Throughout the next 1,000 years, Egypt and Iraq competed for dominance in the region.

Rapid Ascent, Rapid Decline

Baghdad's control over the Empire steadily decreased. Almost as quickly as they had been conquered, the farthest reaches of the Abbasid Empire began to break away from the central authority of Baghdad.

Turks and Persians Behind the Throne

The caliph's ability to rule independently was steadily eroded, as more and more territories challenged the political authority of Baghdad. The weakened caliph, coupled with internal dissent of the Shiites, allowed others to take a more prominent role in affairs of state. By the 830s, the court at Baghdad was really run by the *Mamluks*, who played king-makers. The Mamluks decided who would be caliph and maintained the office to provide legitimacy for their rule. However, the caliph became a religious figurehead only.

Desert Diction

The **Mamluks** originally were Turkic slaves (not Arabs) who came from Central Asia. Initially they were slave-warriors and palace guards. Gradually, they became officers and even administrators in the Baghdad bureaucracy. Finally, they assumed actual control of political affairs in Baghdad, keeping the caliph as a front. As the power behind the throne, they determined who would be caliph, and what policies he would pursue.

In 945, the weakened Abbasid administration succumbed to the Buwayhids, a powerful military clan that originated in Shiite Persia (modern-day Iran). Like the Mamluks before them, the Buwayhids allowed the caliph to remain as a puppet. The Buwayhids, in turn, were superseded in 1045 by the Seljuks, a Turkic group from Central Asia. The Seljuks were Sunni Muslims, and so were welcomed in Baghdad as a preferable alternative to Shiite Buwayhids.

The Seljuk Empire lasted until 1155, and at its height, the area that was to become Iraq experienced a minor renaissance. Infrastructure was rebuilt, and science and cultural institutions were refounded in the major cities. However, the Seljuk line was not able to maintain its grip on power for very long. By 1100, local strongmen were already carving out states of their own within the Seljuk territories. Petty dictators rose and fell almost routinely. For example, between 1118 and 1194, nine Seljuk sultans ruled Baghdad. What's more, only one died of natural causes. The rest were killed by the one who came next. Gradually, the Seljuks gave way to local strongmen, who battled among themselves for supremacy in the region. But before anyone could solidify control in the region, the party was crashed by some very unwelcome guests.

Mongol Destruction

In 1258, the first wave of Mongol invaders crossed into Mesopotamia. Led by Hulagu *Khan*, the grandson of Ghengis Khan, the Mongol horde took Baghdad and plundered the riches of the city.

The Mongol invaders weren't interested in adopting the best of local culture and learning. While not the ravaging savages history often portrays them to be, the Mongols were certainly interested in sacking and destroying … and sack and destroy they did. They flattened the major cities they came through, and legend has it that the Khan made a mountain of skulls from the scholars and leaders of Baghdad. They even wrecked the irrigation canals and city walls. Baghdad and the region that would become Iraq were ruled by the Khan from the city of Tabriz, in modern-day Iran.

> **Desert Diction**
>
> The **Khan** was the ruler of a Mongol horde, or army. The Khans also were the political rulers of their empires.

As occupiers, the Mongols eventually converted to Islam, and they became some of its greatest proponents. As the Mongol Empire extended farther and farther, Islam spread as far as western China on one end and into Europe on the other.

> **Desert Diction**
>
> An **atabeg** was a regent who served a prince under the Mongol system of administration. The atabeg was usually in charge of a city or region that then was controlled by a prince, and ultimately, by the Khan. The atabegs had great autonomy within their own administrative control.

The Mongols themselves were unable to maintain control over Mesopotamia for very long. After the death of the last great Khan, in 1355, the region fell to a local dynasty called the Jalayirids. The Jalayirids ruled until about 1400, when they in turn lost their grip on power by another invader from the East (coming out of Central Asia), whose military savagery rivaled that of the Mongols, themselves.

A Lame Invader

A Turkic *atabeg*, or regent, named Timur, emerged from Samarkand, in modern Uzbekistan.

Timur rallied an army of his own and swept out of Central Asia into Mesopotamia, killing as he went. Timur was lame in one leg, and was known as "Timur the Lame" or "Tamerlane."

In 1401, Tamerlane's armies captured Baghdad. Tamerlane made his own mountain of skulls in Baghdad, and succeeded in wiping out much of the culture that had survived the Mongol invasion a century and a half before.

Tamerlane was not a Mongol, but was a Turk. Tamerlane was also, at least on paper, a Sunni Muslim. However, he didn't do much for Islamic culture in Baghdad. Instead, he pillaged most of the cities he conquered and brought the riches and the scholars that survived the initial invasion to his capital. In fact, the city that really flourished was his capital of Samarkand, where magnificent building ensembles like the famous Registan, caravanseries, and madrasas (Islamic schools) were built.

Tamerlane's empire was short-lived; it declined in the years after his death in 1405. Like the Mongols, long-term administration of an empire was not his goal, or his real talent.

> **Increase Your Iraq IQ**
>
> Today, the Uzbeks have a statue of Tamerlane in the center of the capital city of Tashkent, where he is a national hero ... one man's marauder is another man's savior!

Local Bosses Reign for a Time

As Tamerlane's empire disintegrated, local strongmen again rose to fill the void of power in Mesopotamia. Islam took firm root, as the local people struggled to recover what had been lost or taken by the Mongols and Tamerlane. These local rulers were unable to consolidate much more than a small area or a single city. No one emerged to assume control over the whole region.

The area that would come to be called Iraq became a battleground between two neighbors: the Ottomans and the Persians.

By the start of the sixteenth century, the region was in chaos, and a series of small tyrants came and went in the confusion. Into this mix, the Ottomans—about whom you'll be learning more in a minute—and the Persians began to fight for control of the region. The front line in this fight was the border between Ottoman-controlled, Arab territories (now called Iraq) and Persia (now called Iran). This fighting set a pattern that exists to this day: Iraq as the "bulwark" of the Arab world against the Persian world of Iran.

This parallel has deep historical resonance. Although both sides are Muslims, the Arabs are ethnically different from the Persians and speak a different language.

What's more, today most Arab Muslims are Sunni, while most Persian Muslims are Shiite. By the end of the sixteenth century, after the Persians converted to Shiism, the Arab-Persian struggle took on a Sunni-Shiite element as well. The region that became Iraq was a front-line in this struggle, with Sunni and Shiite groups coexisting uneasily (as they still do today).

In This Corner ... the Persians

After Shiite/Sunni split rocked the Abbasid Empire, and the empire began to weaken, outlying territories broke away from Baghdad's central control; the Shiites concentrated in Persia and southern Mesopotamia. The Sunnis were just about everywhere else in the Islamic world.

When Tamerlane left other Turkish groups moved into the vacuum left and took control of the region in 1508. These groups were known as the Safavids, and they were Shiite Muslims. They invaded, in part, because the two Holiest Cities of the Shiites, Najaf and Karbala, are in modern Iraq.

Again: Most of the population of southern Mesopotamia was (and still is) Shiite. The neighboring Ottomans, however, were Sunni Muslims, and they were not happy about the prospect of a new Shiite state on their doorstep.

And in This Corner ... the Ottomans

The Ottomans were a Turkic people who created an empire that emerged from the Byzantine Empire—the old eastern half of the Roman Empire. Initially Christian, the Byzantine Empire eventually gave way to Islamic forces and became the Ottoman Empire. The Ottomans saw no choice but to invade in order to repel the Persian (Shiite) threat to their Turkish (Sunni) Empire.

Increase Your Iraq IQ
The Ottoman Empire lasted from 1301 until 1918. The Ottomans renamed the Byzantine capital of Constantinople as Istanbul when they conquered it in 1453. They created an Islamic empire that stretched across the Bosporus strait into southeastern Europe (stopping at Vienna along the Danube River), and across the Middle East, eventually encompassing Mesopotamia (present-day Iraq) and stopping at Persia (present-day Iran).

The Ottomans, led by Sultan Sulyeman the Great, began to invade from the north and east, and they took control from the Persians by 1534. The Ottomans held a tenuous control of the region that would become Iraq for the next 100 years. In 1623, the Persians were able to capture Baghdad. Under Sultan Murad IV, the Ottomans drove the Persians out for good in 1638. They retained control of the region until World War I.

CAUTION **Oil Spill Ahead** _____

It's easy to get confused about minorities and majorities in the Middle East. Remember that Sunni Muslims are, and have historically been, the majority group throughout the Arab world — but they are and have been for centuries a powerful *minority* in Iraq. Iraq's dominant Sunni Muslims have been compared (by Shiite Muslims, it's worth noting) to white South Africans in the apartheid period.

Occupying Powers and All That

So it was that the Sunnis living in the territory around Baghdad, in the center of what would soon be known as Iraq, held authority over the Shiites in the south and the Kurds (and rural Assyrians) in the north.

These Sunnis found themselves running the show.

The Sunnis didn't have the blessing of either the Shiites or the Kurds to be in charge, but they did have the backing of a powerful foreign occupying power—in this case, the Ottomans. Later on, the British would play a similar role in maintaining Sunni authority. And, interestingly enough, the United States now appears to be doing the same thing today.

Ottoman Control, Kind Of

It's important not be confused into thinking the Ottomans had an iron grip on the region. They ruled loosely for most of the period up through 1830, when they finally solidified their hold over the region under a string of more able (and less corrupt) administrators.

For most of their time in Mesopotamia, the Ottomans were fighting in Europe and against the Persians, and they devoted little time and attention to internal improvements to the part of the region that would become Iraq. There were periods under

Desert Diction

A **sultan** was a ruler in the Ottoman Empire. The sultans assumed political authority over their territories, unlike the Abbasid caliphs who claimed both religious and secular authority.

certain *sultans* where the region would get a greater-than-normal share of attention, but for the most part the old cities languished and power shifted to the rural tribal leaders.

The Ottomans divided the ancient region of Mesopotamia into three administrative districts, called vilayets. The vilayets were Mosul in the north, Baghdad in the middle, and Basra in the south. Mosul had a majority of Kurds, and along with Baghdad was a Sunni region; Basra was Shiite. Taken together, these three vilayets are the forerunner to modern Iraq.

The Ottomans Settle In

From 1750 to 1830, the Mamluks reemerged in the south and established a stable government in the Basra and Baghdad vilayets. (Remember that the Mamluks were the king-makers whose maneuverings at court determined who would be the next caliph.) The Mamluks were able to check the tribal chieftains, but they were not able to extend their control further northward, toward Kurdish territory.

The Ottomans put their foot down in 1831, and pulled the three vilayets together under central control. However, they were not able to exercise real governance until 1869, when Midhat Pasha took control. During his three-year reign, he cleaned up Baghdad, repaired infrastructure, and pacified the tribal chieftains. Midhat also introduced more persistent taxation on the region. (Up to then, the whole idea of taxation had been a hit-or-miss proposition once you got outside the walls of a city.)

Iraq Fact

Midhat Pasha was a powerful Turkish figure of the nineteenth century. Having served effectively as the Ottoman governor of Bulgaria from 1864 to 1869, he was transferred to Baghdad. After three years, Midhat left Baghdad and rose to a position of prominence within the Ottoman Empire, leading a reform-driven revolution in 1876. He was eventually exiled, sent to prison, and killed.

The Rise of Arab Nationalism

The firmer Ottoman grip on the province of Iraq resulted in growing Arab resentment toward the Turkish rulers.

The Arab Iraqi elites in the cities began to identify themselves as Arabs first—in contrast to the Ottomans who were Turkish, and the Persians who were, well, Persian … and Shiite to boot. These tribal leaders weren't able to generate a broad sense of Arab nationalism in Iraq, but the concentrated populations in the cities began to yield a new and influential brand of resentment against foreigners … a resentment deeply connected to one's (Sunni) Arab identity.

These elites didn't lead a popular rebellion against the Ottomans. This was due mainly to the fact that Ottoman authority over the region was still, for many people, a matter of abstract, and not particularly meaningful, political theory—rather than an important fact of everyday life.

The Ottomans, however, were not the only empire seeing to their interests in the region. There was another group of foreigners to contend with; the British invaded during World War I as part of their conflict with the Ottomans.

> **Increase Your Iraq IQ**
>
> The forerunners to the Arab nationalists (who emerged in the 1930s) in the province of Iraq were wealthy urban merchants, scholars, and religious leaders. It was the members of these elites who chafed most at the presence of Ottoman (and later, British) outsiders who "administered" their lands.

Superpowers Screw Up in Iraq: The Beginning of a Very Long Story

One of the most striking themes of life in post-Ottoman Iraq is the extraordinary series of mistakes and miscalculations made by Western superpowers seeking power and influence in the region without concern for (or knowledge of) ancient social groups and institutions. These errors compounded a steadily more irreparable "disconnect" between local peoples and the Western governments. This is the Big Theme known as the "Compound Error." We will look at this Big Theme more in later chapters.

The destabilizing pattern got its start under the British in the early part of the twentieth century. The Brits viewed Iraq essentially as a geographic means to an end: the development of a land route to India. The United States would make similarly shortsighted mistakes as the years progressed, resulting in a rising tide of Iraqi resentment against the West.

Enter the Bulldog

By the start of the twentieth century, the Ottoman Empire was failing—and was widely known as the "Sick Man of Europe." European powers, notably Britain and Germany, began to covet Ottoman holdings. Along with the Ottoman administrators, the British began to make their presence felt in Iraq, much to the dismay of the budding Arab nationalists.

Imperial Britain was interested in protecting the jewel in its crown: India. The most obvious hurdle, beyond the sheer distance between London and Bombay, was the fact that there was no easy land route to India from Britain.

The British had set up a steamship company in 1861 that ran from the Gulf up the Shatt-al-Arab to Basra. This company would be able to transfer people and material more easily across Mesopotamia to Iran, Afghanistan, and ultimately to India.

Further, the British wanted to maintain a secure air route to India, and they needed secure refueling stops in the Middle East. Remember that airplanes in the early part of the twentieth century navigated more by ground landmarks and flew much shorter distances between refueling stops.

England and Germany: The Major-Power Shuffle

The British also had to contend with the Germans, who were pushing their own agenda in Iraq. The Germans wanted to build a railroad from Berlin to Baghdad that would have given Germany the commercial and strategic advantage in the region. The Germans succeeded in getting a concession from the Ottomans in 1899 to build a railroad from Konya in modern Turkey, to Baghdad. They were able to extend this concession from Baghdad to Basra by 1902. Their ultimate goal was to run the railway all the way to the Persian Gulf port of Kuwait.

The British tried to block this deal, but could do little to prevent it in the end. Ultimately, the British simply worked around the official Ottoman concession to Germany; they struck treaties with the tribal chieftains in Basra vilayet, with an eye toward keeping their own steamship route open … and slowing down German rail construction.

Black Gold: The Beginning of the Oil Economy

Then there came a fateful twist in the story. It was black and it oozed from the ground.

The British realized, around the turn of the century, that there were extensive oil deposits in the region, and their interest in the area duly increased. Over time, the problem of controlling oil reserves became as important as, if not more important than, the problem of maintaining a link to India. The problem of building good relations with the people actually living in the region, however, never seemed to rise very high on the list of priorities.

In 1901, the British obtained a concession from the Ottomans to take oil from Ottoman territories. Under the terms of the concession agreement, the British exacted favorable terms from the Ottomans for exporting the oil they took from the region. In 1912, the British created the Turkish Petroleum Company to pump oil in the Ottoman territories (including the province of Iraq), and the Anglo-Persian Oil Company to extract oil from modern-day Iran.

These two companies quickly built up oil fields and refineries in the region. The main production areas were in modern-day Iran, but oil was also discovered around Mosul, in northern modern-day Iraq.

British oil concessions with the Ottomans and others in the Middle East typically included an agreement that Britain would provide military protection for the sheikhdoms that signed on. Of course, protecting the local kingdoms also meant protecting British investments there, so the military protection was an easy commitment to make. Even before the military protocol had been signed, Britain had had no problem sending in troops when its interests were threatened in the Middle East.

Iraq Fact

Britain has no oil of its own, and its new industries were demanding more and more of the stuff. In addition, the new Lord of the Admiralty, Winston Churchill, decided that the Royal Navy should use oil in its ships instead of coal, so oil suddenly became a key interest of the British.

The Great War Brings a New Boss

The practice of Western military intervention in the Middle East to ensure the steady flow of oil to the West did not start in 1990. The British patented the idea 76 years before the Americans perfected it.

The Ottoman Empire entered World War I as an ally of Germany and Austria-Hungary in 1914. The British were deeply concerned by this development, because their Turkish Petroleum Company holdings were now in enemy territory. In response, the British landed a division of troops from Iran and India in the southern part of Iraq, at Faw on the Persian Gulf. This division marched north up the Shatt-al-Arab, reaching Basra in November 1914. Despite intense Ottoman resistance, the British division managed to reach Baghdad by March 1917.

Even after the armistice between the British and Ottomans was signed in October 1918, the British continued their expansion northward toward the oil-rich areas around Mosul, eventually occupying that city in November 1918. From that point forward, the Ottomans ceased to be the authority in Iraq.

After 500 years of occasionally distracted dominance in Iraq, the Ottomans were out, and Britain was in. The question was, how would this latest outsider respond to the emerging challenges of the Arab world?

The British Stoke the Fires

In the next chapter, we'll look in depth at the nature and consequences of the British military intervention in Iraq, and we'll see how British imperial policies in Iraq helped to foster a growing Arab nationalism and an increasingly anti-Western outlook. Both developments, of course, would continue to play out for decades—intensified, frequently, by Western bluster and shortsightedness: what I call the "Compound Error."

The Least You Need to Know

- The Arabs brought Islam to Iraq, and Baghdad flowered under Arab Islamic culture from 700 C.E. to about 1100 C.E.

- The Mongols and Tamerlane destroyed much of the accomplishments of the earlier Arab culture.

- The Ottomans and the Persians battled for control over Mesopotamia. The region was the border between the Arab and Persian worlds and the Sunni and Shiite sects of Islam.

- As the Ottoman Empire weakened (the infamous "Sick Man of Europe"), Britain and Germany began to extend their imperial reach into the region.

- The British (and other West European powers and eventually the United States) obtained oil concessions and set up oil companies in the region to export the oil at very favorable terms.

- The British took over from the Ottomans at the end of World War I and started a cycle of mistakes that would intensify Arab nationalism and anti-Western feeling for decades to come.

Chapter 6

Lines on a Map

In This Chapter

- ◆ World War I
- ◆ The birth of the modern state of Iraq
- ◆ The British tend to their interests

The story of Western colonialism and imperialism in Asia, Africa, the Middle East, and the Americas is long and sordid. It involved Western powers such as Britain, France, Germany, and the United States taking economic and political control over weaker or underdeveloped countries in order to exploit their natural resources. Such practices had profound, and often negative, impacts on the weaker countries, many of which haven't fully recovered to this day.

We'll only be touching on a small part of the wretched history of imperialism by taking a look at how the British consolidated their power in the soon-to-be-founded state of Iraq.

British Imperialism

British imperialism in Iraq accelerated three important processes that would play out for decades to come:

♦ Sunni control over the territory now called Iraq—despite the Shiite majority within the new country's borders

♦ Increasing local Iraqi resistance to non-Iraqi rulers placed over them

♦ The emergence of increasingly violent anti-Western sentiment

World War I

In the previous chapter, we saw how the British became interested in Mesopotamia, first as a link in their communications chain to India, and then as a source of newly important oil.

However, things got messy for the Brits when the Ottomans entered World War I on the German side. The Turkish Oil Company holdings in Mesopotamia were immediately threatened by the Ottoman action. In response, the British moved troops into the region to protect their oil operations and their link to India.

The military action in the province of Iraq was fierce. In 1916, the Ottomans captured the entire British 6th Division (of thousands of men) after a bloody 140-day siege at Al Kut.

General Maude, who led the British troops, declared that the British would support Arab independence after the end of the war, in return for their support against the Ottomans during the war. The Arabs agreed, throwing their support behind the British to fight off the Ottomans who ruled over them. The British regrouped and took Baghdad and Mosul by 1918.

Lawrence and the Arabs

British military fortunes were aided by the efforts of T. E. Lawrence, also known as Lawrence of Arabia, who organized Arab tribal fighters into an effective force. In 1918, Lawrence and his Arab allies succeeded in capturing Damascus before the British army even got there.

An idealistic and energetic man in his 20s, Lawrence embodied the promise of British imperial support to the Arabs in the region. Like the Arabs, he grew disillusioned when the British did not make good on their promises of Arab independence after the Great War ended. The concept of "Arabism" was a relatively recent invention of the late nineteenth and early twentieth centuries, one that paralleled the emergence of other national identities. The British appealed to this sense of being "Arab" to help rally support against the Germans.

Increase Your Iraq IQ

Thomas Edward Lawrence (1888–1935) was a British Military Intelligence Service officer stationed in Cairo at the start of World War I. Lawrence cultivated a strong bond with Prince Faisal (later King Faisal of Iraq), a member of a powerful Hashemite family. During the war, Lawrence organized and fought alongside these Arab allies against the Ottoman armies in the region. After the war, Lawrence remained in the region, in the Middle East division of the British Colonial Office. Disillusioned when the British did not grant independence to their former Arab allies, Lawrence resigned his commission and spent the next few years out of the spotlight. Probably looking for new adventures, he enlisted in the Royal Air Force under an assumed name in 1925. After his discharge, he died in a motorcycle accident in England in 1935. His story was the basis of a number of popular works, including the Oscar-winning film *Lawrence of Arabia*. Lawrence authored several books expressing his views on the Arab world at that time, including *Seven Pillars of Wisdom* and *Revolt in the Desert*.

Mandate, Not Independence

At the end of World War I, the Ottoman Empire was defeated, and the British were in control of former Ottoman holdings in the Middle East. In Iraq, British imperial troops occupied the main cities of Basra, Baghdad, and Mosul (these three cities were the capitals for the Ottoman vilayets that bore their names).

After the Treaty of Versailles that ended World War I was signed, the future of the Middle East (including Iraq) was settled at the San Remo Conference. The League of Nations took over the administration of the territories of the defeated German and the Ottoman Empires. These territories were called Mandates, and were placed under the control of a European ally until the country could govern independently.

Europeans Divide the Spoils and Draw (Dumb) Borders

The French got control of what was soon to be called Syria, while the British got Palestine, Saudi Arabia, and Iraq. They already had control of Persia (later known as Iran).

The borders of these regions were drawn in blissful ignorance of local realities. The Europeans drew straight lines for most of the boundaries, assuming that the deserts they were drawn through were unpopulated. They were wrong on that account, and the new countries were immediately saddled with tribal strife as members of the same clan were divided by national boundaries, while rival clans were joined within the same region.

The boundaries that were drawn for Iraq were particularly disruptive of traditional trading and tribal patterns. To the south, the border between Saudi Arabia, Kuwait, and Iraq was a series of straight lines. The border included a diamond-shaped "Neutral Zone" between Saudi Arabia and Iraq, and an almost diamond-shaped Kuwait next to that.

The line between Iraq and Kuwait separated the city of Basra from its long-time trading partner, the coastal city of Kuwait (for which the new country of Kuwait was named). Furthermore, the Neutral Zone became a source of friction over potential oil reserves there. Further northward, the boundary between Saudi Arabia and Iraq sliced through the old Baghdad vilayet, and divided traditional tribal territories with an international border.

CAUTION **Oil Spill Ahead** _____

If the British had set up a formal committee to find a mistake that would amplify their initial alienating approach to Iraq—treating it, in essence, as a convenient doorway to India—that committee couldn't have come up with a more high-handed alternative than the British policy choices that immediately followed World War I. Arab leaders were denied the independence they had been promised as incentive to fight alongside British forces, and borderlines that ignored social and cultural were instituted. As a result, local aspirations and cultural allegiances were effectively ignored.

The British also cobbled together the Sunni Baghdad vilayet and Shiite Basra vilayet. At first, the Mosul vilayet was not part of Iraq, but the British became alarmed by Turkey's claims to the Mosul vilayet—Turkey had recently been formed from the remains of the Ottoman Empire—and so included Mosul in the Iraq Mandate by 1925. The boundaries and ethnic and religious makeup of modern Iraq were set.

The Iraqis received "Class A" Mandate status according to Article 22 of the League of Nations Covenant, which meant that it was intended to become an independent country in a few years' time.

Iraqi Reaction

The Iraqi leadership—the wealthy elites in the cities, who were Ottomans (non-Arab), and the tribal leaders, who were Arab—was dismayed by the broken promises of the British. They had expected that the 1919 Paris Peace Conference that resulted in the Treaty of Versailles would also result in the immediate creation of independent

Arab states. Instead, the Paris Peace Conference left it to a later conference, at San Remo, to define borders of the Arab Mandates that would eventually become modern states.

The British appointed Sir Percy Cox to serve as high commissioner, or leader, of the Iraq Mandate, and he was assisted by Colonel Arnold Talbot Wilson. Cox was soon embroiled in all the local problems of the Iraqi state, from infrastructure repair to tribal conflict. Cox eventually was dispatched to Iran from 1918 to 1920, leaving Wilson in charge. Wilson originally came from India's imperial administration, and he promoted a number of Indians to responsible positions in the Iraqi government. In retrospect, this was a foolish and high-handed choice that further alienated the Iraqis.

The Mandate was strained from the beginning. A British officer, for instance, was ambushed and killed in the Shiite Holy City of Najaf, leading to bloody reprisals.

Repercussions

The Iraq Mandate was finalized at the San Remo Conference, on April 25, 1920. In July 1920, the local Iraqi nationalist leadership learned of the Mandate's final adoption, and they attacked the British troops still stationed in Iraq.

Led by secret societies made up of scholars, religious leaders, and merchants, the *Rebellion of July 1920* started in Mosul and soon spread across the territory.

The rebellion failed, but that was almost beside the point. The new state was bringing tribal leaders together, but hardly in the way the British had hoped.

Iraq Fact

Prince Faisal, one of the Hashemite Arab heroes of the rebellion against the Ottomans, attended the Conference expecting to participate in the planning of Arab independence. Instead, Faisal was largely ignored.

Oil Spill Ahead

The British failed to incorporate local Iraqi elites into their new government in Iraq. Instead, they imported still more foreigners (this time Indians) to assume roles in the new bureaucracy. Needless to say, this move did nothing to endear the British commissioners to the local population.

Desert Diction

The **Rebellion of July 1920** was an important event in modern Iraqi history. The British ultimately put down the rebellion, but the uprising featured Sunni and Shiite leaders, and cities and rural dwellers, working together against the occupying British.

The British Abandon the Mandate

After the Rebellion, the British decided, for both logistical and financial reasons, that the Mandate period had to end, and that the time had come for Iraq to be in charge of its own affairs. (In name, at least. Britain still hoped to be able to control Iraqi policy from behind the scenes.)

To lead the new nation, the British selected Prince Faisal, the friendly son of the *Hashemite* Hussein ibn Ali. Prince Faisal had become King Faisal of Syria in 1920, but was removed from that role by the French when they assumed control of the Syria Mandate in 1920. The British plucked Faisal off the bench, and put him in charge of Iraq in 1921. The British arranged a plebiscite, with only one question on the ballot; it resulted in Faisal's "election," with 96 percent of the vote.

While the Hashemite claims of descent from Mohammed probably helped with the Sunni portion of the population, they didn't inspire allegiance from the Shiite majority in Iraq, who didn't recognize the authority of the sharif of Mecca, anyway. The British, however, decided that it was more important to appeal to the Sunnis.

The new Hashemite monarchy immediately entered into a treaty with Britain that guaranteed the monarchy would "consult" with the British on foreign affairs, and any affairs that related to British oil concessions.

> **Desert Diction**
>
> The *Hashemite* royal family installed in Iraq was, not surprisingly, pro-British. The family included the sharif of Mecca, and claimed to be descended from Mohammed. The British assumed, somewhat naively, that this fact would somehow legitimize the monarchy. However, the Hashemite kings were not from Iraq, and this fact alone doomed the monarchy from the start.

> **Increase Your Iraq IQ**
>
> Hussein ibn Ali (not related to Saddam) was sharif of Mecca. The sharif was considered to be the descendent of Mohammed, and his family was powerful and well respected in the hijaz (the area that would later become part of Saudi Arabia). Hussein's son, Faisal, was a prince alongside Lawrence during the march into Damascus. This same Faisal later became King of Syria (for a year) and then King of Iraq. Faisal's son Ghazi and his son Faisal II also ruled in Iraq.

The British Make a Fateful Choice

When the British determined to set up a king in Iraq, they also decided to prop him up with a locally recruited army, rather then rely on British imperial troops. This decision was critical, as the Iraqi army became a vital force in the decades leading up to the overthrow of the Iraqi monarchy (see Chapter 9). In an attempt to accommodate the Sunni majorities in the countries surrounding the new Iraq (every other Arab country and Turkey), the British set up Sunnis in leadership positions in the army and government bureaucracy. The Shiites, the majority in the new state of Iraq, made up the rank and file of the army—but they were commanded by Sunnis.

Guiding principle: The British weren't particularly big on listening or inclusiveness at this point in their imperial history.

The army would prove to be a critical force in modern Iraq. First, the new army officer corps provided stability to the (foreign) monarch the British selected. (Later in Iraqi history, however, the military would provide the leaders of a series of coups.)

Faisal's Uneasy Rule

King Faisal ibn Hussein I ruled from 1921 to 1933. As you might imagine, Faisal suffered from a chronic legitimacy problem. He was not granted full authority (the British also created a national parliament), he was not Iraqi, and he was considered (with some justification) to be a British puppet. Faisal's regime was wracked by outside pressures from Turkey (still coveting Mosul) and internal resistance from tribal leaders who had never really been totally subdued during or after World War I. (Remember that during the Ottoman period, the tribal leaders were essentially left to their own devices.)

The treaty that Faisal signed with the British basically dictated that Iraq would remain economically and politically dependent on Britain. The treaty also earned the disdain of the Iraqi elites, who considered their leadership to be traitors to the Iraqi nationalist cause.

Iraq Fact

The British took care not to fully enfranchise the Shiite majority. The British figured that a Sunni-controlled state was more palatable to Iraq's neighbors, and would ultimately support the uninterrupted flow of oil.

Oil Spill Ahead

The British didn't bother to discuss important matters with affected local Arab leaders when Iraq was formed. Instead, the British allied themselves to the old Ottoman elites who remained in the area. This disregard for local Arab desires eventually contributed to open rebellions against Britain and the governments it maneuvered into place in Iraq.

Leaving the Kurds Out in the Cold

Flashback time: During World War I, British victory in the Middle East was far from certain, and British policy makers were looking for support wherever they could find it. The British had told the Kurds that they would get Mosul vilayet as part of an independent Kurdish state.

However, once oil was discovered in the Mosul area, and with the Turks threatening the Mosul vilayet from the north, the British incorporated Mosul into the new Iraqi state in 1925.

CAUTION

Oil Spill Ahead

In yet another compound error, the British made conflicting promises that could never be honored. During the height of the fighting in World War I, the British had promised the Kurds that they would have an independent state in return for their support against the Ottomans. However, the British had also promised the Arabs that they would gain their independence. It was, of course, impossible to give the same land to two different groups of people.

The Kurds were left out in the cold, and were denied their independence. Indeed, the disgruntled Kurdish minority found itself subject to a new (and utterly alien) monarchy.

The Kurds found themselves spread among Iran, Iraq, and Turkey, with no homeland of their own. This "solution" was to have profound consequences for modern Iraq.

Including Mosul meant oil wealth for the Iraqi state, but it also meant a large group of angry Kurds inside Iraq's borders. This situation further necessitated a powerful domestic (Sunni-led) army to help keep the country together.

Desert Diction

Levies were indigenous troops considered part of the British armed forces. The levies were conscripted soldiers (literally "levies" were placed on the local population to provide recruits). The levies were not considered as fully skilled as their British counterparts.

Leaving the Assyrians Out in the Cold, Too

Like the Kurds, the Assyrians in northwest Iraq had been promised independence if they supported the British against the Ottomans. The Assyrians were Christians, and because of this, the British assumed that they were somehow superior to the Muslim Iraqis.

The Assyrians were formed into separate army units and allowed to keep their weapons after the British dissolved the old Iraqi *levies* in place of the new Iraqi army. Assyrians fleeing from a brutal Turkish regime were given lands in the historic Kurdish homeland to settle on. The Assyrians, armed and hostile to the Kurds, relied on the British to help them gain their own homeland. However, like the Kurds, the Assyrians were shut out during the country-creating San Remo Conference.

Iraq and a Hard Place

It all added up to a nearly impossible-to-manage domestic political situation.

Faisal I did his best to moderate between British demands and local realities. He was mindful of how the French had tossed him out of Syria, and he wanted to stay in power in Iraq as long as possible. He made sure the British wishes were carried out, and that the oil kept flowing. The nationalists were too busy competing amongst themselves for power to mount effective resistance to the monarchy.

The treaty with Britain called for a nationally elected assembly, a first for Iraq. The elections were held, and the National Assembly convened in 1925. As it turned out, the Sunnis and some Kurds held authority in the executive branch and the army, while the Shiite tribal leaders held power in the National Assembly. As a practical matter, the National Assembly enacted laws that did little more than create prolonged, regional debates.

The British maintained their control through the divide-and-conquer policy: a semi-strong monarch, an ineffective parliament, and internal power struggles among the potential opposition. While this policy might have appeared to make sense at the time, it didn't address the growing resentment of the British role in Iraq.

Independence, at Last

After years of lobbying and negotiations between the British and the Iraqi monarchy, Iraq was finally admitted to the League of Nations on October 13, 1932, as a fully independent nation. Of course, the British still had a stranglehold on the economy and the political organization of the state, but Iraq had won its place in the community of nations.

In 1933, however, the picture changed dramatically. The pro-British Faisal I died, and his son, Ghazi ibn Faisal, an Arab nationalist and anti-British, took the throne. Ghazi was an adherent of pan-Arabism (discussed in Chapter 1), and he favored an alliance of Arab countries. The new king signed a nonaggression treaty with Saudi Arabia in 1936. (Remember that Ghazi's family was related to the sharifs of Mecca, so the agreement with Saudi Arabia was easily signed.)

Even Ghazi's Arab nationalism didn't save him from the same illegitimacy that haunted his father's regime. In fact, Ghazi continued his father's practice of making decisions behind closed doors. Rather than reach out to the local elites, he excluded them from policy making.

The First Coup

Ultimately, Ghazi's regime was rocked by a *coup d'e'tat* (Iraq's first of many) in 1936. The army officers, led by Bakr al Sidqi, staged the coup that put in place a coalition government that included Kurdish and Shiite leaders, along with the Sunni elites.

Desert Diction

Coup d'e'tat is French for "state stroke." A coup, or change of government, is initiated by a small group and almost always involves military officers. This small group suddenly takes power, displaying and using enough force to remove (usually kill or exile) the current leaders, and inserts a new leader instead. Coups occur by surprise; coup leaders don't consult with the general population before taking power.

Ghazi had no choice but to accept the new government in order to keep his throne. This coalition government was the first truly pluralist government in Iraq. It wasn't popularly elected, but it did include the main constituencies that comprised the new state. The post-coup coalition had two factions: the Shiite and Kurdish leaders who wanted to focus on internal reforms such as land ownership and laws, and the military leaders, who wanted to expand the power of Iraq. There were no pan-Arabs in the new government to argue for brotherhood with fellow Arab states.

The coalition government reached a treaty with Iran that recognized the border between Iran and Iraq to be the middle of the Shatt-al-Arab channel. Up to that point, the border was the Iranian shore, an arrangement that had given Iraq at least nominal control of the waterway.

The coalition didn't survive very long. The Shiite leadership simply could not tolerate Sidqi's policies, and eventually he was assassinated by a group of army officers in 1937. The new nationalist government also made plans for the first Iraqi invasion of Kuwait in 1939. The Iraqi leadership saw Kuwait as a former province of Iraq—even though the British had created an independent monarchy there as well. In the Ottoman days, the region had been closely connected with the Basra vilayet, and the Iraqi nationalists felt that the British had unjustly withheld Kuwait from their new state.

The Ghazi regime was preparing the invasion of Kuwait when the king was killed in, of all things, a car accident. The invasion was postponed in the confusion, and the plans were dropped altogether when World War II broke out.

The Least You Need to Know

- The British established a Mandate in Iraq following World War I to maintain control of the oil in the region.

- The British withdrew from the Mandate in a few years' time; formal independence for Iraq, however, did not come about until 1932.

- The British set up a non-Iraqi Sunni monarch in Iraq, with a weak national assembly to check his power.

- The monarchy and the post-coup government took a decidedly anti-British bias in the 1930s.

- The British intervened in Iraq when it suited them to safeguard their oil interests.

Chapter 7

West Is West: The British and the Americans

In This Chapter

- ◆ The errors and weakness of the pro-British regime in Iraq
- ◆ The rise of anti-British political and revolutionary groups
- ◆ The push to keep more of the oil riches in Iraq
- ◆ The Americans step in

Nationalism can take odd forms in a newborn country whose borders are determined by centuries of overseers from other lands, and whose residents are deeply suspicious of one another even at the best of times.

In this chapter, the uneasy balancing act that is modern Iraq comes into clearer view … as does a deeper understanding of its steadily intensifying hostility toward the West.

Arab Nationalism: Convenient to the West (for the Moment)

As we'll see later in the book, the quickening fire of Arab nationalism helped Lawrence of Arabia rally an Arab army to the British cause in World War I, when the British promised Arab independence in return for Arab military support.

In the end, however, the British did *not* deliver the independence they had promised. At the end of World War I, England was triumphant, but the people of the Middle East were still being ruled by outsiders.

The failure by the British to follow through quickly on the expectations of independence they had manipulated during World War I was among the most serious of their errors during the period. This failure, in fact, was one of the chief reasons that British policy alienated Arab nationalists in the period following World War I.

Iraq Fact

Eventually, Arab nationalists in Iraq came to see the objective of getting the British out of the Middle East as similar to the earlier effort to get the Ottomans out of the region.

Western mistakes in the Middle East in general, and in Iraq in particular, were starting to gather a kind of cumulative force.

In this case, the escalating "value" of Western errors in the region could eventually be calculated in lost diplomatic opportunities, the alienation of key Iraqi elites, and (scariest of all) a tilt toward Hitler.

The foundation for an serious "disconnect" was being laid.

Another War, a Different Attitude

By the beginning of World War II, a coalition government had taken control in Iraq. It was led by Premier (and Sunni Iraqi Army General) Nuri as-Said.

This coalition was the first-ever governing combination of the three groups that constitute the modern state of Iraq. There were Shiite tribal leaders, Sunni officers and merchants, and Kurd leaders in the coalition.

In March 1940, though, Said's government was replaced through election by a stronger Arab nationalist coalition led by the new premier, Rashid Ali al-Gailani. Gailani, a Sunni, was one of an emerging group of nationalists dedicated to an independent Arab nation ... and to getting the British out of the region.

As a result, Gailani's government immediately adopted an anti-British stance, and stopped implementing the full terms of the 1930 Anglo-Iraqi friendship treaty.

Iraq Defies the British

The British pressed Gailani's government to fulfill the terms of the alliance treaty. In response to this affront to their national independence, the Iraqi military leadership (made up of Sunnis, and many Arab nationalists) revolted April 30, 1941.

The army leadership installed Gailani as the head of a new regime that was now openly pro-Axis, and defiantly anti-British. Gailani then alarmed the British (who still garrisoned troops in the country) by trying to impose limits on British troop movements inside Iraq. (From the nationalist Iraqi point of view, of course, limiting the troop movements of a foreign army stationed inside one's own borders seemed a perfectly appropriate exercise of national sovereignty.)

> **CAUTION** **Oil Spill Ahead** _____
>
> The mistakes that compounded after World War I, including the failure to deliver quickly on expectations of independence, contributed to the rise of Iraqi nationalism. That nationalism, in turn, led to a decidedly pro-Axis government in Iraq at the start of World War II. The British were faced with the same problems they had encountered in Iraq in World War I: a hostile government threatening both the flow of oil and communications with India.

The Bulldog Barks

Britain responded to Iraqi resistance in the same way it had during World War I: British troops from Iran and India were dispatched to Iraq.

They arrived at Basra, and on May 2, 1941, war broke out between British and Iraqi forces. In a remarkably quick capitulation, the Iraqis surrendered on May 31, 1941, just four weeks after the fighting began. (Sound familiar?)

Compounding a by-now familiar error, the British perpetuated a local government that was not led by locals. Instead, the British continued to throw their weight behind a Hashemite, non-Iraqi, monarch whose biggest political handicap, among a torrent of competing handicaps, was probably his age. (More on that in a moment.)

Increase Your Iraq IQ

On June 1, 1941, in the aftermath of the British victory, a campaign of terror by Iraqi "soldiers and civilians" was unleashed against a small delegation of Jews who had journeyed to Baghdad to greet the regent there. The violence followed an abortive attempt by one Yunis Al Sabawi, a Nazi sympathizer, to slaughter all Jews in central Iraq. (He was deported before he could carry out the plan.)

The spasm of violence was part of a two-day descent into chaos now known in Iraq as the *Farhud* (dangerous collapse of order).

A Foreign Monarchy

Remember, the Hashemite royal family installed in Iraq when the British abandoned the Mandate was, not surprisingly, pro-British. However, the Hashemite kings were Saudi, not Iraqi, and this fact alone doomed the monarchy from the start.

Iraq Fact

The British were willing to fight in Iraq in World War II when there were so many other battles raging because Iraq was important to the Allied War effort as a source of oil, and as a transshipment point for war materials going to the Soviet Union.

Look once again at the situation the British had engineered: An artificial country found itself with artificial leadership imposed from the outside—leadership incapable of commanding the respect of the majority of its citizens.

During World War II, the defects of the puppet-show became steadily more obvious … and steadily more difficult for nationalist forces in Iraq to stand.

Iraq and the Allies

In addition to throwing their weight behind the Hashemites, the British installed a provisional pro-British government (excluding the recently elected anti-British National Assembly). Later the British backed a new government formed by Nuri as-Said, the long-time friend of Britain.

The Said government promptly declared war on Germany and its allies on January 17, 1943, and was touted by the Allies as the prime example of an "independent" Arab state fighting against the Axis.

And a Little Child Shall Lead Them ... Not

What was the biggest problem the Hashemite royal family faced during this period? It had to do with the calendar.

At the death of his father, Gazhi ibn Faisal, in 1939, Faisal ibn Gazhi (Faisal II) was informed that he was the new king of Iraq. However, at the time of his father's death, Faisal was only three years old, and only nine at the end of World War II. The monarchy was controlled by a regent, Amir Abd al Ilah, who was Ghazi's first cousin.

The authority of the regime was diminished for a number of reasons, among them the fact that until Faisal, the peoples in question had not been ruled by a king for more than 1,000 years.

Even a strong, capable, shrewd, and occasionally visible monarch would have had a tough time asserting authority in this situation. A nine-year-old boy had no chance. The national assembly, controlled by the military, commercial, and religious leadership, did its best to assert daily authority in Iraq.

This was not always easy, given the predations of the British.

"Sure, You've Got a Government. Just Don't Do Anything We Don't Approve of ..."

Most attempts at Iraqi self-government during this period were effectively undermined by the British.

Under the terms of the 1930 agreement between the two countries, the British essentially controlled the Iraqi transportation system and several key ministries, including, not surprisingly, those that oversaw oil production.

The Iraqi government was obliged to consult with Britain on foreign affairs, and was forbidden to take any foreign policy actions of which the British disapproved.

Cracks in the Facade

Although the government was dominated by Britain, that hold was tenuous. The National Assembly had bitterly debated the 1930 Treaty with Britain—but eventually ratified it. There had been fights in the parliament chambers during the debates.

The same Iraqi elites who dominated the parliament in 1930 (Shiite and Sunni tribal leaders) and the military (Sunni city leaders and a few Kurdish leaders), and had united in the 1936 coup, were in power during the 1940s. Their affection for Britain was certainly strained, and the British could not rely on the local leadership for very much support.

The clock was ticking.

Britain Gets the Postwar Imperial Blues

The truth was that after World War II concluded, the British found the Iraqis increasingly difficult to control. The support of the parliament and army was lukewarm at best, the monarch was a child, and the regent, Amir Abd al Ilah, turned out to be an Arab nationalist.

Here and elsewhere in the world, British imperial authority went into severe decline, due to the costs of maintaining an empire, coupled with the staggering costs of the just won victory in World War II.

CAUTION **Oil Spill Ahead** _____

As they had in World War I, the British made conflicting promises to a number of parties during World War II. The offer: greater independence in return for support against the Axis. This time the promises were made to both the Palestinians and the Jews living in the Palestine Mandate. This promise to Arab and Zionist groups, coupled with moral revulsion at the scope of the Holocaust, led to the creation of Israel after the war, and the next defining element of modern Iraq: opposition to Israel.

Previews of Coming Attractions: Nationalism Rises ... and a Strongman Holds Court

After the war, the leadership in Iraq was made up of wealthy merchants, scholars, clerics, and army officers. Many of them were Arab nationalists whose goal was true Iraqi independence from the West. Some nationalist groups were inspired by movements in other countries, some groups represented local divisions of international movements (the Ba'th Party was an example) and some, like the Kurds, agitated for their own independence from Iraq, and thus were against its current regime.

The prime minister, Nuri as-Said, however, suppressed virtually all overt political activity. The government didn't even allow political parties until 1946. Even afterward, the government was very heavy-handed with opposing parties, and most legal forms of dissent in the press or political arena were not tolerated. Without such avenues of protest, dissent went underground and became more revolutionary. Even the more moderate groups of the intelligentsia were radicalized by the tough tactics of the Said government, which was the ruling government for most of the post-WWII era.

The Iraqi leadership, ever conscious of its weak grip on power, responded by closing off debate and making policy decisions behind closed doors. The leadership circle effectively cut out the majority of the officials in the government who represented the Iraqi people.

This closed decision-making process was a portent of things to come.

Tough Times for the Hashemite Monarchy

The alienation of the Iraqi elites occurred at several levels. The intelligentsia were more inspired by pan-Arabism than by any Iraqi-developed political movements. The army had attempted an abortive coup during World War II, and had suffered chronic underfunding and close scrutiny by the government ever since. Even before World War II, the Free Officers Movement—a group of officers dedicated to full Iraqi independence—had been strong among the military leadership. And the Shiite tribal leaders, for their part, were dismayed by the heavy-handed Sunni leadership.

The one thing *all* the leading Iraqi players seemed to agree on, though, was a distaste for the Hashemite (Saudi) monarchy.

The alienation of the general population went even deeper. They saw their standard of living sink by the day, with little hope for improvement. The country's economic situation had been bad before World War II and only got worse in the decade following the war, as oil revenues spurred inflation—but not real wages.

Economic Woes, Economic Colonialism

The government's legitimacy was sorely tested by economic troubles. The domestic economy was beset by high inflation, bureaucratic corruption, and an increasing rift between the Regent (Abd al Ilah) and the Nuri as-Said government. The two could not agree on common economic policies and political initiatives that could have led to meaningful infrastructure improvements, and public works devolved into petty squabbling between the tribal factions in the parliament.

Meanwhile, marginal harvests and a land policy that allowed the tribal leaders to export most crops to the British (rather than feed their own people) compounded the misery of the rural population.

In the cities, an emerging middle class found little economic opportunity, and inflation attacked the real value of salaries.

Economic policy centered on the oil industry, which was now controlled by the British, French, and Americans. The Iraq Petroleum Company (IPC) continued to be dominated by a consortium of British, French, and finally U.S. oil companies. To the Iraqi resistance movements, the oil concessions that enabled these Western oil companies to develop Iraqi oil fields were just a thinly veiled form of colonialism.

This pattern was the same in the other countries in the region. Iran, Saudi Arabia, Kuwait, and the other Gulf states all had Western-dominated oil companies.

While oil revenues gradually climbed over time, they didn't help the vast majority of ordinary Iraqis. After the Said government renegotiated the Iraqi share from 20 percent to 50 percent of revenues in 1952, Iraqi oil receipts jumped from $32 million in 1951 to $112 million in 1952. The increased cash flow, however, only lined the pockets of government officials. Little was devoted to infrastructure projects or development programs. Iraq's oil boom stood in stark contrast to the poverty of its people.

> **Increase Your Iraq IQ**
>
> The export economy, both for oil and food, was a signature element of colonialism. The colonial power (in this case Britain), takes raw materials from the colonized country, without compensating that country to the full value of the materials extracted. The Iraqi economy simply could not support that kind of strain, particularly in drought years, when crops failed.

> **Oil Spill Ahead**
>
> High-handed Western dominance of the Middle Eastern oil industry, based on past concessions, inflamed passions in Iraq and many other countries in the region. Anti-Western feeling grew.

Open Rebellion

The Portsmouth Treaty, signed in 1948, once again defined the relationship between Iraq and Britain in a way that was completely in Britain's favor. The agreement required Iraq and Britain to reach an agreement on all matters pertaining to Iraqi defense. Basically, Iraq could not make any defense treaties on its own. The Treaty severely compromised Iraqi sovereignty, and outraged Iraqi nationalists.

Opposition openly erupted in 1948, in what came to be called the Wathbah Rebellion. The nationalists were outraged by the Portsmouth Treaty signed earlier that year; they had finally had enough of decisions being made without their agreement.

The rebellion probably had as much to do with Iraq's increasing economic woes as the lower oil revenues due to the closing of the Haifa pipeline during the *Israel War*.

More than 40 percent of oil receipts that were left were earmarked for either the army or to support the Palestinian refugees who flooded into Transjordan and Iraq. There were bread shortages and high inflation. Widespread riots broke out in the cities, and there was fighting in the countryside.

Eventually, Said put down the rebellion, but his relationship with the nationalist regent became even more strained. The British supported Said and his oppressive tactics. They saw him as the best way to maintain stability (and the flow of oil) in Iraq.

Iraq Fact

The **Israel War** (or Israeli War of Independence) occurred between 1948 and 1949. Egypt, Transjordan (now Jordan), Iraq, Palestine, and Syria waged war against the new state of Israel; the Arab states eventually negotiated separate armistice agreements after the Israelis established clear air supremacy.

Nationalism Gets a Boost

In order to get peace with the rebels, Prime Minister Said was forced to repudiate the Portsmouth Treaty, and the nationalists were encouraged by their results.

The simple fact that factions from all facets of Iraqi society had coalesced and rebelled signaled continued trouble for the Hashemite monarchy and the British-backed parliament.

Five years later, on January 17, 1953, a direct election (the first in Iraq) took place. A new, constitutionally elected government was seated on January 29, 1953. This government was also pro-British—but it didn't last long.

Enter the U.S.A.

U.S. oil companies had begun to take a larger and larger role in the Iraqi oil industry. (You'll learn about the U.S. oil industry and Iraq in Chapter 11.) At the time, Iraq and Iran each played key roles in the U.S. policy of containment of the Soviet Union. With, at least on paper, a democratic process in place and the oil flowing, the United

States was able to point to Iraq as a model ally in the Middle East. The Eisenhower Doctrine, instituted by the United States in the early 1950s, promised U.S. aid to any country that resisted Communism, and the Eisenhower administration decided that Iraq fit the bill. However, this was a surface perception: the Communist and Socialist Parties did exist under the surface in 1950s Iraq. They were never as powerful as the Nationalists, but the Communist Party persisted into the 1960s, until it was outlawed by the Ba'th Socialist Party. Nonetheless, the Eisenhower administration decided to provide military aid to Iraq in 1954.

Like the British before them, the Americans' interest in the region was not welcomed by the Iraqi elites who ran the parliament. By the summer of 1954, a new parliamentary election resulted in anti-U.S. groups gaining the majority, threatening the military aid package—and the power of the seated, pro-Western Said government.

Before the new government could take control, Said dissolved the parliament on August 4, 1954, and new elections were held. This time, the main opposition party, the National Democratic Union, found itself suppressed by the government. This led the Socialist Party to walk out of the elections in sympathy. When the new elections were held in September 1954, the pro-Western government won in a landslide.

At this time, the United States took the baton from Britain in Iraq. Unfortunately, as we shall see, the Americans also took on the British propensity for superpower mistakes.

The Least You Need to Know

♦ For much of the twentieth century, Iraq was governed by a shaky, pro-British monarchy and heavy-handed government.

♦ The combination of Sunni-controlled parliaments and a Hashemite regent challenged the legitimacy of the government, which was largely ineffective.

♦ Western oil concessions, treaties, and maneuvering by Britain, and later the United States, only increased simmering anti-Western sentiment.

♦ The United States took over for Britain in the mid-1950s, as the Eisenhower Doctrine (and U.S. thirst for oil) pulled the United States into the region.

Chapter 8

Iraq During the Cold War

In This Chapter

- ◆ Iraq between the U.S. and the U.S.S.R.: what have you done for me lately?
- ◆ Iraq and Israel: the continual flashpoint
- ◆ Iraq and Egypt: struggle for leadership of the Arab world
- ◆ Iraq and Iran: bulwark of the Arab states

During the Cold War, Iraq's foreign policy resulted in a series of frustrations for the Iraqi leaders, and a growing frustration with the Western superpowers. British and U.S. errors in policy toward Iraq certainly strengthened Iraq's anti-Western outlook. Those errors, however, are not the only reason Iraq has developed and reinforced the kind of culture, outlook, and leadership history that it has.

Foreign Policy Frustrations

Much of Iraq's focus during the Cold War was on its relations with Turkey, Iran, Israel, and Egypt. We will see how Iraq's kings and later its dictators, have consistently latched on to these enemies—and Great Britain and the United States—in an attempt to bolster their own shaky authority at home.

This is not to suggest that actual conflicts and disagreements with these countries do not exist—only that the legitimacy of the Iraqi leadership is often deeply invested in an adversarial relationship with *some* enemy, and that the struggle against that enemy serves an important unifying (and distracting) purpose.

Specifically, we will look at Iraq's rivalries with …

- **Turkey.** The rival claimant for former Ottoman territories that would make up the modern state of Iraq. In addition to the territorial rivalry, the Turks are not Arabs and represent the old Ottoman oppressors.

- **Israel.** A long-standing focus of the Iraqi leadership, and the main rallying cause of the collective Arab states. Iraq's Ba'th Party tenets included a stated objective of destroying Israel and establishing a Palestinian homeland in its place.

- **Egypt.** A rival for about 1,000 years for leadership of Abbasid culture and commerce, Egypt is the chief rival for control of the pan-Arab movement. (See Chapter 2 for a quick overview of the pan-Arab movement, and Chapter 10 for more details.)

- **Iran.** The ancient enemy to the east. The Iranians are Farsi-speaking Persians, not Arabs. Also, Muslim Iran is Shiite, like the southern majority in Iraq. This Shiite connection makes Iran a neighbor who can (and perhaps does) create a destabilizing influence in Iraqi internal affairs. During the Ottoman Era, the Iraqi vilayets of Basra, Baghdad, and Mosul were the bulwark of Arabism against the Persians. We will look in greater depth at the on-again off-again hate affair with the Iranians in Chapter 12.

- **The United States.** The latest Western imperialist (taking the place of Britain). We will look briefly at the role the conflict with the United States has played in recent years. (The United States' status as enemy number one in Iraq is covered in greater detail in our discussion of Saddam Hussein, in Part 3). The United States had been following the British lead in compound errors since the end of World War II. U.S. companies began to get serious about Iraqi oil and, using the vehicle of the Eisenhower Doctrine, the U.S. government had become increasingly involved in Iraqi internal affairs.

A Common Thread

Over the years, Iraqi leadership (Hashemite kings, regents, prime ministers, and dictators) have been repeatedly frustrated in their foreign policy forays. Their foreign policy efforts were usually intended to increase their domestic stature. This pattern was already in place when Iraq was born as a state, and the new state began to squabble with Turkey over the Mosul vilayet.

Turkey, the Kurds, and the Contest for Mosul

In the period immediately following World War I, you may recall, the modern nation of Turkey was carved out of the Ottoman Empire.

The former Ottoman vilayets of Basra (now southern Iraq) and Baghdad (now central Iraq) were combined to create the Hashemite Kingdom of Iraq. The vilayet of Mosul (north of the Baghdad vilayet, bordering Turkey and Iran) was not originally part of the post-WWI state of Iraq. Mosul's status was undetermined at that time, as the British tried to figure out what to do about the Kurds (who occupied a significant portion of the Mosul vilayet).

When large amounts of oil were discovered in the Mosul region, the British were keen to control those assets. The post-WWI country of Turkey began to make serious claims for Mosul, however, and the Kurds also were arguing for this territory.

Faisal Finds a Unifying Cause

King Faisal, the Saudi clan member and newly installed king of Iraq, was looking for some cause to rally the people of his new country (new as a state, and new to him). The aggressive rhetoric of the Turks over Mosul was the perfect opportunity.

Faisal used this issue to create a sense of rivalry with Turkey, and by so doing, hopefully ingratiate himself to the Iraqi Sunni elite in Baghdad.

He was only marginally successful. Many of the Baghdad elites were enamored by the Young Turks movement (a progressive group of army officers in Turkey, dedicated to reforming the Turkish government and breaking away from Western dominance), and saw it as a blueprint for their own independence from British authority. Furthermore, most of the people in the Baghdad vilayet had more in common with the tribes in Syria and Jordan than with the people (including a lot of Kurds) up in Mosul. For that matter, most of the people in the Basra vilayet in southern Iraq had more in common with the people in Kuwait and the Shiite in Iran.

A Hollow Victory

As noted in Chapter 6, in 1925, the British, who were also alarmed by Turkish overtures regarding incorporating Mosul into Turkey, had the League of Nations agree to assign Mosul to Iraq. So Faisal had his foreign policy "victory" over the enemy (Turkey).

Unfortunately, most Iraqis never bought into the argument that Turkey was the enemy, or that Mosul was worth fighting for in the first place. In fact, given the way the British forced the solution through the League of Nations on behalf of Iraq, most Iraqi elites (the people Faisal was trying to impress) saw the annexation of Mosul as a sign of Faisal's weakness, not as a sign of strength. Furthermore, as a result of the Mosul annexation, Iraq inherited a large minority of Kurds, whose own goals for autonomy would vex Faisal and all the leaders to follow.

Increase Your Iraq IQ

The "Cold War" is the name for the competition between the West (mainly the United States) and the Soviet Union for primacy in the world. While the United States and Soviets never fought directly, they battled each other through proxy wars fought by allies and client states, covert operations, foreign aid, propaganda, and technology. Both sides labored under the MAD (mutually assured destruction) principle, which stated that neither side would deploy a national missile defense system (as a guarantee that neither side would use its nukes). The Cold War lasted from the end of World War II, to the collapse of the Soviet Union in 1989.

The Cold War Comes to the Desert

At the end of World War II, Britain became concerned by the Soviet Union's increasing attention to the Middle East. In a rekindling of the old *Great Game* played by the British and Russian Empires in Central Asia, both sides made moves to shore up partners in the oil-rich Middle East.

Desert Diction

The **Great Game** is the name for the maneuvering between the British and Russian Empires in the late nineteenth and early twentieth centuries. The British wanted to protect their northern frontier in India, and the Russians wanted to extend their southern frontier toward India. The two superpowers invaded, plotted, and spied throughout Central Asia during this period.

The Bulldog Brings in Uncle Sam

As the Cold War deepened, Britain did its best to prop up pro-Western Arab governments in its former Mandates, and promoted their participation in the United Nations.

Iraq joined the UN in 1945. Even before World War II, Britain had maneuvered to promote a stronger Iraq in the region—the better to contain other rivals.

In 1945, one of those rivals was the Soviet Union. However, after the end of World War II, Britain's resources were exhausted, and the old British Empire was crumbling. Britain found itself spread too thin to manage the growing Soviet threat. The United States emerged as the leader of the Soviet *containment* effort.

The first real test of the containment policy (and thus the beginning of the Cold War) occurred in 1947, when the Soviet Union became involved in a civil war in Greece. Communist rebels were attacking the pro-Western monarchy there, and the Soviet Union was backing the rebels. Also, the Soviets were pushing Turkey to grant them naval base concessions on the Bosporus. (The only route Soviet ships had to get into the Mediterranean was to exit the Black Sea via the Bosporus.) The Soviets were offering cash to Turkey, which Turkey sorely needed.

Britain was unable to match the Soviet offer, but U.S. President Harry Truman could. So Truman trumped up the Soviet threat to something greater than it actually was.

By "scaring the hell out of the country" (as Senator Arthur Vandenberg so eloquently put it at the time), Truman was able to get the United States Congress to appropriate a $400 million aid package for Greece and Turkey. The Greek communists were defeated, and the Soviets never got their naval base on the Bosporus. The Cold War was on, and it quickly reached into Iraq.

Desert Diction

The **containment** concept, which is credited to George Kennan, a senior diplomat at the U.S. Embassy in Moscow in 1946, outlined the need and methods for containing Soviet expansion.

The Arab League

Although weakened after World War II, Britain continued to maneuver to protect its position in the region. They moved to contain the Soviets by encouraging the formation of a coalition of Arab countries into a larger, unified entity. This concept eventually became embodied in the "Arab League."

The British favored the Arab League, as it represented a bulwark against Soviet expansion into the region. Over time the Arab League would become less sympathetic to Britain, but early on, the League was pro-British.

Increase Your Iraq IQ

The Arab League (formally called the League of Arab States) includes Egypt, Transjordan (now Jordan), Lebanon, Saudi Arabia, Syria, Yemen, and Iraq. The League exists to this day, but it doesn't represent all the Arabs in the region, and it has not worked toward a unified Arab state in decades. Its mission now focuses more on issues that affect the collective Arab states.

Iraq was a founding member of the Arab League in 1946. As an Arab League member, Iraq became an active proponent of the pan-Arab movement. Iraq's Premier Nuri as-Said went so far as to suggest that Iraq and Transjordan (now Jordan) should be united. While the idea did not go very far at that time, the Said government signed a treaty of mutual defense and friendship with Transjordan in 1947.

Pan-Arabism's First Test

The first test of the pan-Arabism, and the new alliance treaties, came in May of 1948, when the State of Israel was proclaimed. Anti-Zionism had been a long-time tenet of Arab leaders, and the Arab League member countries all adopted the same policy.

The Hashemites Find a Unifying Cause

The Hashemite monarchy in Iraq saw the founding of Israel as an opportunity to bolster their own domestic position. The Hashemite regent Abd al Ilah seized the opportunity to put Iraq in the forefront of the fighting against Israel. (The king, whom the regent represented, was 12 years old in 1948.)

Iraq Fact

The Hashemite monarchy had, of course, been created by the British. Britain had also led the way in the creation of the state of Israel from the Palestine Mandate. The British did not want the Arab states to attack Israel. Ironically, it was their own creation—the Hashemite monarchy in Iraq—that became one of the most violent opponents of Israel.

Immediately after the creation of the Israeli state in 1948, Iraq and Transjordan invaded Israel. Even after the other Arab forces had withdrawn from the fighting, the Iraqis stayed on. The Iraqis fought with particular fury all that summer and into the fall.

Finally, when it was apparent the Israeli defense forces were going to win (or at the very least, the Iraqis were not going to win) the Transjordanians negotiated a cease-fire with the Israelis on behalf of themselves and the Iraqis. Even after the cease-fire agreement was signed on May 11, 1949, Iraqi troops continued to fight against Israeli troops in central Palestine. On April 3, 1949, the Transjordanian army replaced the Iraqis, and the fight finally stopped.

A Hollow Defeat

Back at home, the regency had failed to score the points it wanted to with the Iraqi elites. The engagement in Israel was a failure, and the prominent role that Iraq played was a source of embarrassment at home, not pride. While the Iraqi military would participate in the 1967 and 1973 wars against Israel, the Iraqis didn't play the leading belligerent role they had in 1948.

Given that the attempt to prevail against Israel, or to even assume a leadership role in the fight against Israel, had fallen flat, the Iraqi leadership needed a new enemy to fight, the better to rally support and gain prestige.

They found the competition they needed within the arena of the pan-Arab movement, in a renewed rivalry with Egypt.

> **CAUTION**
>
> **Oil Spill Ahead** _____
>
> The Iraqi government's continued antipathy to Israel would emerge again during the Gulf War, when the Iraqis launched missiles at Israel in an attempt to draw Israel into the war, and turn the conflict from a U.S.-Arab coalition vs. Iraq to an Arab coalition against a U.S.-Israeli alliance. Again, the attempt failed.

Competing with Nasser

What country would lead the Arab world? In the late 1940s and early 1950s, the most prominent candidates were Egypt and Iraq.

In 1948, Abd al Ilah (the regent for the Iraqi boy king) proposed an Iraqi-Syrian union. Nuri as-Said, the prime minister, opposed the idea, and a rift between the two Iraqi leaders began to widen. The matter was settled by the Syrians, themselves, when Syrian strongman Adib Shishakli took over that government in a coup in 1949.

Shishakli was opposed to a union with Iraq. Even though he was overthrown (with Iraqi help) in 1954, the plan was dropped. By then, Syria was closer to Egypt, anyway.

Under Gamal abdel Nasser, Egypt was presenting itself as the alternative to Iraqi leadership of the Arab world. A dominant personality, with ambitious international goals of his own, Nasser moved away from Britain early and often.

As part of his own anti-British leaning, Nasser targeted Iraq's policy parallels with Britain, and used them to win greater credibility for himself within the Arab world.

Consider, for instance …

The Baghdad Pact

In 1955, Iraq was a founding member of the Baghdad Pact, a mutual defense treaty with Iran, Pakistan, and Turkey. The simple fact that the treaty was signed in Baghdad indicates the leadership position that Iraq was trying to maintain.

Nasser saw the Pact as a clear challenge to Egyptian dominance in the Arab community. The Baghdad Pact was supported by Britain, and was signed with non-Arab states. The British and Americans assembled the Baghdad Pact nations as an anti-Soviet coalition. The British didn't think they needed Egypt to participate, and this troubled Nasser.

Nasser knew that if more Arab states joined the Pact, Egypt's standing would suffer. He responded to its creation by calling on the Iraqi military to overthrow the monarchy.

This call was not as far-fetched as it may sound. Remember that the Iraqi monarchy was ruled by a Hashemite family from Saudi Arabia—they were not Iraqis. Consider, too, that the king himself was only 16 at that time. The monarchy was run by a regent, the king's uncle, Abd al Ilah. The government was run by Nuri as-Said, who owed his position to the British and almost always carried out their wishes regarding foreign policy. Nasser's call cannily appealed to the growing anti-Western sentiment in Iraq.

The Iraqi military didn't actually rise up at that time, but the Pact wasn't a popular treaty with the Iraqi elites, who identified more with Nasser's style of Arab nationalism over their own government's notions of international relations.

And Then There Was Suez

Things only got worse for the Iraqi government during the Suez Crisis.

The crisis started when the Egyptians nationalized *the Suez Canal.* The British responded by invading the Sinai, supported by the French … and the hated Israelis. As an ally of the British (at the government level, if not among the country's elites), Iraq had to stand by and not openly oppose the British initiative.

> **Desert Diction**
>
> The **Suez Canal** connects the Mediterranean Sea to the Gulf of Suez, and then out to the Indian Ocean. The canal is located in Egypt; transit through the canal saves ships the much longer and more arduous journey around the Cape of Good Hope and the African continent.

Before war could break out, the United Nations brokered a truce, and the British, French, and Israelis withdrew. After the settlement, Nasser's standing only increased among the Arab world, at the expense of Iraqi prestige. After all, the Iraqis had done nothing (except be the lapdogs of the British) while Egypt (led by Nasser, of course) had struck a blow for Arab autonomy and prestige.

Struggles for Pre-Eminence

The competition over leadership of the Arab political world carried over into the pan-Arab movement. Nasser promoted the United Arab Republic (UAR), as we saw in Chapter 1. The UAR was intended to become a single Arab power, and was supposed to incorporate the Arab nations in the Middle East (under Egyptian moral leadership, of course).

Syria and Egypt joined up in February 1958, and Yemen tentatively joined soon after. However, no one else joined, and the UAR fell apart a few years later. Yemen never completely joined in, and Syria dropped out. Egypt kept the UAR as its name, even though it was the only member of the Union after the Syrians dropped out.

The Iraqi Leadership Searches for a Unifying Cause

Iraqi leaders were not to be outdone by the Egyptians. They responded by forming their own version of the UAR, the Arab Union (AU), in 1958. Iraq and Jordan joined up (there was a Hashemite monarchy in Jordan), and Iraqi Prime Minister Nuri as-Said was brought off the bench to head the new state. Said had been in retirement at that time.

The newly crowned king, Faisal II, was only 22 (he had formally assumed the throne at the age of 18 in 1954) at the time, and he was still taking orders from his uncle, the regent. The Arab Union was formed with British and American blessings. Like the Baghdad Pact, the AU was a controversial move, initiated almost exclusively by the government of Iraq instead of the Iraqi people, and it didn't have unanimous support from the Iraqi National Assembly.

Egypt's (the UAR) Nasser portrayed the Arab Union as another Western affront to the Arab world. The Egyptians argued that the only reason the AU was created was because the British were trying to defeat a true Arab union, the United Arab Republic. Nasser called again for the Iraqi people to overthrow the new Arab Union government.

Increase Your Iraq IQ

The Hashemite monarchy was simply unable to generate the loyalty and passion that Nassar could excite in Egypt. The Iraqi government couldn't count on the military's full support. The monarchy was alone, cut off from the Arab nations because of its pro-British stance, cut off from the Iraqi elites because of its non-Iraqi roots, and cut off from the Iraqi people because of its privileged background.

Good-Bye to the Hashemites

This time, Nasser's ploy worked. On July 14, 1958, Iraqi General Abdul Karim Kassem led a coup d'état. Ostensibly, Iraqi troops were moving into Jordan as part of a joint military exercise. Instead, the battalion stopped in Baghdad and seized control of the government.

King Faisal II, Abd al Ilah, and Nuri as-Said were all killed. The next day, on July 15, 1958, the new government declared its support for the UAR and announced the termination of the Arab Union.

The pro-British Hashemite monarchy was gone, and it would not be replaced. Its repeated attempts to gain sufficient legitimacy for survival through foreign policy victories had failed. There were in fact very few Iraqi foreign policy victories in the decade following World War II.

Iraq Fact

Prime Minister Nuri as-Said was captured trying to escape Baghdad dressed as a woman.

With the successful coup, Iraq had entered the next phase of its journey to the twenty-first century. Iraq was now a self-governing state, Arab-focused, and run by a Sunni military elite more than willing to focus public attention on an external enemy (such as Israel or the United States) to bolster its legitimacy.

This structure would survive to the present. It is the formula that rules Iraq.

The Least You Need to Know

- ◆ The Iraqi monarchy never had the support of the Iraqi elite or people.

- ◆ The Iraqi monarchy and later dictators attempted to legitimize themselves by finding an enemy. (The Turks, Israelis, and Egyptians all played that part.)

- ◆ The Iraqi monarchy ultimately failed in each of its major foreign policy initiatives.

- ◆ The British, following the principle of Compound Error, repeatedly placed the monarchy in no-win situations, and abandoned them in the end.

- ◆ The Hashemite monarchy ultimately fell to a coup lead by the Sunni-controlled Iraqi army leaders.

Part  3

Saddam Hussein

What made Saddam Hussein's reign possible? The answer involves at least a century of global conflict, superpower diplomacy, ancient rivalry, and modern geopolitics. (There were some disagreements about oil along the way, too.)

In this part, you'll get an introduction to the world that made Saddam possible—and get an understanding of the man himself.

Three Coups: The Rise of the Ba'thists

In This Chapter

- ◆ The 1958 coup
- ◆ The 1963 coup and the first Ba'th government
- ◆ The 1968 coup that entrenched Ba'th rule in Iraq

The Arab Ba'th Socialist Resurrection Party gained power through a series of coups over a 10-year period between 1958 and 1968. All the coups were led by Iraqi generals, who were just as alienated from the common Iraqis as the Hashemite monarchs had been.

We're Closed!

An important theme that unites all three of these coups is the notion of the *closed society*.

In a closed society, power is concentrated within a small group. Other groups that manage to maneuver their way into a position to challenge the ruling group can quickly take over power from the ruling group, without the rest of the society being able to do much about it.

Open societies take longer to make fundamental political changes, are less likely to undergo coups and revolutions, and are less prone to rapid changes in the central authority group. In an open society, more groups share power and wealth. Each group holds some power—and no one group has virtually *all* the power.

Desert Diction

A **closed society** is one where information, power, and decisions are controlled by a small central authority and are only shared within a tiny ruling circle. Closed societies don't allow for a pluralist government or meaningful open debate on issues. Open societies, by contrast, share information, power, and decision-making across a much broader spectrum of the population.

In closed societies, changes in leadership and policy may happen in sudden, violent shifts (like a coup d'état). Open societies, on the other hand, tend to process social change more easily, with fewer violent spasms and fewer dramatic, unexpected political upheavals.

In Iraq in the 1950s, power resided with a very few groups—the fragile leadership structure set in place by the British excluded important sections of the population.

Demagogues, Dictators, and Chaos

To understand Iraq's political situation in the 1950s and early 1960s, it helps to understand power shifts in other closed societies in the twentieth century.

One of the ways a *demagogue* becomes a dictator is by promising to bring order when there is chaos. This is the technique that Hitler, Stalin, Mussolini, and others used to justify taking total control in Germany, Russia, and Italy, respectively.

Desert Diction

Demagogues are leaders or prominent figures within a society who preach a specific philosophy. They gain prominence by preying on the fears or prejudices of the population.

Hitler's Nazi Party, for instance, actually joined forces with the communists (even though the two groups were complete opposites on the political spectrum) in order to destabilize the Weimar Republic government in the 1920s and 1930s. By joining voting blocs with the communists, the Nazis were able to help bring about vote after vote of "no confidence" in the seated government in the Reichstag (parliament).

The combined efforts of the communists and the Nazis resulted in dissolved governments, hectic reelection campaigns, and ineffective decision-making, creating an atmosphere of chaos within the government—and deep resentment in a population facing economic crisis.

Hitler was finally given the opportunity to form a government in 1933. In the name of stability, he then cracked down brutally on all opposition (including the communists, who had been the Nazis' partners in chaos).

Similarly destabilizing maneuvers were in evidence in Iraq in the 1950s and 1960s.

The Army Elite Gains Power

Emerging as a power center to challenge the unpopular, foreign-born monarchy and the ineffective parliament was an increasingly powerful military officer corps.

You'll recall that the British had created a local, Iraqi army to prop up the Hashemite monarchy. This was because the British realized the Hashemites might have a tough time of it—not being Iraqis and all—and would need a tool to help maintain control of the country. Remember that the tribes in the countryside, and the Kurds in the north, were essentially operating independently within Iraq. The army, the British reasoned, was needed to control these restless and potentially destabilizing groups.

Recall, too, that the British wanted to maintain ties with other Arab leaders in the region; hence the Sunni (minority) monarchy. The Sunni monarch, of course, would need Sunni support in the army. So even though the majority of the population in Iraq was (and is) Shiite, the British made sure the officer corps was made up of Sunnis, while the rank and file was Shiite.

It was this Sunni military elite that became the key lever in prying out existing governments and setting up new ones in their place. The principal method of change was the coup d'état.

> **Oil Spill Ahead**
>
> The coups of the 1950s, while important, were not the only leadership spasms in Iraq; there had been several coups and rebellions over the preceding 20 years, including the 1936 coup, the 1941 military takeover, the 1948 Wathbah Uprising, and smaller uprisings in 1952 and 1956.

Times Change

Power in Iraq in the 1950s was concentrated into the hands of the British-leaning monarch (Faisal II), and the prime minister (Nuri as-Said) and his immediate circle. The other power elites, including the Iraqi officer corps, were not included in the decision-making process, and they were becoming increasingly unhappy at this state of affairs.

The officers, in particular, were unhappy over several things. They were Arab nationalists who resented the pro-British puppets who ran their state. The officers didn't necessarily identify themselves with the rest of the Iraqi population, especially the Shiite majority, the Kurds, or the Assyrians. Their interest was focused on themselves, and their pan-Arab brethren in other countries.

These officers resented the non-Iraqi monarchy, they resented the foreign policy blunders of their government, and they resented its heavy-handed approach to decision-making. Most of all, they resented the British manipulation of their nation.

A Fateful Party

Iraq was fertile ground for the Ba'th Party in the 1950s. Founded in Syria, the Ba'th Socialist Party was pan-Arab; it had local branches in each Arab country, and its members were dedicated to a pan-Arab state.

The Ba'th Party originated during World War II, formed by two Syrian students, Michel Aflaq and Salah ad-Din al-Bitar. It was formally founded on April 7, 1947, as the Arab Ba'th Socialist Party.

Aflaq and al-Bitar were keenly aware of British and French imperialism throughout the Middle East. They were fans of the pan-Arab ideal, and they were enamored with the political ideology of *socialism*.

Desert Diction

Socialism as a concept was first described by Friedrich Engels, and then extended by Karl Marx in the end of the nineteenth century. Both were reacting to the situation that early industrialization had created. Workers (labor) were paid subsistence wages and had little to no hope of social advancement. Owners (or the capitalists) controlled the means of production and exploited workers. Socialism argued that workers should own the fruit of their labors, not the capitalists. The ideology envisioned workers owning the means of production, with higher living standards for all.

Socialism had emerged as a vibrant political ideology in the 1920s and 1930s, and a wide range of socialist parties became powerful before and immediately after World War II. Socialism took many forms depending on where it took root, but its emphasis on equity, political rights, and state ownership of property had a strong pull on young idealists in universities around the world.

The Ba'th Party in Iraq

The Ba'th Party emerged as a viable organization in Iraq in 1952, when a charismatic leader named Fu'ad ar Rikabi founded the Iraqi branch of the Arab Ba'th Socialist party that year. Even though Rikabi was a Shiite, he was able to attract Sunnis to the party. However, over time, the Sunnis took control of the party.

The Ba'th Party tenets included adherence to socialism (including state ownership of the key segments of the economy), political freedom (an inclusive process), and pan-Arab unity. These tenets took root amongst the Iraqi intelligentsia, who were suffering from the poor economic environment in Iraq, and who were alienated by British imperialist policies and the closed decision-making style of the Iraqi leadership.

The members of the Iraqi intelligentsia drawn to the Ba'th Party were generally Sunnis of some privilege. Like the officer corps, they identified more with other Sunni intelligentsia in other countries, and less with their own countrymen who represented far different religious and economic realities than their own.

During the next five years, some army officers joined the party ranks, but membership was still very small within Iraq. Like the national socialists in Weimar Germany, and the communists in Tzarist Russia, the Iraq branch of the Ba'th Party started as a small group on the outside, looking in.

> **Increase Your Iraq IQ**
>
> Across the Arab countries, memberships in local Ba'th Party branches grew rapidly during the 1950s and 1960s.

Wathbah, Revisited

Look once again at the challenge that *preceded* the coup that swept away the Hashemite monarchy described in Chapter 7.

Prime Minister Nuri as-Said and the Hashemite regent, Abd al Ilah, negotiated the Portsmouth Treaty with Britain. The Treaty stipulated that Iraqi leadership had to consult Britain on any military matters, through a board of Iraqi and British "advisors." The nationalists were outraged, and without a legal political option, they rebelled. The rebellion spread quickly and tapped into popular unrest over high bread prices and continued economic malaise.

The Wathbah uprising was violent. It was suppressed violently, and the rebel groups were all but eliminated (at least in the forms they had taken at that point). However, the strife didn't end until the Said government openly repudiated the Portsmouth Treaty.

The result: The rebels were defeated and repressive measures were heightened, but a segment of the rebels' wishes were granted (namely, the treaty was abandoned).

In order to retain power, the ruling government had accommodated some opposition demands, but had redoubled its efforts to avoid any further challenges to its authority. Such challenges, however, would prove impossible to avoid.

Rumblings

What have we got so far? A state of general political chaos, economic hardship, resentment of the British, and widespread alienation of Iraqi elites excluded from participating in policy decisions. All of this was bubbling in the pressure cooker of a closed society.

Something had to give.

July 14, 1958

And give it did, on July 14, 1958. On that morning the Iraqi army toppled the royal regime. According to official Iraqi accounts of the event, the regime the army overthrew "had opened the door wide for monopolies to plunder the country's oil wealth under unjust concessions, tied Iraq to imperialist alliances, especially the Baghdad Pact, and turned the country into a center of conspiracy against the revolutionary movement of the Arab homeland."

Was the 1958 coup a just uprising by an oppressed people ... or, a coup staged by members of the Sunni officer elite to topple the Said government they despised?

However it's categorized, the July 14, 1958, coup followed the Hashemite monarchy's creating the Arab Union with Jordan (in response to the Egyptian-sponsored United Arab Republic, or UAR). The Iraqi parliament ratified the union on May 12, 1958, but the Sunni officers got together enough supporters to bring the union—and the Iraqi government—down only 60 days later. They were led by General Abdul Karim Kassem.

King Faisal II, the regent, and Said were all killed immediately. The next day, July 15, the new government (now calling the country the Republic of Iraq) abandoned the Arab Union, and announced its intention to forge closer ties to the UAR.

Kassem continued the new government's anti-British policies by withdrawing from the Baghdad Pact in March 1959 and pulling out of the *sterling bloc* in June 1959. Remember, the Baghdad Pact was a mutual defense treaty that included Iraq, Turkey, and Iran. It was sponsored by the British, and was intended to stave off the Soviet expansionism.

Kassem was forced to carry out a delicate balancing act. A child of Sunni-Shiite parentage, Kassem tried to keep the various groups happy, but he wasn't always successful.

For example, under pressure from the nationalists, Kassem's government revoked about 99.5 percent of the Iraq Petroleum Company (IPC)'s concession rights. However, this move didn't really change much, as the existing IPC facilities were located on the remaining 0.5 percent of the original concession area. So by nationalizing the concession, Kassem looked like an Arab nationalist to the nationalists by defying the foreign powers, and he looked like a socialist to the Iraqi Communist Party by nationalizing a key industry. His action helped him gain prestige from both groups at home. At the same time, he really didn't seize any physical plant from the IPC, though he did take value from the IPC by taking away its concession areas.

Desert Diction

The **sterling bloc** was the group of nations who tied their currencies to the pound sterling. Iraq withdrew from this group in 1959.

Oil Spill Ahead

Once Iraq pulled out of the Baghdad Pact, the treaty group really couldn't refer to itself that way anymore ... after all, there was no Baghdad in the pact! So the remaining countries (including Turkey and Iran) called themselves the Central Treaty Organization. This name was safer, in case anyone else decided to drop out.

Red Bedfellows

Kassem wasn't really pro-Communist, but his government did reach an aid agreement with the Soviet Union. Because of that agreement, Kassem was diplomatically obliged to tolerate the Iraqi Communist Party (ICP)—a rival of the Ba'th socialists—in order to get the aid the Soviets were promising. The ICP was a more established party than the Ba'th Party, and it had successfully agitated against previous governments. The ICP was, in a way, much less violent than the Ba'th, and more extensive. The ICP had, in a sense, paved the way for the Ba'th Party in Iraq, even though the Ba'th were ideologically opposed to the ICP.

The issue of the UAR membership involved another balancing act. The Ba'ths wanted to join the union, but Kassem and the Communists did not.

The Kuwait Conflict (1960)

The Kassem-controlled Republic of Iraq wasn't done throwing off the British yoke. In June 1960, the British ended their protectorate over Kuwait and declared it an independent state.

With the British out, Kassem's troops moved into Kuwait. The Iraqis claimed that Kuwait had been part of the old Basra vilayet, and so it really belonged to Iraq. The British rejected this claim, stating that the League of Nations had sanctioned the current borders, and that the vilayet borders were not material to the current situation. Warranted or not, the Iraqis used the ancient vilayet boundaries to justify their claim (and they would do so again).

The British sent troops to Kuwait in July 1960. Kassem tried to get the United Nations to order the British to leave what he claimed was Iraqi territory. (You'll recall that the Iraqis were poised to invade Kuwait in 1939, as well.)

The United Nations refused, and even the Arab League rallied to support Kuwait. (Does any of this sound familiar?)

The Iraqis backed off. Like the Hashemite monarchs before him, Kassem saw his prestige (and his grip on power) suffer a debilitating blow through a failed foreign policy initiative. Kassem responded by cutting of relations with most of his Arab neighbors, deepening his isolation.

Pressure from the Kurds

The Kurds saw their chance during all the confusion. They initiated a rebellious uprising in northern Iraq. Kassem responded brutally, and unsuccessfully, continuing the previous regime's protracted campaigns against the Kurds. His inability to contain the Kurds only hastened his own demise, as his prestige with the army took another blow.

February 8, 1963

So in the environment of internal chaos and foreign policy failure, the Iraqi officer corps decided to try again.

They first attempted a coup in March of 1959, but Kassem got wind of it, and rallied the Communists to his side. Iraqi Communists organized a huge rally in Mosul; it got out of hand, and members of the Iraqi Communist Party attacked and killed well-to-do Mosul families and nationalists.

Later, the Iraqi Communist Party led attacks on upper-class Turkoman groups in Kirkuk during another rally. Kassem finally responded by cracking down on the ICP, and jailing some of the rank and file membership. Despite these actions, the Ba'th officers attempted to assassinate Kassem in 1959, having concluded that he had lost effective control of the country and was letting their enemies, the Communists, get too powerful.

Saddam Takes Aim

General Saddam Hussein (yes, *that* Saddam Hussein) attempted the assassination, but he only wounded Kassem.

Predictably, Kassem responded by cracking down on the Ba'th Party. Undeterred, the Ba'th tried again on February 8, 1963. Despite his enormous popularity with the vast majority of his country's population, Kassem was alienated as a leader from the ruling elites, and so was removed and killed. (Kassem purportedly was on an unofficial CIA hit list, but the Iraqis finished the job before the Agency could get to him). According to the official Iraqi account of events:

> On this day the Arab Ba'th Socialist Party carried out its great Revolution, which brought down the dictatorial regime. It was a socialist, democratic, and nationalist revolution in which all the civil and military formations of the Party took part, which elicited the hostility of imperialist forces. The latter combined in conspiring against it on 18th November, 1963, while it was only a few months old.

Increase Your Iraq IQ

Thus, the 14th July Revolution was a historic event, but it soon suffered a set-back when it was dominated by the dictatorial rule of Abdul Karim Kassem. The Arab Ba'th Socialist Party therefore had to continue the struggle to restore the revolution to its genuine path.

—*Official Tourist Guide to Iraq, from the Saddam Hussein regime*

This coup involved the Ba'th elements of the Iraqi officer corp. They succeeded in killing Kassem, but the Ba'th were not strong enough to hold onto power.

The Backlash

There were about 1,000 members of the Iraqi branch of the Ba'th Party at that time. Now, this seems like too small a number to mount an effective government, but remember that in a closed society, relatively small numbers of well-placed people can topple a shaky regime.

However, when Kassem was overthrown, millions of Iraqi urban poor and rural peasants rallied to his support in a fruitless attempt to save his life and restore him to power. Kassem's own poor origins had made him a hero to the common people who made up the bulk of Iraqi society.

The simple fact that Kassem could be so easily removed from power despite popular wishes shows just how illegitimate the Iraqi political process was in the eyes of the people of the country. From the Ottomans, through the Hashemite monarchs, to the military-led republic, the leadership of Iraq had steadily moved apart from the people it was supposed to govern. This process continued with Ba'th leadership.

Moreover, the Ba'th had gone on a nine-month purging spree during their time in power. They arrested, imprisoned, and killed Communists and other political challengers to their power. Some 5,000 Iraqis, mostly ICP leaders, were killed. Increasingly isolated, and increasingly unpopular, the same factors that allowed the Ba'ths to take power allowed the next officer clique to take it from them on November 18, 1963.

Rapprochement?

The Ba'th group was pushed out in November 1963 by a group led by General Abdul Salam Arif. The Ba'th were big enough to unseat Kassem, but were just too small to effectively run the state. Arif represented a broader base of followers who were more moderate than the Ba'th. Once in control, Arif attempted a rapprochement with the West and his Arab neighbors.

Arif was killed in a helicopter crash in April 1966, and his brother, General Abdul Rahman Arif, took over as president. The Arif(s) government was no more open or embraced than the first Ba'th or Kassem governments had been. Salam Arif was also a supporter of the United Arab Republic's Nasser, and his plan included eventual membership in the UAR. (The target date was 1966.)

Arif continued to maneuver pro-Nasser people into his inner circle, much to the dismay and concern of the Iraqi pan-Arabists, who still saw Iraq as the leader of the Arab world. For them, union with Egypt would surely mean domination by Nasser, and that was unacceptable.

The Ba'ths, meanwhile, continued to recruit new members and extend their reach deeper into the officer corp. Five years after their first attempt, they seized power again.

According to the official Iraqi account of the events: The 17th July 1968 Revolution, under the leadership of the Arab Ba'th Socialist Party, is the most important event in the history of modern Iraq. A progressive Revolution, it succeeded in liberating Iraq from all forms of subservience, in rescuing the country's oil wealth from the control of international oil monopolies by the historic decision of Oil Nationalization of June 1, 1972.

The events that led up to the July 17 coup came to a head during the 1967 Arab-Israeli War.

Why It Happened

In 1967, Iraq had joined other Arab countries in declaring war on Israel. Iraq had also closed pipelines used to send oil toward Western nations. Diplomatic ties were cut with the United States, which supported Israel during the conflict.

The result of the economic effects of closing the pipeline, and the anger that arose from losing another showdown with Israel, combined to encourage a group of Iraqi officers to make their move.

The Arab Revolutionary Movement

The Arab Revolutionary Movement, comprised of a group of young army officers, was increasingly disillusioned by the Arif government's reliance on Nasser supporters within the government.

Led by Colonels Abd ar Razzaq an Nayif and Ibrahim ad Daud, the Arab Revolutionary Movement ousted the Arif government.

Taking Over Someone Else's Coup

The Arab Revolutionary Movement officers acted independently from the Ba'th when they launched the coup. However, it quickly became clear that Nayif and Daud did not have the backing within the army to remain in power. In less than a month, the Ba'th levered Nayif and Daud out of power, and took over the government again.

The new Ba'th government was led by General Ahmed Hassan al-Bakr. Official Iraqi accounts of events claim that the Ba'ths united the competing constituencies within

Iraq, but this is far fetched. The al-Bakr government was just as isolated as the Arif and Kassem governments had been. It was still a case of closed-society, leading groups fighting amongst themselves. The average Iraqi was not considered.

The stage was set for the Ba'th government's consolidation of power, and for General Saddam Hussein's rise from would-be assassin to leader of Iraq.

The Least You Need to Know

- ◆ The coups that led up to the Ba'th seizure were a result of shaky provisional governments taking over for the ones that preceded them.

- ◆ The coup governments took increasingly anti-Western positions.

- ◆ All the coups were led by Iraqi generals, who were just as alienated from the common Iraqis as the Hashemite monarchs had been.

- ◆ The Ba'th Socialist Party persevered against Communist rivals during the 1950s and 1960s.

- ◆ The Ba'th Socialist Party attempted to take power in 1963, but was edged out; they themselves did the edging out in 1968.

Meet the New Boss: Saddam's Ascent

In This Chapter

- ◆ Saddam's early years
- ◆ His role in the Ba'th rise to power
- ◆ His campaign to consolidate his authority
- ◆ His move to the top

The lack of industrial development in Iraq meant the Ba'th leadership had to look to the oil industry to finance its regime.

In order to get the necessary money from the oil industry, the government assumed full control over that industry. Iraq's first "republic" governments nationalized the Iraqi Petroleum Company (IPC). By nationalizing the IPC and its Basra Petroleum Company subsidiary, the Iraqi leadership created a huge source of revenues for the state.

The oil revenues were used to prop up undeveloped and inefficient local industries in Iraq. Oil money also bought food to supplement local agriculture. The money also was a way for the Ba'th to reward its supporters, punish foes, and buy off everyone else. Perhaps most important of all for the Ba'th leadership, the oil money funded a strong police force. This group later grew into a force that was fiercely loyal to the man who headed the secret police, Saddam Hussein.

Saddam's Ascent

Saddam Hussein was born into a rural farm family in the village of Auja, in the Tikrit region north of Baghdad. He was born into the al-Khattab clan and so as a youth he had three blue dots tattooed onto his right hand. This tattoo was a sign of his clan roots, and marked him for life as a member of that clan and the rural community.

Saddam Hussein.

Saddam's career and mentality reflected far more of a clan leader's roots than those of a socialist visionary. His rise and consolidation of power followed the patterns of village power politics, where the strongest leader's family ruled the village and so took the best for themselves at the expense of other families. In Saddam's case, the village eventually became the entire country.

Country Mouse, City Mouse

An enduring defining characteristic of Iraqi society has been the split between rural tribal culture and urban culture.

In the cities, people identify more with the state and with the services it provides to make life in the city possible.

In the countryside, on the other hand, state ties are less pronounced. The population is connected more directly to a number of tribes. Each tribe consists of a number of clans. Each clan is centered around a number of villages. Each village consists of several families. Each family is led by a patriarch.

The strongest patriarch's family holds sway in the village, commandeering the best resources and land. In the rural areas, one's identity is with the family, the village, the clan, and more loosely, the tribe.

Missing in Action

Saddam's father abandoned the family prior to his birth, leaving Saddam to be raised by his mother.

In subsequent years, Saddam's mother remarried. Saddam's stepfather was abusive toward Saddam, and the little boy had an unhappy early childhood.

Saddam was sent to live with his uncle when he was 10 years old. It was (and is) not uncommon for an elder in an Iraqi tribal group to take in a young child in need of direction.

> **Increase Your Iraq IQ**
>
> The name Saddam means (aptly enough) "One who confronts."

Enter the Rich Uncle

The uncle who took in Saddam was one Adnan Khairullah Tulfah. Tulfah was a devout Sunni, and he introduced Saddam to members of the Sunni elite who were playing a leading role in Iraqi politics.

Tulfah himself eventually became the governor of Baghdad, and Saddam gained first-hand exposure to how power was gained and wielded in Sunni ruling circles.

Saddam was instructed early in two concepts that would become pillars of the Ba'th Party: Pan-Arabism and anti-Zionism. Many young Arab men of the era, of course, were trained in the same ideas. These two concepts were deeply ingrained into contemporary Arab attitudes, and still are to a great extent. Saddam happened to have, in his uncle, a particularly able and energetic instructor.

> **CAUTION**
>
> **Oil Spill Ahead**
>
> Saddam's uncle gave Saddam an early education in ethnic prejudice; Uncle Tulfah wrote a pamphlet titled: "Three Whom God Should Not Have Created: Persians, Jews, and Flies."

Contempt for the British

As a teenager, Saddam watched as Gamal abdel Nasser toppled the British-backed regime in Egypt. Nasser became the symbol of Arab power and pride to Arab nationalists in the other British-run Arab nations, including Iraq.

Saddam was 15 years old in 1952 when Nasser staged his takeover. Like many young Arab men of the period, he doubtless held the (formerly) powerful British empire in contempt for its past arrogance and current influence within Iraq.

Young Saddam lived in the household of a high-ranking Sunni official in Baghdad, and thus had access to a variety of news, books, and broadcasts that brought events in the world to his doorstep.

A Member of the Elite

Saddam was raised into the Sunni, anti-Israel, anti-British, pan-Arab, Iraqi elite. He was able to network with others in Baghdad who shared his beliefs and to learn about important new ideas and political movements in the Arab world.

> **Increase Your Iraq IQ**
>
> As in many countries where communist and socialist parties vied for control against other political groups (nationalists, fascists, and so on), the communists and socialists saved their most savage violence for each other.

One of the political movements that was captivating Iraqi urban elites in the 1950s was the Arab Ba'th Socialist Renaissance Party. As we have seen, this party synthesized pan-Arabism and socialism into one ideal, and preached the resurgence (resurrection) of the Arab nation.

Young Saddam saw the Ba'th Party, and its dedication to overthrowing the existing Iraqi government, as a path to power. Saddam jumped onto the Ba'th bandwagon with both feet, proving himself a worthy revolutionary at every opportunity.

Previews of Coming Attractions: A Death in the Family

At the age of 20, Saddam officially joined the Ba'th Party. He took part in Party demonstrations and was a prominent fighter alongside the street toughs whom the Ba'th used to fight their battles against rival parties.

No rival party was so detested by the Ba'th as the Iraqi Communist Party (ICP).

Saddam gained stature in the Ba'th movement by killing a Communist activist. The activist happened to be his brother-in-law.

A Murderous Ascent

In 1959, Saddam led an attempt to kill Prime Minister Kassem. Saddam was wounded in the leg but was able to escape to Syria.

Like the unlucky Nuri as-Said (the last prime minister under the Hashemite monarchy), Saddam went disguised as a woman. (Remember that at the time, most Iraqi women wore veils, and so it was a good way for a person to hide his or her identity.) Of course, considering that Saddam is 6 feet 2 inches tall and more than 210 pounds, he must have cut a fairly striking figure in a country where most people are almost a foot shorter.

Even though the assassination attempt failed and he fled the country dressed as a woman, Saddam's stature within the Ba'th organization in Iraq grew. He had proven himself as committed as any to the success of the Ba'th Party. Saddam traveled from Syria to Cairo, where he met his hero, Egyptian President Gamal abdel Nasser. At that point, Nasser's popularity outside Egypt was extremely strong. He represented the resurgence of Arab culture against the Western imperialists, and his successful nationalization of the Suez Canal was a source of pride for Arabs throughout the Middle East.

Nasser, while not a Ba'th himself, was an Egypt-centric pan-Arabist; he was in favor of overthrowing the Iraqi government because it constituted a rival to his pan-Arab authority. (You'll recall his repeated calls to the Iraqi military to take over the government). Nasser was all too happy to give aid and comfort to the young Ba'th revolutionary. With Nasser's support, Saddam was able to enroll in a Cairo law school in 1962. Saddam's true course of study, however, was the overthrow of the Iraqi government.

Back Home Again

On February 8, 1963, the Ba'th Party staged a coup and ran a short-lived, violent regime.

During this nine-month tenure, the Ba'th killed thousands of people and imprisoned thousands more. The Ba'th resorted to torture to punish their captives and to gain information and confessions from them. (In so doing, they were setting a precedent that would be followed in later years under Saddam's rule.)

Saddam returned to Baghdad and quickly was given command over a Ba'th prison where, not so surprisingly, most of the tortures were conducted. He again demonstrated his willingness to do whatever was needed—including murder and torture—to support the Ba'th Party's power, and by doing that, increase his own power.

You'll recall that the Ba'th Party only held power for nine months in 1963. A coalition of officers, led by General Abdul Salam Arif, threw out the Ba'th in November 1963. The Ba'th officials were all removed from power, and many were imprisoned. Saddam managed to survive the Arif sweep, however, and he began to work with the Ba'th Party leadership to prepare for the next opportunity to seize power.

Saddam himself oversaw the creation of a secret police force and an intelligence apparatus that would be used during the next coup—whenever it came—to consolidate the Ba'th grip on power. The Ba'th leadership would not leave the door open again for another group to undermine their position.

A Tale of Two Coups

The Ba'th Party in 1963 had been heavily influenced by Nasser and less focused on domestic realities inside Iraq than it should have been. The 1963 Ba'th leadership had taken power riding popular discontent with Iraqi foreign policy moves, but they lost power because of their own clumsy dealings with domestic resistance and their inability to assume a sustaining control of the daily functions of government.

By 1968, the Ba'th Party was older and wiser. Nasser's influence had begun to wane. The Ba'th Party leaders were focused, prepared, and (thanks to a new intelligence network) better informed about their adversaries.

The next opportunity came in July 1968. By that time, the Arif government was reduced to an uneasy alliance of senior officers trying to maintain their grip on power. As described in Chapter 9, the disastrous economic and political results of the 1967 Arab-Israeli War, the mounting corruption in the leadership, and fracturing of the central ruling group, opened the door for the Arab Revolutionary Movement to take power from the Arif government.

Increase Your Iraq IQ

Saddam Hussein was a key figure in the 1968 Ba'th campaign to take power. He was everywhere in the early days, rallying support, directing the secret police, and demonstrating his leadership.

Saddam had helped build the Ba'th's secret police force, and he was a respected leader inside the Ba'th Party. He was one of the up and comers in a party that commanded the attention and the imagination of the Iraqi intellectual elite in Baghdad. Saddam was not from that crowd—as his tattooed hand betrayed—but he was still able to move among them, thanks to his uncle's teachings. More importantly, he was able to gain their acceptance through his tireless support of the socialist and pan-Arab ideals of the Ba'th Party.

However, the Arab Revolutionary Movement was just as unprepared in 1968 as the Ba'th were in 1963. In less than two weeks, the Nayif-Daud government was overwhelmed by the Ba'th, thanks in large part to their secret police and intelligence agents.

Led by Saddam Hussein, the Ba'th moved swiftly, and they did not repeat their 1963 mistakes. They took power, and they held it.

He Took All of Us In

Initially, Saddam's rural background was seen by the early Ba'th intellectual leadership as an asset. Because he came from the "other side of the tracks," he was even more qualified in their eyes to keep the amalgamation of peoples, religious sects, and rural/urban backgrounds together.

Dissolution of the Iraqi state was—and still is—a real fear of the elites in Iraq. They were well aware of the diversity and constant antagonisms within their artificial boundaries, and they realized that a strong hand would be needed to keep it all together. Truth be told, the elites may have been happy to have a "low-born" person (although certainly one capable of taking on refined airs) to handle their dirty work for them.

Hamed al-Jubouri, an early member of the Ba'th Revolutionary Command Council, put it this way in a recent interview in *The Atlantic Monthly:*

> In the beginning the Ba'th Party was made up of the intellectual elite of our generation. There where many professors, physicians, economists, and historians—really the nation's elite. Saddam was charming and impressive. He appeared to be totally different from what we learned he was afterward. He took all of us in. We supported him because he seemed uniquely capable of controlling a difficult country like Iraq, a difficult people like our people. We wondered about him. How could such a young man, born in the countryside north of Baghdad, become such a capable leader? He seemed both intellectual and practical.

As al-Jubouri and his peers learned, Saddam's inscrutable character and urbane manners were the poses of a ruthless clan patriarch who would do whatever was necessary to preserve and extend his own power.

The Ba'th Party Triumphant

In late July, the Ba'th Party scooped power from the Arab Revolutionary Front and installed Ahmed Hasan al-Bakr, a former Army general, as the country's new leader. Al-Bakr was the chairman of the Revolutionary Command Council (RCC) that exercised real political authority in Iraq. (The positions of president, and prime minister of the cabinet, while important, did not carry the authority that membership in the RCC did.) Almost all the top spots were held by military officers, increasing the likelihood of military support for the new regime.

Iraq Fact

The Tikriti tribe was centered in a region just north of Baghdad. They were located in and around the city of Tikrit. Saddam Hussein's village, Auja, was near Tikrit. Saddam surrounded himself with members of his tribe as a measure of loyalty and protection.

Note the clan influence: The ruling circle of the Ba'th Party was dominated by Tikritis. The Tikritis were from the town of Tikrit (close to where Saddam was born). Ahmed Hassan al-Bakr, the leader of the Ba'th Party in 1968, was a Tikriti. Three of the five-member Revolutionary Command Council were Tikritis: al-Bakr, Hammad Shihab, and Saddam Hussein. All three were related, as well. Furthermore, the president, prime minister, and defense ministers were Tikritis.

Why Not Saddam?

If Saddam Hussein was so capable and so well positioned within the Ba'th leadership, why wasn't he placed in charge in 1968? The answer is twofold:

- ◆ In 1968, Saddam was not yet willing to take power.

- ◆ He was not strong enough to hold power if he had taken it.

Saddam probably remembered the short-lived 1963 coup; a careful man, he probably wasn't ready to stick his neck out as the head of a precarious fledgling government. Saddam had managed to survive the November 1963 power transition, mainly because he was not that visible outside the Ba'th Party itself.

Saddam Hussein was, in short, the consummate behind-the-scenes man.

Another point to bear in mind is that the other Ba'th leaders, and Iraqi elites who indulged them, were still not quite prepared to have a tattooed country boy in charge. Early in 1968, before the purges that Saddam and al-Bakr pursued with a vengeance over the next five years, there were still solid power blocs outside the fledgling Ba'th regime. These power elites would have to be mollified, or destroyed, before Saddam would be able to wrest and hold on to power in Iraq.

Saddam Repels a Counterattack

The members of the Ba'th leadership that took over in 1968 were not Nasser sycophants, but there were still many Nasserites in the Iraqi elites. These Nasserites saw the Ba'th government as being too independent and as promoting a brand of pan-Arabism that was not espoused by Nasser. These Nasserites felt strong enough to try their own coup in September of 1968. However, this time the Ba'th secret police, under Saddam's direction, sniffed out the plotters and foiled the coup. The Nasserites were purged from the party and from any positions of responsibility. Their families were dispossessed of their homes; women and children were sent into the street, and men were imprisoned.

Justice, Clan-Style

This style of justice was totally in keeping with the clan-type power preservation methods that were perfected by Saddam and al-Bakr in their early years. Families would take revenge … so families had to be destroyed.

Saddam, like Joseph Stalin before him, was a master of the *purge*.

Removing the Rivals

Using the Nasserite coup attempt as a pretext, Saddam and al-Bakr relentlessly purged competitors, power groups, and opponents from the government. Purges became a method of removing opposition and instilling a state of terror that enabled the leadership to assert tighter and tighter control of the government, and through it, the people of Iraq.

Setting the Stage

After a decade of purging, power plays, and consolidation, Saddam had assumed an aura of populism and authority with the people, and a practical control of power within the government, that strongly recalled the position of Joseph Stalin at a similar stage in his career.

The reality was as follows: al-Bakr brought popular legitimacy and army ties to the Ba'th

> **Desert Diction**
>
> A **purge** is the removal of a set of individuals from a group. In the case of Iraqi politics, purges meant imprisoning and perhaps killing groups of people who were seen as threats to the ruling circle. Typically, a purge needs a reason, such as an attempted coup. The Soviet dictator Joseph Stalin excelled at the purge; he staged elaborate show trials to justify the removal of former party favorites.

> **Iraq Fact**
>
> The 1968 Nasserite coup attempt wasn't the last that Saddam Hussein batted down. He successfully oversaw the response to yet another coup attempt by a dissident Ba'th faction in July of 1973.

administration; Hussein brought a genius for counter-operations and eliminating opposition. Over time, al-Bakr and Hussein took effective control of the Party.

By most accounts, Saddam was the real driver. He organized party structures and established a Ba'th militia, which later became the Republican Guard. (This militia would grow to over 50,000 men before the end of the 1970s.)

Troubles with the Kurds

Saddam continued to do the dirty work of the Party. He directed operations against the Kurds during the early 1970s.

The Kurds were rebelling against the central government in Baghdad. After the Ba'th takeover, they continued to agitate for autonomy, if not outright independence.

The Kurds were led by Mustafa Barzani. In March 1970, the RCC (with Saddam Hussein representing the council) and Barzani agreed on an elaborate, 15-article peace plan. The agreement allowed the Kurds to keep a 15,000 man fighting force. The agreement defined these Kurdish fighters as the Pesh Merga, meaning "Those Who Face Death."

The agreement did not define the status of Kurdish territory. It was not defined as independent, or autonomous, at least on paper. However, in reality the Pesh Merga controlled a broad swath of northeastern Iraq. Provisional Kurdish governments were established in this zone. Furthermore, Barzani's faction in Kurdistan, the Kurdish Democratic Party (KDP), was appointed as the only legal representative of the Kurdish people. Not all Kurds belonged to the KDP, however, and dissenting Kurds began to assail the agreement (and Barzani's Pesh Merga). By 1973, the agreement was basically defunct, and the Kurds were as rebellious as ever.

Saddam Seeks Soviet Support

At this point, the Ba'th government resorted to an assassination attempt against Barzani and his son, Idris, in 1974. The assassination attempt failed, and the Kurds reacted with increased fury. Saddam responded with an agreement with the Soviet Union that managed to isolate the Kurds in Iraq.

Barzani responded by getting military aid from the Shah of Iran and the United States. The United States—like the Shah—was concerned by the Soviet inroads into Iraq, and they were working together to counter that influence by strengthening the Kurds. Also seeking to weaken the Ba'th government, Syria and Israel contributed weapons to the KDP.

Seeing the forces arrayed against them, the Ba'th leadership (with Saddam again leading the way) negotiated an agreement with the Shah of Iran. Basically, the Shah agreed to stop supporting the Kurds if Iraq would recognize that the boundary of the Shatt-al-Arab Waterway was the thalweg, or mid-channel, and not the Iranian shoreline. The thalweg boundary would allow both countries to utilize the waterway equally. This was a critical—and short-lived—compromise; the dispute over the waterway would eventually be the pretext that erupted into an epic and bloody war between the two nations.

Iraq also dropped its claims to some islands at the mouth of the Shatt-al-Arab and to Khuzestan (a region along the Iran-Iraq border in the mountains). The Shah agreed to cut off arms shipments to the Kurds. This agreement, signed on March 6, 1975, by Saddam and the Shah, was finalized in Algiers, and came to be known as the Algiers Agreement.

A Carrot and an Even Bigger Stick

With Iranian assistance cut off, the Iraqi military moved in on the Kurds. Most of the Pesh Merga surrendered, but a significant number faded back into the hills and continued to fight—or fled over the border to Iran. Saddam offered to create three autonomous areas for the Kurds and provide them some constitutional protections. At the same time, he ordered the Kurdish villages on the Iranian border destroyed. He also forcibly relocated Kurds out of the Kurdish homeland and relocated Arab settlers into the Kurdish homeland.

This carrot and stick policy only led to more fighting and to the weakening of the KDP legitimacy in Kurdistan. In June 1975, Jalal Talabani created the Patriotic Union of Kurdistan (PUK). The PUK and KDP devolved into a violent internecine battle through the end of 1979, effectively ending their resistance to Iraqi countermeasures. So by the end of 1978, Saddam was able to claim a "victory" in the Kurd campaign. Once again, Saddam's reputation increased.

On the Home Front

In the name of socialism, the Ba'th Party unveiled an industrial modernization program in 1976. Using revenues from the newly nationalized oil industry, including the quadrupling of oil prices during the oil shock in 1973, the government plowed subsidies into Iraqi industry. The government strategically located factories to create patronage and loyalty to the ruling group.

The land reform campaigns (see Chapter 11) that redistributed much of the shaykhs' lands to the farmers who actually worked them was also an effective means of strengthening the Ba'th Party, as rural communities benefited from the land reforms. Clan leaders' power was diminished, as individual families were able to take title to lands that had belonged to absentee landlords for decades.

The Ba'th leadership also invested heavily in hospitals and infrastructure projects like irrigation and roads. By judiciously meting out the cash, the Ba'th leaders were able to secure loyalties by granting economic resources through specific projects to chosen people. More cash, from higher oil prices, meant more patronage, more loyalty, and (not incidentally) more power for Saddam, as most ordinary Iraqis credited him with making the changes given his authority over the projects.

There was also an aggressive literacy campaign, and state education reforms that resulted in an almost universal literacy rate. The number of schools increased, as the state founded a public school system (which allowed girls and young women to be taught) alongside the existing religious ones. The United Nations even gave Saddam an award for his efforts in this campaign. The program secured more loyalty for Saddam, thanks to the careful placement of the schools and hospitals.

During this period, some wealth was redistributed, education rates increased, and health standards increased. Saddam's power also increased. Domestic unrest was at least contained, and Saddam looked to foreign policy as the next step on his path to power. Saddam started by reaching out to his neighbors.

> **Increase Your Iraq IQ**
>
> Saddam Hussein was presented as the primary architect of domestic reforms (education, agriculture, and industry) for the Ba'th Party in the 1970s. Al-Bakr, the chairman of the RCC and leader of the country, allowed (and probably encouraged) Saddam to take the public spotlight and credit for these populist moves in order to set the stage for Saddam to assume a leadership role.

> **Desert Diction**
>
> The peace agreement between Israel and Egypt was known as the **Camp David Accords**. Israel agreed to return the territory in the Sinai that it had occupied at the end of the Six-Day War in 1967, and Egypt agreed to recognize Israel's right to exist. The agreement constituted the first time that a Middle Eastern Arab nation formally recognized Israel's right to exist.

The Break with Egypt

Saddam's big break on the foreign policy front came with Anwar Sadat's signing of the *Camp David Accords* with Israel in September of 1978. The Accords were reviled by the Arab countries, and Egypt's stature as leader of the pan-Arab movement was immediately destroyed. Saddam seized the opportunity to convene an Arab summit meeting in Baghdad that resulted in a condemnation of the Accords. The other Arab countries imposed sanctions on Egypt. (The Egyptians, now major recipients of U.S. aid, managed to get along without Arab support.)

Still not yet a formal head of state, Saddam had nevertheless taken the lead in denouncing Egypt. Iraq's stature—and Saddam's—increased among its neighbors.

Saddam Takes Center Stage

By early 1978, the ties that bound the Ba'th rulers were as tight as ever. Saddam, al-Bakr, and the new Defense Minister General Adnan Khairullah Tulfah were all related to Khairullah Tulfah, Saddam's uncle and mentor. All of these men were Tikritis, and all were tied to the same clan.

Around this time, al-Bakr, older than Saddam, found himself in increasingly poor health. His own grip on power was loosening, while Saddam's was tightening. In July of 1979, Saddam made his move. He placed his relative, al-Bakr, under arrest.

Officially, al-Bakr resigned. In fact, he had been in political decline for some years. Saddam, the ultimate behind-the-scenes man, was ready to step without hesitation to the forefront of Iraqi politics.

So it was that Saddam Hussein assumed control of the government and proclaimed himself the new leader of Iraq.

The Least You Need to Know

- Saddam Hussein was born to a poor rural family, but he was sent to live with a rich uncle who introduced him to the elites in Baghdad.

- Saddam was steeped in the pan-Arab, anti-Zionist, anti-British beliefs that defined the Iraqi intelligentsia.

- As a young man, Saddam joined the Arab Ba'th Socialist Resurrection Party and became a capable lieutenant.

- Saddam gradually rose to prominence through a steady campaign of power consolidation and ruthless suppression of enemies that strongly echoes the career of Joseph Stalin.

- After the Ba'th takeover in 1968, Saddam steadily expanded his influence behind the scenes before assuming control of the government in 1979.

Oil, Guns, and Money: Iraq's Economy Supports the Tyrants

In This Chapter

- ◆ Socialism in Iraq creates a fragile economy

- ◆ The oil industry gets nationalized to fund political power

- ◆ The ins and outs of OPEC

The Arab Ba'th Socialist Resurrection Party took control of Iraq on July 17, 1968. As the party name suggests, the Ba'th added their own brand of socialism and foreign policy to the economic mix they inherited.

To understand current Iraqi economic challenges we have to understand how Ba'th-led Iraq dealt with its economic challenges, its Middle Eastern neighbors, and its role in the international community in the years following the 1968 coup. Some 40 years of socialism and subsidy have created a major challenge for Iraq's current economic ministers.

Socialism, Iraqi-Style

As we've seen, the Arab Ba'th Socialist Resurrection Party was founded by Michel Aflaq and Salah ad-Din al-Bitar, a pair of Syrian students who were steeped in the concepts of socialism, which included the following:

♦ Land reforms

♦ Trade unions

♦ Public ownership of natural resources

♦ Public ownership of factories

♦ Worker involvement in the management of companies

♦ Inclusion in the political process

Socialism in Open and Closed Societies

Historically, socialism has evolved very differently in open societies than in closed societies. The socialism that emerged in countries like Britain, Germany, and Sweden was based on a much more inclusive political process than the socialism that was practiced in the Soviet Union. The Western European model involved steady but sure politically mandated reforms to an existing (and thriving) economic system. The governments created socialist institutions and nationalized various industries and services, but they did so as a result of the mandate of the voters in those countries.

In other words, socialism did not occur outside the democratic process. These countries had a vibrant democratic process that was essentially stable. No coups took place.

Socialism in closed societies, on the other hand, looks very much like another code-word for dictatorship. The Soviet system had only one political party (the Communist Party of the Soviet Union); and although the system claimed universal suffrage, there was no tolerance, dissent, or political challenge to the ruling party. Power and decision-making was concentrated in the Politburo, which consisted of fewer than 20 people. Changes were mandated from the top, not from the will of the populace.

STICKING Socialism to the People

The socialism that emerged in Iraq resembled the Soviet version far more than it resembled the West European model. Like Tsarist Russia, Iraq was a closed society prior to the coup in 1968. The Iraqi populace was almost completely alienated from the process of governance. Any socialist institution-building (nationalization of industries and collectivization of agriculture) happened *to* the people, not *by* the people.

And Now, a Word from Your Friendly Neighborhood Economic Theorist ...

Industrialization is the process of creating specialized production processes in a centralized location, like a factory. In an industrialized society, workers perform specific functions that contribute to a complete product or service. Each function is a specialized activity that is unique and separate from the other specialized activities that also make up the product.

Industrialization requires capital formation. In other words, people need to have excess capital (money) to invest in factories and machinery, or to buy stock in companies that make things.

The standard theory about industrialization runs something like this:

- Agricultural resources are concentrated into efficient farms.

- The increased farm output generates excess capital for the farm owner— money that the farm owner later invests in industry. The more efficient farm frees up people to move from farm work to factory work.

- The key ingredients—extra money and extra people (and, incidentally, extra food to feed them)—all have to be in place for industrialization to take place.

Oil Spill Ahead

Until recently the agricultural sector in Iraq could support the population. The combination of wartime damage to irrigation infrastructure and increased urban population means that Iraq must now import food.

The underlying assumption to this theory is that investment in industry yields higher results for the landowner than investment in agriculture. However, in Iraq at the time of the Ba'th Party takeover, it had long been more profitable for landowners to continue to invest in agriculture than in industry.

Landowners had to pay the rural peasants very little, and infrastructure improvements (such as

Desert Diction

A **shaykh** was the traditional tribal leader in Iraq. Tribal groups were made up of families, and the leader of the family groups was the shaykh. The position was hereditary.

new irrigation systems) greatly increased output, and thus money. So most ruling *shaykhs* were content to continue to plow their profits back into farming, rather than into industry.

Flashback: Private Sector Growth (Or Lack of It) in Iraq

At the turn of the twentieth century, Iraq was not a particularly good place to build a factory. Transportation was primitive, electricity was rare, and local demand was small. So most manufacturing remained at the artisan level, with work done in small shops.

During World War II, local demand for manufactured goods increased, as deliveries from other countries were curtailed. Local industrial investment took off in the post-World War II era, when state oil revenues were devoted to investments in private industry. From 1950 to 1959, the output of manufactured goods grew at a brisk 10 percent annually. Of course, that was from a very small initial base, but the numbers still signified the potential for Iraq to develop a significant value-added industrial sector.

A common pattern in socialist economies is that private sector investments tend to slow down as state investment picks up. The same happened in the post-1958 coup Iraq. As the new leaders invoked socialist principles and began to return land to the peasants, private money began to flee the country.

The process was gradual at first. The Abdul Karim Kassem government focused on returning land to the peasants and initiated the first phases of nationalizing the oil sector. Still, beyond these few measures and allowing trade unions, he basically ignored the industrial sector, which was hardly the orthodox Communist approach to economic planning. Communist orthodoxy included complete control over industry.

However, the emphasis changed in 1964, when the post-1963 coup government of Abdul Salam Arif, taking its cue from Nasser's Egypt, nationalized (that is, established government control of) the 27 largest private industrial companies in Iraq. The Arif government also instituted other socialist concepts similar to those the Ba'th espoused. These included limiting private ownership in non-nationalized industries, mandating worker participation in governing boards of factories, and requiring a

> **Iraq Fact**
>
> The Iraqi version of socialism was at first heavily influenced by Egyptian socialism, as developed by Gamal abdel Nasser. The Arif government that took control during the 1963 coup followed Nasser's lead; it began the process of nationalizing industries, starting with insurance companies and banks, and moved on to assume state control of many other industries.

25 percent profit-sharing program. Under such a plan, 25 percent of the profits from the enterprise would be allocated to a workers' fund, for distribution to the workers at some later date, in some future determined manner (direct payments, investments in worker's health and recreation facilities, and so on).

The result was predictable: Most able administrators and factory managers left Iraq, and they took a lot of capital with them. Industrial output slowed compared to earlier years.

The Whys and Wherefores of Socialism in Iraq

Why did Iraq's leaders pursue these policies? There were a number of reasons.

For one thing, many Iraqi officials truly believed in the socialist doctrines they preached. For another, leaders had convinced themselves that they should follow suit with what was happening in Egypt and other countries. There was also an attempt to appeal to popular sentiment by exacting some degree of retribution against those who had prospered under British protection. Once political power had been attained, nationalization of industry was seen as the remedy to ongoing economic domination by the old British-backed power elites. Land redistribution was used to break the stranglehold of the monarchies the British had established and to displace the groups who had benefited from the system and kept largely landless peasants in servitude.

Probably the main reason for the nationalization, though, was that by removing a class of well-educated, well-off industry owners, the government was eliminating a significant threat to its tenuous authority.

> ### Increase Your Iraq IQ
>
> Many communist and socialist regimes include a "central planning" agency, where a single ministry directs all economic activity. In the Soviet Union, this organization was called GOSPLAN (State Planning Agency). In Iraq it was called the Ministry of Planning. The central planning agency creates a five-year plan that sets targets for production and investments during the following five-year period. In general, Iraq's five-year plan goals were usually not met, and much economic development still occurs outside the scope of the plan itself.

The Ba'th Regime Keeps on Nationalizing

The Ba'th regime continued previous governments' socialist policies and extended the nationalization reach to just about all industry during the 1970s.

Iraq was not (and is not) an exporter of industrial goods to any large extent. The total size of the Iraqi nonoil industrial sector is basically limited to serving domestic demand. The part of the Iraqi industrial economy that doesn't produce oil isn't particularly efficient; it has been subsidized by oil revenues for years.

The Ba'th government used the five-year plan method for managing Iraqi economy, but that system was disrupted by the Iran-Iraq War, the Gulf War, and the subsequent sanctions. The post-Saddam Iraqi government has abandoned any sort of annualized macroeconomic plans.

It is true that, in the 1980s, due to the tremendous economic strains of the Iran-Iraq War (see Chapter 12), Saddam Hussein allowed more private enterprise to meet domestic demand. (In a similar way, Lenin launched the New Economic Program in the 1920s to stimulate local industry that had been devastated by socialization in the years before.) Still, the main way that Iraqi industry continued to function was by means of an infusion of subsidies from oil revenues.

Iraqi Oil: From Concessions to Nationalization

The timeline showing the movement toward nationalization of the oil industry in Iraq is as follows:

1912: Turkish Petroleum Company (TPC) formed

1914: Anglo-Persian Oil Company (British owned) takes 50 percent stake in TPC

Iraq Fact

The concessions granted to the British in 1901 resulted in only 5 percent of the country's oil revenues remaining in Iraq. The Hashemite monarchy managed to improve terms somewhat, but not much; Iraqi elites seethed for years about concessions granted to the Iraqi Petroleum Company (IPC), and this resentment was a major impetus toward nationaliza-

1925: Hashemite monarchy grants first oil concessions for TPC in Iraq; oil-rich Mosul vilayet added to modern state of Iraq

1928: Gulf Oil Company joins TPC; the first U.S. oil company to enter Iraqi oil fields

1929: TPC changes its name to Iraqi Petroleum Company (IPC)

1932: Mosul Oil Company formed to manage northern IPC concessions

1938: Basra Oil Company formed to manage southern IPC concessions

1966: Iraq government repeals 99.5 percent of original IPC concession; Mosul Oil nationalized

1972: Al-Bakr government repeals remaining IPC concessions

1973: Iraq nationalizes Basra Petroleum Company

Pipeline Politics and the Road to Nationalization

Formed in 1938, the Basra Petroleum Company (BPC) had responsibility for the southern portion of the IPC concessions. The BPC opened a pipeline to Faw on the Persian Gulf in 1951. In 1952, another pipeline was laid across Syria, linking the huge Kirkuk fields to the Syrian port of Baniyas. With these two pipelines working, Iraqi oil exports doubled from 10 million tons in 1951 to 20 million tons in 1952. The increased oil revenues to the Iraqi government went to industrial investment, military expenditures, and (last but not least) the cause of lining the pockets of the ruling group.

Up to this point, the ruling Iraqi group did not interfere with the IPC, or with its foreign owners. The money was rolling in, and there was no need to rock the boat.

As oil revenues dramatically increased, however, Iraqi governmental leaders focused on domestic supplies. As part of the concession, the IPC was supposed to provide all of Iraq's domestic demand for gasoline and distillates. The IPC operated a small refinery near Kirkuk for this purpose, but it couldn't meet demand on its own. The IPC also relied on an Iranian refinery to help. The Iraqi leadership did not like the strategic disadvantage of this arrangement.

Their fears were proven when the Iranian government nationalized its oil industry in 1950 and cut production of the refinery used to produce Iraqi oil. The Iraqi government bought the Kirkuk refinery from the IPC and commissioned another to be built at Baghdad. This move signaled the beginning of the Iraqi leadership becoming directly involved in its own oil industry.

Let Me Tell You How It Will Be: Oil Taxes in Iraq

In 1952, the Iraqi leadership demanded, and received, a 50 percent tax on the oil profits. The government was simply following the example of Saudi Arabia, which had increased the tax it charged on oil profits. The old tax had been around 25 percent, so the change again increased oil-related revenues for the ruling group.

Still the IPC limited overall production from Iraqi fields, because there was more than enough oil available by 1960. The major oil companies that controlled IPC lowered the prices they charged for Iraqi oil, which reduced the profit tax. Even more frustrating to the Iraqis was the fact that the IPC treated Iraq as a strategic reserve, using only a fraction of the massive oil resources available … and essentially "calling the shots" in a way that had a profound effect on the Iraqi economy.

Enter OPEC

In response to the situation, the Iraqi leadership convened a meeting, in Baghdad, of the major oil producing nations in the region. In September 1960, this group formed the Organization of Petroleum Exporting Countries (OPEC). This single move was a critical step on the path to nationalizing Iraqi oil. OPEC membership meant the Iraqi oil production was added to that of a bloc of oil producing countries. By working together, these oil-producing countries could dramatically affect oil prices by controlling oil production.

The next such step, as we have seen, occurred in December 1961, when the Kassem government repealed a huge (undeveloped) portion of the IPC concession. This move did not take over working assets, but it did signal the impatience of the Iraqi leadership with the relatively small output of the IPC.

> **Increase Your Iraq IQ**
>
> The 11 countries that form OPEC are Algeria, Libya, Nigeria, Indonesia, Iran, Iraq, Kuwait, Qatar, Saudi Arabia, the United Arab Emirates, and Venezuela. OPEC countries exert a measure of control over world oil prices by determining oil production levels for its members.

In February 1964, the Arif government set up the Iraq National Oil Company (INOC). INOC was state-owned, and did not include any of the Western major oil companies who were invested in the IPC.

However, INOC lacked the experience necessary to effectively develop oil fields on its own, and the IPC continued to generate most of the oil revenues from Iraq at the Kirkuk field it controlled.

In 1966, despite the higher taxes, the repeal of 99.5 percent of the oil concessions, and the formation of a state-owned oil company, the foreign dominated IPC still controlled how much oil would be pumped and shipped out of Iraq. On top of this situation, OPEC member countries negotiated individually with the major oil companies, rather than as a group, so there was little benefit yet to OPEC membership.

The situation worsened for Iraq in 1966 when Syria raised its transit rates on the oil passing through the pipeline across its territory. The Arif government refused to pay, and the Syrians cut the pipeline. The loss of revenue to the state was enormous.

The Arif government felt that the IPC was selling its oil at lower prices and limiting production to punish the government for the previous repeal of the 99.5 percent of the original concession. Arif reached out to the French, and later the Soviet Union, to help develop domestic oil for itself. Eventually, these two outside players were able to help get Iraqi oil production moving without the help of the IPC.

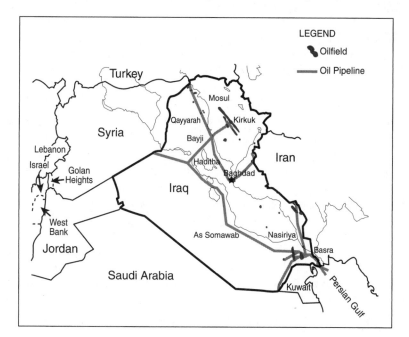

Iraqi oil fields.

Nationalization Under the Ba'th

By 1972, when the Ba'th party was in power, the success of the INOC finally brought the IPC to the bargaining table. The IPC offered to increase output and raise prices "if the original concession area was restored. But, by now, the al-Bakr government, emboldened by the successes of INOC in developing the huge Rumalyah field, responded by nationalizing the remaining 0.5 percent of the old IPC concession. They created the Iraqi Company for Oil Operations (ICOO) to manage the Kirkuk fields. The Basra Petroleum Company was allowed to continue operation in the south.

The IPC and Iraqi government settled their grievances in February 1973. The IPC paid $350 million to the government as compensation for charging low prices, and the government gave the IPC 15 million tons of Kirkuk crude, valued at $300 million.

The following year, the al-Bakr government nationalized the Basra Petroleum Company interests. They were reacting to the October 1973 Arab-Israeli War; they wanted to avoid shipping oil to any country that supported Israel. To do this, it was necessary to control all of Iraq's oil. By 1975, the process was complete, and Iraq controlled 100 percent of its oil industry.

Increase Your Iraq IQ

On October 6, 1973, the Jewish holy day Yom Kippur, the Arab states around Israel attacked. Egyptian forces drove across the Sinai, and Syrian forces attacked from the north. Iraqi troops joined with the Syrians, and Iraqi planes attacked alongside the Egyptians. After some initial success, the Egyptian forces were pushed back across the Sinai. Then the Syrian, Iraqi, and Jordanian forces were pushed back beyond Jerusalem.

U.S. and Soviet diplomacy, along with a rapidly deteriorating military situation for the Arabs, forced a cease-fire on October 23, 1973. Egypt and Israel signed a peace treaty in November, but Syria and Iraq kept fighting until 1974. As a result of the war and subsequent cease-fire discussions, U.S. ties with Egypt (that had been broken after the Six-Day War in 1967) were resumed. (U.S. diplomacy stopped the Israelis from destroying a marooned Egyptian army group during the fighting, and that may have contributed to the warming relations between the two countries.)

Al-Bakr was the nominal leader of the Ba'th government, and gets the credit for nationalizing the Iraqi oil industry in the early 1970s. However, al-Bakr was just the front man for another Ba'th leader, who also took part in the 1968 revolution, and was steadily assuming more and more power inside Iraq.

This leader proved to be quite adept at channeling the newly controlled oil revenues to domestic infrastructure projects that increased agricultural output and improved transportation—as well as his own popularity. This new leader also succeeded in channeling more resources into internal security, otherwise known as the secret police. This enlarged security apparatus eventually became his stepping-stone to ultimate power.

His name was Saddam Hussein, and his next step was to secure his place in Iraqi and Arab history by promoting himself on the international stage with a bold stroke. That bold stroke would almost become his downfall.

The Least You Need to Know

- Industry in Iraq was gradually nationalized from 1963 to 1980.
- The oil industry was nationalized by 1975.
- Oil revenues allowed the Iraqi governments to subsidize their nationalized non-oil industries.
- Saddam Hussein tried to use the riches of his oil-based, socialized economy to prop himself up, at home and abroad.

Rivers of Blood: The Iran-Iraq War

In This Chapter

- ◆ A brisk consolidation of power
- ◆ Saddam's miscalculation
- ◆ A crisis averted

As though eager to take yet another page from the Joseph Stalin playbook, Saddam moved swiftly, vigorously, and dramatically to neutralize people in two groups: enemies and potential enemies.

In July 1979, Saddam was vice chairman of the RCC and vice president of the Republic. He was planning to assume the chairman and president roles as a matter of course. Other Ba'th Party leaders wanted a party election to select the next leader. Saddam would not risk losing that election process.

The Purge: Saddam Takes Charge

On July 18, two days after al-Bakr's resignation, Saddam summoned the RCC and many other senior party officials to a meeting. With cameras rolling, Saddam appeared before the group in full military regalia and declared that there had been a Syrian plot to overthrow the government. Before anyone could protest, Saddam produced the secretary general of the RCC, Muhyi Abd al-Hussein Mashhadi.

Increase Your Iraq IQ

In assuming power, Saddam was simply manifesting his tribal background and the tribal way of dealing with one's rivals. By those rules, eliminating your enemies is the only way of being absolutely sure that they are no longer a threat. By being publicly ruthless, Saddam also made it quite clear to the nation—and the world—that he was capable of, and willing to use, terror in order to maintain power and authority.

A broken Mashhadi confessed his role in the plot and started naming members of the audience as co-conspirators. As each person was singled out, armed guards descended on him and dragged him away. Later, these "conspirators" were tried in secret and executed.

At the end of it all, Saddam circulated film of the spectacle throughout Iraq, publicizing his "rightful" ascent to power. Outside of the ruling circles, the military, and the urban intellectual elites, however, it is doubtful that Iraqis were overly concerned with the leadership change. In fact, considering all the reforms Saddam had instituted, they probably were happy he was now in charge. Saddam, not content with domestic authority, now sought to establish his international authority (at least with his fellow Arabs).

The Background Story: All the Stuff That Led Up to That Deal with the Shah

The gradual departure of the British from the region in the decades following World War II left Iran and Iraq jockeying for dominance in the Gulf. Before 1975, the two countries had operated under the terms of a 1937 British-mandated treaty governing the Shatt-al-Arab. That treaty placed the international border at the Iranian shore, instead of in the middle of the channel. Thus, Iraq had nominal ownership of the waterway. The treaty also required Iraq to maintain the waterway for navigation, while requiring "other nations" (namely Iran) to pay a transit fee for use.

With the British pulling their military forces out of the Gulf states, Iran became bolder. The Shah said that Iraq was not fulfilling its end of the treaty and abrogated the 1937 treaty. To prove his point, the Iranians cruised the waterway and did not pay the fees. The Iraqis responded by aiding dissidents in Iran, and Iran returned the favor by aiding the Kurds in Iraq. In other words, things were getting ugly between the neighboring states.

Increase Your Iraq IQ

The Persian Gulf is separated from the Indian Ocean by the narrow **Strait of Hormuz.** Tankers and navy vessels going to or from the upper Gulf (where the oil loading terminals of Iraq, Iran, Kuwait, Bahrain, Qatar, and the UAE are located) must pass through this strait. Iran makes up the entire northern shoreline, and the islands of Abu Musa and the Greater and Lesser Tunbs are across the Strait. The country that controls these islands can more easily interfere with shipping through the Strait.

In November 1971, Iran occupied the Gulf islands of Abu Musa and Greater and Lesser Tunbs. These islands had been controlled by the two Emirates in the United Arab Emirates. Without British military support, there was little the UAE could do about the move. However, the Iraqis viewed the move as a clear challenge; they saw Persians trying to take over the Gulf and threaten Iraqi oil shipments through the strategic *Strait of Hormuz*. They didn't like what they saw. But they couldn't do much about the incursion, thanks to the vexing Kurd rebellion back home, which required their full attention.

Iraq Fact

Born in 1900, Ruhollah Khomeini was educated in the Shiite faith. In 1950, at the age of 50, he was dubbed "Ayatollah," a title that designates status as a supreme religious leader. There are a number of ayatollahs in the Shiite legal hierarchy; the Shiite faith places great emphasis on their leadership. Khomeini, like many Shiite clerics, was outspoken in his criticism of the secular regime of the Shahs. He was exiled from Iran in 1964, and spent the next 15 years in Najaf, the Shiite holy city in Iraq. At the request of the Shah, Saddam Hussein deported the Ayatollah in 1978. After a year in exile in Paris, the Ayatollah Khomeini returned to Iran during the Islamic Revolution of 1979. He was proclaimed leader of the Islamic Republic of Iran in 1979. The final decade of his life was filled with turmoil, notably the hostage crisis at the former U.S. Embassy in Tehran and the Iran-Iraq War.

As we have seen, the Ba'th finally sought rapprochement with the Shah in 1975. The Shah's support for the Kurds was threatening the very stability of the Ba'th government. By agreeing to move the international boundary to the thalweg (or mid-channel) of the Shatt-al-Arab, Iraq got Iran to stop supporting the Kurds. The trade-off worked, in so far as the Iraqis were then able to suppress the Kurds, who were left hanging without Iranian arms shipments. But it was only a matter of time before Iran and Iraq would be back at each other throats.

Relations between the two countries were cool throughout the late 1970s. At one point, however, the Iraqis granted a special request of the Shah: Saddam expelled an Iranian Shiite cleric, Ayatollah Ruhollah Khomeini, from Najaf (the Shiite holy city in southern Iraq) in 1978. The Shah was leery of the Ayatollah's fundamentalist influence on the Shiites in Iran. Saddam, similarly leery of the Ayatollah's fundamentalist influence on the Shiites in Iraq, was only too happy to comply.

The Ayatollah went into exile in Paris, only to return to Iran in 1979, with the onset of the Iranian revolution. The Ayatollah proclaimed the Islamic Republic of Iran and assumed absolute power in that same year, 1979. Saddam was thus faced with a resurgent Shiite ruler in Iran whom he had booted out of the most holy Shiite city scarcely 12 months before. Rather than a secular, pragmatic (if belligerent) Shah, Iraq's new leader had to deal with a hostile revolutionary cleric who commanded the religious attention of over half the population of Iraq—and virtually all the Shiites in Iran.

So what did Saddam do? He picked a fight with the Ayatollah ... a fight that eventually led to an epic and bloody war.

Why Pick a Fight with Iran?

To understand why Saddam waged war against Iran, you have to understand the challenges and the opportunities he faced once the Ayatollah assumed power in Iran.

The Challenges

Saddam feared that the Ayatollah would resume arms shipments to the Kurds in the north, and worse, maybe even to the Shiites in the south. Already, Iraqi Shiites were rioting, thanks to the government's refusal to allow a procession of Shiites to cross into Iran to congratulate the Ayatollah. To make matters worse, Saddam's remarkably efficient secret police had uncovered a Shiite group named al-Da'wah al Islamiyah (the Islamic Call, usually referred to as al-Da'wah) that called for an Iraqi fundamentalist Shiite state—on the Iranian model. Finally, the Ayatollah's regime was every bit as despotic and aggressive as Iraq's. Already, Iranian Shiite leaders were preaching an expansionist theme. Who knew what it would do next?

The Opportunities

Iran could have been weakened by the cataclysm of fundamentalist revolution, and therefore, have been a ready target for attack. Saddam could increase his stature within Iraq (meaning within the Sunni elites), and within the Arab world, by beating up on the non-Arab Shiites in Iran. Second, shutting down the Ayatollah meant shutting down the Kurds. Saddam had not really put the Kurd problem to bed, and a Kurd truce was vital to his personal hold on power. Third, the Iranian region of Khuzestan bordered Iraq. It had an Arab (not Persian) majority, and was rich in oil. Saddam thought it possible that he could either carve that region off of Iran, or at least incite the Arabs there to join his march on Tehran.

Countdown to Battle

In April of 1980, the al-Da'wah attempted to assassinate Iraqi Foreign Minister Tariq Aziz, and then, a short time later, made an attempt on the life of the minister of culture and information, Latif Nayyif Jasim. The attempts failed; and Saddam responded by deporting thousands of Shiites with Iranian blood back to Iran and jailing al-Da'wah leaders.

Baqir as Sadir, the al-Da'wah leader, was executed, as was his sister. Things remained tense, and in September 1980, Saddam decided to make his move. The decision looks worse in hindsight than it did at the time; relations with Iran were bad for all the Arab states at that time, and the historical enmity between the two nations meant he could expect some support from the Arab world. What's more, he doubtless saw war with Iran as a golden opportunity to increase his power at home (remember that *dictators need enemies!*), while increasing his stature as a pan-Arab leader.

A Pretext for War

Saddam found all the justification he needed for war in the Algiers Agreement he had negotiated with Iran. The Iraqi government took the position that the 1975 agreement—the one that had given Iran joint control over the Shatt-al-Arab—was only a truce, and not a permanent treaty.

In late September of 1980, Saddam officially rejected the Algiers Agreement and announced that the Shatt-al-Arab had reverted to full Iraqi authority. Iran was incensed at the change of terms, and almost immediately both sides prepared for war. On September 21, the Iraqis lobbed some artillery into Iran, and Iran responded in kind. The next day, both sides sent aircraft on bombing raids into each other's territories. On the day after that, Saddam sent troops into Iran, and the serious fighting was underway.

Act I: Iraq Attacks (1980–1981)

In the early stages of the war, it seemed as though the Iraqi army would win in a walk. They were well equipped with Soviet weapons, had high morale, and were ably led. They had 12 divisions, with tanks, to throw at the Iranian army.

The Iranians, on the other hand, were suffering from low morale; most of their experienced officers had been purged during the revolution; and they were now led by clerics with no military experience. Their mechanized equipment (obtained during the Shah's rule from the United States) had not been maintained, and there was little hope of getting spare parts from the Americans in the war's early stages.

Originally, the Iranians had two divisions in the central border region, but these had been degraded to the point where they only had some poorly outfitted battalions and a handful of undermanned tank companies. The rest of the Iranian equipment was not operational, due to lack of parts. The Iranian air force still was operating some of the latest American fighters, and they had shown they could use them during the foiled hostage rescue attempt in April 1980.

Iraq Fact

On November 4, 1979, Islamic revolutionary "students" seized the U.S. Embassy in Tehran, taking 71 captives. After releasing 19 of the hostages on November 19, they held the remaining Americans hostage for a total of 444 days. The Carter administration attempted a rescue in April of 1980 that failed completely. The failure was due to several factors, including too few helicopters, mechanical problems, dust storms and low visibility, and a collision between a C-130 and a helicopter at a desert refueling point. The hostages were released on the eve of Ronald Reagan's inauguration in January 1981.

The Iraqis attempted a massive air strike against Iranian airfields on September 22, 1980, but the strikes were ineffective, and the Iranians quickly responded with air strikes of their own.

Saddam Gains Ground

Initially, things went well for Saddam. On September 23, six Iraqi army divisions invaded the Iranian territory of Khuzestan. This region held a sizable Arab-speaking minority and was oil-rich. Saddam wanted at least to be able to carve out this section of Iran, and he hoped the Arab minority would rebel against the Ayatollah. The rebellion never happened; however, the initial Iraqi attack drove 8 kilometers into Iran within a matter of days.

To the north, an Iraqi mechanized mountain division took the Iranian border town of Qasr-e Shirin. In the center of the front, the Iraqis drove on Mehran and severed the main north-south road along the Iranian side of the border.

The invasion in the south pushed more than 80 kilometers into Iran after only a few weeks of fighting. In response the Iranian president, BaniSadr, freed many of the fighter pilots who had been jailed due to their loyalty to the Shah. These skilled pilots, using the latest American aircraft, were able to blunt the Iraqi attack.

By November 3, 1980, Iraqi forces reached the city of Abadan, but were stopped there by an Iranian Revolutionary Guard unit, called the Pasdaran. At its height, the Iraqi army had secured the Shatt-al-Arab and occupied a 40-kilometer swath of Iranian border territory. However, the Iranians stopped all the talk of a quick Iraqi victory by calling on the Pasdaran military units, and a new force, called the *Basij*.

> **Desert Diction**
>
> The **Basij** were referred to as the "Army of Twenty Million" or the People's Militia. They eventually numbered in the hundreds of thousands. The Basij were poorly trained and equipped, but they were religious zealots. Many went into combat carrying their own shrouds, because they expected to die in battle and achieve martyrdom.

Saddam Extends an Olive Branch

Iran's counterattacks finally stopped the Iraqi advance. Iran also responded by convincing Syria to close the Iraqi oil pipeline and by seizing the Iraqi oil terminal in al-Faw. The Iraqi army began to dig in and build an impenetrable defensive line (a tactic they would employ again in the Gulf War in 1990).

Perhaps realizing that he may have overplayed his hand, Saddam offered a peace settlement to Iran early in the war. The offer was rejected, and Iran began to counterattack by January 1981. The first attacks were clumsy and failed in part because Iranian President BaniSadr insisted on commanding the troops himself. BaniSadr did not coordinate the regular army units with the Pasdaran troops, and the Iraqis were able to push the Iranians back.

In late 1981, at the Karun River, the Iranian clerics unleashed their "human wave" tactic that used thousands of Basij to break Iraqi positions. The Basij (often unarmed, many of them children), simply ran at the Iraqi troops, absorbing whatever bullets or bombs the Iraqis fired at them. Any survivors who reached the enemy (the Basij were too numerous to be completely obliterated) would fall upon the Iraqis with whatever they had, often their bare hands. The Iranians had forced the Iraqis out of their northern and central occupations by December 1981. However, the Iraqi army proved unwilling to endure the thousands of casualties that the Basij were willing to take, and so did not mount a serious counteroffensive. To make matters worse, the Iranian air force had almost total control of the skies and was able to bomb literally any target they could find inside Iraq.

Act II: Iraq Retreats (1982–1984)

The Iranians launched a new offensive, Operation Undeniable Victory, in March 1982. The attack forced the Iraqi army to retreat, and it wrecked three Iraqi divisions in the process. By May 1982, the Iranians had the Iraqis on the run all over the front. Saddam ordered the Iraqi army to return to the national border. He hoped that Iran would be happy to go back to the status quo and even repeated his offer to negotiate a peace settlement in June 1982. Iran again refused to negotiate, and instead launched a major offensive (this time inside Iraqi territory) on Basra.

Still using the human wave strategy, and after suffering enormous casualties, the Iranians succeeded in capturing a small slice of Iraq. Throughout 1983, Iran continued to use the human wave with some success. However, with their superior armor, Iraq had been able to stop the Iranians. Still, Iran was prepared to fight and win a war of attrition with Iraq.

CAUTION

Oil Spill Ahead

Don't overlook the element of personal animus in the war waged by Saddam Hussein and the Ayatollah Khomeini. The Ayatollah no doubt still resented Saddam for kicking him out of Iraq in 1978.

During 1984, Iraq concentrated on defending its own territory, rather than on attacking Iran. As part of this effort, and due to the large number of Iranian attackers, Iraq resorted to chemical weapons in 1984, in an attempt to stop the Iranians. Again in April 1984, Saddam offered to meet personally with the Ayatollah, but the Ayatollah again refused to negotiate with the Iraqi leader.

Iraq Fact _____

Iran's human wave tactic used people in huge numbers to attack the Iraqi enemy. The casualties were enormous. An east European reporter, watching the battle from February 29 to March 1, 1984, wrote that he "saw tens of thousands of children, roped together in groups of about twenty to prevent the fainthearted from deserting" during the attacks. The Iranians made little, if any, progress despite these sacrifices.

Act III: The War of Attrition (1984–1987)

By 1984, some 300,000 Iranian soldiers and 250,000 Iraqi troops had been killed or wounded. The Iranians were still more than willing to take the immense casualties, and the Iraqis were not; thus it was that the Iranians waged a war of attrition in the hope of pressuring the Iraqis to accept defeat.

In just two days, between February 29 and March 1, over 25,000 combatants died on both sides during one of the largest battles of the entire war. In this battle, the human wave performed a new role. They ran through the minefields, to clear a path for the Iranian tanks.

Finally, the Ayatollah started to use regular army units instead of his Pasdaran and Basij volunteers. Still, the losses mounted. During one four-week stretch, the Iraqis lost 9,000 troops, and the Iranians lost 40,000. Part of these casualties were the result of chemical attacks—though Iraq denies having used these weapons of mass destruction.

On February 9, 1986, the Iranians succeeded in taking al-Faw, where Iraqi oil was pumped into waiting tankers. The Iraqis attacked furiously, and finally regained al-Faw in 1988. However, the oil facilities were out of commission.

Iraq Fact _____

In March 1986, the United Nations formally accused Iraq of using chemical weapons, namely mustard gas and nerve gas. There was little doubt about it, given the large number of Iranian burn victims who were flown to Europe for treatment. The British representative to the Conference on Disarmament estimated that more than 10,000 people were injured in chemical weapons attacks.

The land fighting continued, though it was basically a stalemate. Both sides extended the war to the Gulf and attacked neutral shipping that was carrying supplies to the belligerents as well as each other's oil facilities. The "tanker war" eventually damaged or sank over 111 neutral ships in 1986 alone.

In January 1987, Iran launched Operation Karbala Five, aiming at Basra. By the time that battle was over, Iraq had lost 20,000 men and 45 planes. The Iranians lost more than 65,000.

Despite coming close to breaking the last ditch defense of the Iraqis, Iran called off the offensive on February 26, 1987. Heavy fighting erupted in the north in May of 1987, but no definitive gains were made by either side.

The West Gets Involved ... Sort Of

The attacks on oil shipping were making Western countries concerned. Seventy percent of Japanese, 50 percent of west European, and 7 percent of American oil imports came from the Persian Gulf in the early 1980s. No one wanted to lose those ships or see a reduction in oil exports from the Gulf region.

While both sides attacked shipping, experts estimate that Iraq attacked three times the number of ships as Iran during this period. Iraq had anti-ship missiles in its arsenal and knew how to use them. Finally, Iraq began attacking Arab-flagged shipping that was moving Iranian oil. Kuwaiti ships were attacked at this time, and they appealed to both the Soviet Union and the United States for help.

Both countries charted some tankers, and the United States sent some naval vessels into the region. On May 17, 1987, the Iraqis accidentally hit the guided-missile frigate USS *Stark* with an anti-ship missile, killing 37 crewmen. Iraq apologized, and did not attack U.S.-flagged ships after that.

> ### Increase Your Iraq IQ
>
> In 1985, the United States had been arming Iran, to counter the earlier Iraqi successes. (These clandestine arms shipments eventually came to be known as the Iran-Contra Affair.) But as fortunes shifted, so did superpower support. After Iran began to make progress through 1986, the United States and the Soviets became concerned about regional stability. Both countries started to arm the Iraqis during 1987, and stopped arming the Iranians. The superpowers were concerned about the possibility of a pro-Iranian Shiite state forming in southern Iraq. Such a state, they reasoned, could create serious instability in the region, and result in a further protracted war.

Within a few weeks of the *Stark* incident, the Americans drafted UN Security Council Resolution 598 on the Gulf War, which the Security Council passed unanimously on July 20. Resolution 598 called for Iran and Iraq to suspend hostilities immediately and return to prewar boundaries. The resolution also promised potential

UN aid to help rebuild the two countries' infrastructure (a step meant to result in increased oil exports from the region and lower oil prices). Tehran rejected the resolution because it did not meet Iran's terms for ending the war, and instead insisted that Iraq should be punished for initiating the conflict. By the beginning of 1988, 10 Western navies and 8 regional navies were patrolling the area.

Finale (1988)

As the land war remained static, and the superpowers were putting a damper on tanker attacks, the Iranians resorted to missile attacks on Baghdad. In what would later be called the War of the Cities, Iraq launched some 190 missiles into Iran in response to the Iranian missile attacks on Baghdad. The ongoing stress of these missile attacks, and the fear that the Iraqis would launch chemical warheads next, brought the Iranians to the negotiation table at last.

The Iranians came to the table for another reason, as well: The Iraqi army, now reequipped with Soviet and French equipment, was a much more effective fighting force than the same group four years earlier. During the first half of 1988, Iraq defeated Iran in four major battles. In the battle to retake al-Faw, the Iraqis used chemical weapons yet again. Facing those defeats, the continued missile terror, and the threat of chemical weapons, the Iranians agreed to negotiate a peace settlement with Iraq. The Iraqis, by this time, had regained some Iranian turf, but Saddam had had enough.

The Iran-Iraq War lasted nearly eight years, from September of 1980 until August of 1988. It ended when Iran and Iraq accepted UN Security Council Resolution 598, resulting in a cease-fire on August 20, 1988.

A Bloody Toll

Iraq had about 375,000 people killed or wounded in the war, a staggering figure for a nation of 16 million. This ratio equates to about 1 casualty for every 42 people in Iraq. Iran may have endured as many as one million dead or wounded. To put those numbers in perspective, consider that Iran had 60 million people in 1988—meaning there was 1 casualty for every 60 people.

When it was all over, the issues that led to the war were still unresolved. The borders were the same, and the combatants were bloodied, but unbowed. Iraq did come out of the war with a military superiority over Iran, but that superiority was lost after Iraq's Gulf War defeat three years later.

At the end of the Iran-Iraq War, Iraq had an army of one million well-equipped, hardened fighters, with extensive combat experience. It had the largest Arab army in the region (and was second only to the Israeli Defense Forces in terms of overall power). By contrast, neighboring Kuwait had virtually no army or air force to speak of, and certainly had no combat experience.

At the same time, Iraq emerged from the war in dire economic trouble. It was supporting an army of one million men. Oil deliveries had been dramatically reduced, so money wasn't coming in. In fact, Iraq owed billions to Arab neighbors who had loaned Iraq money to battle the Iranians. It owed the most money to tiny Kuwait ... and had little prospect of making its payments.

What to do?

The Least You Need to Know

- Saddam picked a fight with Islamic Fundamentalist Iran for a variety of reasons, among them a desire to increase his own stature at home and in the Arab world.

- Iraq began the war well, but almost lost it all during the mid-1980s.

- Finally, when the war began to threaten oil shipments, the United States and the Soviet Union got involved and mandated a ceasefire that took place in August of 1988.

- When the war was over, Iraq faced enormous debts to its neighbors, most notably Kuwait.

- Iraq had also built the largest, most experienced army in the region.

13

Shifting Sands: Iraq Between the Wars

In This Chapter

- ◆ Saddam's debt
- ◆ The quest for Arab leadership
- ◆ Iraq's idle, but powerful, military machine

The years that immediately followed the end of the Iran-Iraq War were fateful ones. The policies that Saddam Hussein followed during that period put the country on a collision course with the United States—and with history.

Iraq's Economy: Black Gold, Red Ink

By the end of the Iran-Iraq War, Iraq's economy was in shambles. The country owed more than $50 billion to a range of countries that had loaned Iraq the money to fight the grinding, increasingly desperate war with Iran. Iraq had taken weapons on credit from the Soviet Union and France; it had borrowed heavily from Saudi Arabia, Kuwait, and the other oil producing Gulf states.

CAUTION

Oil Spill Ahead

Iraq owed $30 billion to Saudi Arabia and Kuwait alone. It owed the most to Kuwait, their tiny neighbor to the south.

Most of Saddam's industrialization plans had been delayed, and finally abandoned altogether, as the shockingly bloody war steadily drained the government coffers. By 1989, investment in nonpetroleum-related projects had practically stopped. There simply wasn't the money to finance projects, and wartime lenders turned off the spigots when the fighting stopped. As he surveyed the postwar wreckage, Saddam's plans for a robust, independent manufacturing sector were just a memory.

Twisted Pipes, Twisted Dreams: The State of the Oil Sector

It all came down to the oil industry. Saddam needed oil revenues to finance the reconstruction of his shattered economy and to pay back his creditors. Saddam was well aware of the animosity of the Kurds and the Shiites toward his government. Besides using terror tactics to quell revolution, before the war Saddam had relied on relatively steady improvements in the standard of living for everybody—including the Shiites (whose loyalty was questionable given the Shiite regime in Iran)—to mollify the people and thus safeguard his position since the promised prosperity had not been achieved.

Desert Diction

In 1988, oil generated more than one third of Iraq's GNP and constituted 99 percent of export revenues.

During the war, Saddam could blame the decline in living standards on the necessities of war. Now that the fighting was over, he was under pressure to deliver some improvements, or face the prospect of instability and an increasingly hostile Shiite majority.

Infrastructure Blues

The problem was really quite simple: Even if Saddam could get the oil out of the ground, he couldn't get it out of the country very easily. Oil production and exports had fallen off dramatically due to war-related damage to the oil production and trans-shipment infrastructure.

In 1979, prior to the outbreak of hostilities, Iraq had produced 3.5 million barrels per day (bpd) and exported 3.2 million of them. Almost all the oil produced was exported, because Iraqi domestic demand was fairly small. Almost at the very start of the war,

Iran had crippled Iraq's two main offshore terminals at Mina al Bakr and Khawr al Amayah, where oil was loaded onto tankers. These terminals were still not open by the end of the war. Thus, the major Iraqi outlet to the world markets was closed in 1980, and two years later, in April 1982, Syria turned up the pressure by closing the pipeline that ran from Iraq, across Syrian territory, to the Mediterranean.

Why did Syria do this? Recall that Syria was led by a Ba'th regime under Hafiz al-Asad. The Asad regime was almost diametrically opposed to the Iraqi Ba'th regime, and the two countries' relations were strained even in good times. During the Iran-Iraq War, Syria was an ally of Iran. In fact, Iranian martyrs' families were given vacations in Damascus.

> **Increase Your Iraq IQ**
>
> During the Iran-Iraq War, Saudi Arabia and Kuwait, along with other Arab Gulf states, "donated" oil to Saddam Hussein's government in Iraq in order to make up for production shortfalls due to war damage. Throughout the war with Iran, Iraq received almost 300,000 bpd from Saudi Arabia and Kuwait.

With the Syrian outlet cut off, and its own terminals in shambles, Iraq resorted to tanker truck convoys through Jordan and Turkey as an alternative way to get oil to market. About 250,000 bpd were exported via this method from 1983 through 1989. Iraq also expanded an existing pipeline that connected to Turkey, and by 1984 the country was exporting 1 million bpd through that channel. By 1987, the pipeline's capacity had been increased again to 1.5 million bpd. The Iraqis were also expanding a pipeline through Saudi Arabia to the Red Sea at Yanbu that would allow them to export an additional 500,000 bpd.

By 1987, despite the loss of the Gulf oil terminals and the wartime damage to other oil facilities, Iraq was still able to produce 2.8 million bpd (compared to 3.5 million bpd prior to the war) and export 1.8 million bpd (compared to 3.2 million bpd prior to the war). In short, oil production was down, and exports were just over half their prewar levels—but the exports were still reaching the foreign markets.

Adding Insult to Injury: Crude Oil Prices Plummet in 1988

The crash in world oil prices in 1988 made Iraq's internal economic situation even worse. *Spot prices* in 1988 were less than $13 per barrel—compared to prices over $35 per barrel in 1979.

Desert Diction

Spot prices are the current trading price of products in markets where the material is available for immediate delivery. Oil spot prices are standard measurement of current oil product values.

Iraq Fact

Iraq has proven reserves of around 140 billion barrels. Proven reserves are oil that we know to be in the ground. Given that amount, Iraq could pump oil for 100 years at its 1987 rates. On top of that oil (literally) is 850 billion cubic meters of natural gas. Iraq could capture that energy source as well, and had been working on that capability with Soviet assistance in 1989.

So let's review the situation: To attempt to improve domestic economic conditions, and to mollify a population that had endured eight years of war-related privation, Saddam had to get more money. His only realistic strategy for getting money was to sell oil—99 percent of Iraq's export revenues depended on oil.

The only way to sell oil was to get it out of Iraq, either by pipe or truck overland, or by ship through the Persian Gulf, past the Iranian-dominated Strait of Hormuz. (Remember that Iran had occupied Abu Masul and Greater and Lesser Tunb—islands on the south side of the Strait—and Iran also constituted the entire northern shoreline.) Unfortunately for Saddam, the main facilities for getting the oil to market were wrecked, and he could only get out about half of what he could before the war started.

Even if oil prices had remained the same as they had been in 1979, Iraq would only have been able to generate half the money it could have made if its facilities were working at full capacity. But, oil prices at the end of the war were half the levels they had been before the war, so Iraq's export revenues were only at about one-quarter of their pre-war levels.

The Bottom Line

At a time when Iraq needed more money to rebuild its economy, it was making even less. One solution to the problem was to continue to increase export capacities and pump even more oil out of the ground to sell.

The only problem with increasing the amount of oil to sell (assuming it could regenerate its production and export capacities) was that, as a member of OPEC, Iraq was constrained by a quota on its export levels. OPEC instituted quotas to ensure that too much oil was not produced. Too much oil would create a surplus, and that would drive down prices even further. So OPEC members adhered to set quotas for production. The quotas were, and still are, based upon two main factors: negotiations, and a complex formula relating to proven reserves, capacity, and size.

If Iraq felt constrained by its quota, it could try to increase the quotas during OPEC negotiations. However, Iraqi credibility was limited on this score. Given the desperation of its situation in the middle years of the war, Iraq had unilaterally announced in 1986 that it would produce oil at whatever levels it needed to prosecute the war. In 1987, facing pressure from other OPEC members (countries who were not only loaning Iraq billions of dollars, but also donating large amounts oil), Iraq had said it would stick to its quota … if Iran would reduce its quota to Iraq's level. Predictably, Iran refused the offer because the Iranian quota was twice the Iraqi level. For the remainder of the war, Iraq had produced oil inside the quotas—simply because it didn't have enough working oil production capacity to exceed them. However, as time went on, and as Iraq continued to invest in its oil infrastructure, it had begun to bump up against the quota limits.

By the middle of 1989, Iraq was becoming increasingly belligerent within OPEC, demanding an increase in quotas. Saddam needed the money, and the other OPEC members were standing in his way. Quota limits are negotiated at OPEC meetings, and as in any negotiations, other factors can be brought into play, such as emergency need, or the veiled threat of using force.

> **Oil Spill Ahead**
>
> While still powerful, OPEC's ability to effectively manipulate world oil prices has been diminished since the oil shocks of 1973. The reason is simple: OPEC controls less of the world oil market. The biggest wild card has been the entrance of Russian oil into the market. Russia is not an OPEC member, and sells as it needs and as it pleases.

No Respect: Iraq as International Citizen

In 1988, Iraq was looking for respect, and the benefits that came with it. However, that respect was in short supply.

Any gains in prestige that Iraq had made as a leader in the Arab world during the war were tempered by the fear that its army now inspired in its neighbors. Iraq had been struggling to assert its leadership in the Arab world against its long-time Arab rival, Egypt. Saddam Hussein had seized the opportunity of Egypt's détente with Israel to increase his own stature by leading the chorus of Arab outrage over the Camp David Accords. By 1979, Iraq had normalized its relationships with the oil-producing Arab Gulf states and the other Arab countries in the region.

For years, relations with the West—particularly the British and the Americans— had revolved around the issues of oil and Soviet containment. While not as solidly pro-West as the Shah, Saddam had been careful to be more friendly to the United States after the Islamic Revolution in Iran and had leveraged animosity between Iran and the United States to his own advantage.

Increase Your Iraq IQ

While Iraq and the United States did not have formal diplomatic relations during the 1980s, there were established communications between them through a U.S. Interest Section Saddam opened up to U.S. companies who wanted to sell their services and products in Iraq.

When two countries have formal diplomatic relations, they typically open an embassy in each other's country. When the two countries do not have formal diplomatic relations, they resort to the device of an "Interest Section" that is housed in a neutral country's embassy. During the 1980s, the United States had an Interest Section in the Belgian Embassy in Baghdad. A U.S. executive who worked in Iraq during the early 1980s described the building as "a U.S. Embassy with a Belgian flag over it."

Iraq had also been warm toward the Soviet Union in the period immediately prior to the Iran-Iraq War, but not too warm. The Soviet invasion of Afghanistan in 1979 had alienated most of the Muslim countries in the world, including Iraq. However, the ties between the countries became closer during the war: Iraq bought a significant portion of its armaments from the Soviet Union, and the Soviets were providing technical assistance to Iraq for the development of gas processing and transmission infrastructure.

Of course, the Soviets had looked at Iraq as an element in their larger Cold War struggle with the United States during this period. Anything to weaken the U.S. position in the Middle East fit their strategy, and developing closer ties to Iraq certainly fit the bill.

Changes at the End of the War

Most Arab nations had been happy to see Iraq fulfill its ancient role as bulwark of the Arab world against the Persians. They figured that a strong Sunni-controlled Iraq was better than an expansionist, Shiite-controlled Iran in the region. Support was ample, as we have seen, and by the end of the war, Iraq owed Arab nations in general, and Kuwait (its largest lender) in particular, a very large amount of money. Iraq would pay this debt back in a way that nobody expected.

The loans had been used to buy arms from the Soviet Union, France, and the United States during the war. As a result, Iraqi relations with France were fairly strong during the 1980s. Relations with the Soviet Union and the United States warmed when the war went badly for Iraq, and got cooler when the war went better for Iraq. The superpowers, as we have seen, were working toward maintaining a prewar status quo, and in the end, they got more or less what they wanted: Neither Iran nor Iraq had emerged as a clear winner or loser, and both sides had been taken down a peg or two.

In the Arab world, however, the end of the war brought not satisfaction, but concern. By the end of the war, the other Arab countries were increasingly alarmed by Iraq's resurgence and its massive army. At over one million battle-tested men, it was the largest army in the region.

With the Iranians beaten back, there was no other country in the region that could even begin to match the Iraqis for size, experience, and fire power. Without the Iranian threat, what was to stop Iraq from embarking on an expansionist campaign at the expense of other countries in the region?

Exit the USSR, Enter the U.S.A.

The Soviets had continued to play an active role in oil industry investment projects in the period immediately following the Iran-Iraq War, but that all came to a halt in 1989—along with the Soviet Union itself.

The Russians had economic and political problems of their own to attend to, and the Iraqis soon learned that the fading USSR was in no position to continue foreign investment in Iraq.

The U.S.-Iraqi connection continued to develop toward normal relations. However, the United States was not forthcoming with postwar financial aid to Iraq, which is what Saddam most needed in 1989. Still, Saddam acted like a man who believed that the United States was a country he could bargain with. Encouraged by the steady thawing of relations during the war, U.S. diplomats expected that the American relationship with Iraq would continue to blossom. But there was a surprise in store for the Americans—a surprise that grew out of the nearly incomprehensible levels of debt Saddam Hussein had amassed.

Iraq Fact

By 1989, the Soviet Union was crumbling. Central authority in Moscow was unable to maintain its tight grip on the 15 Republics that made up the Soviet Union. With the culmination of declining economic conditions, increased political and personal freedom, and nationalism, the Soviet Union formally ended on August 26, 1991.

A Sea of Debt

By the end of the war, Iraq owed France $1.3 billion and the Soviets about $5 billion for arms purchased during the fighting. On top of that, Iraq owed about $9.3 billion to various export credit agencies (who had financed additional purchases of weapons on behalf of the governments who controlled those agencies). Iraq also owed private companies about $7 billion. These private companies were generally from countries like Turkey and India, who did not have export credit agencies to support their companies in foreign trade. Iraq also owed Western banks about $6 billion.

The most extraordinary debts, however, were owed to the Gulf states. Iraq owed these countries about $80 billion, and Kuwait was the largest single creditor. Countries that had loaned massive amounts of money, like Saudi Arabia and Kuwait, had wanted a "friendly" country between them and the Shiite Islamic Republic of Iran, and they had seen Iraq as that country.

> **Iraq Fact**
>
> On the home front, Saddam had offered a pension and benefits package worth more than $30,000 to each family that lost a soldier killed in action. Saddam had also compensated each Iraqi property owner in full for any property that was destroyed during the fighting.

In all likelihood, the Gulf states did not expect full repayment on the original schedules they negotiated with the Iraqis; they were, however, expecting some repayment, according to some schedule. At the end of the war, Iraq found itself in the position of having constantly to reschedule its debt payments and promise increasing amounts of its oil production to barter deals and debt repayment. This practice left less and less oil available for infrastructure investments and consumer goods imports.

Caught in the Sinkhole

In the years following the war, Saddam found himself trying, without success, to deal with the economic implications of a conflict that had cost far, far more than he had anticipated.

When the war had started, Saddam appears to have assumed that Iran would surrender quickly, and that Iraq could enrich itself with Iranian land and oil at a fairly low cost. Saddam had plenty of money in the bank (about $35 billion in reserves). He figured he could pay for it all, and not risk his position by depriving his people of material comforts.

Saddam had believed that he could shield the population from the heavy casualties, and he spent heavily on expensive material and munitions in an effort to lessen the Iraqi casualty count.

The result: As the casualties had mounted surrealistically, the costs of the war had, too. This is one reason why the borrowing had mushroomed to such fantastic levels.

Building a $300 Billion Tab

As the war progressed, Saddam also continued to invest in domestic infrastructure and factories that could produce consumer goods. As more and more men went to the front, Iraq had been forced to import foreign labor from countries like the Philippines to complete these investment projects, many of which would eventually be abandoned anyway.

In addition to these expenses, the war had cost Saddam something like $25 million each and every day. The act of keeping the army equipped and at the front had drained the country's wallet at a rate that no one, least of all Saddam, had anticipated.

By the end of it all, the total cost of the war had been truly mind-boggling for a country Iraq's size. One estimate placed the total cost of the conflict to Iraq at more than $300 billion.

Saddam simply couldn't afford to pay off the fight he had picked with Iran.

> **CAUTION**
>
> **Oil Spill Ahead**
> The Kurds were not significantly represented in the Iraqi army, as they had resisted the draft throughout the war.

The Army: All Dressed Up with No Place to Go

By the end of the Iran-Iraq War, a major transformation had taken place concerning the status of the Iraqi army. You'll recall that this army had been fighting a grueling, savage war with the Iranians for eight arduous years. Over one million Iraqis (out of a population of 16 million) were in uniform, and most were battlefield survivors.

The army had earned an even more powerful role in Iraqi government and society. It was considered honorable to be in the military, and honorable to fight. Even the Shiites, who made up 85 percent of the army rank and file (but not the officer corps) took pride in their role fighting against the Persian aggressors, despite the shared religion. The officer corps seemed satisfied with being officers, rather than political leaders—as long as Saddam kept the army supplied with goodies—and they did nothing to impugn the honor of the military. Saddam returned the favor by praising his army as the victors in what was essentially a stalemate.

Saddam was in the position of having fully 6 percent of his people in uniform. One out every 16 people was in the army. Iraqi society was fully militarized by the end of the war, and the citizenry was repeatedly told that they had won the struggle against the hated Persians.

Now that the war had been "won," Saddam would have to produce results for these soldiers, and the folks at home. If he did not, further rebellion was likely from the Kurds, and maybe even the Shiites.

So it was that, at the end of 1989, Saddam faced some extremely difficult choices. He needed money, stature, a way of dealing with his massive debt, and some role for his huge military machine. He looked around the region and saw a ripe plum to be picked just next door.

He set his sights on his chief creditor—the tiny kingdom of Kuwait.

The Least You Need to Know

- ◆ At the end of the Iran-Iraq War, Iraq's economy was in shambles, and the oil production was down to half its prewar levels.

- ◆ Iraq did not get the assistance and respect it felt it deserved after the war.

- ◆ Iraq's ties to the United States were slowly warming, and Saddam felt he could work with the U.S. government.

- ◆ Iraq owed billions to other countries, foreign banks, and foreign companies, and had little prospect of meeting its payments.

- ◆ Iraq had over one million men under arms in the years just following the war.

Part 4

The Gulf War, Part 1

In this part, you find out about the origins, the key events, and the aftermath of Iraq's *first* conflict with the U.S.-led coalition. Here you'll find out how and why the Coalition formed, how the war unfolded, and how Saddam lost the war ... but won the peace. You'll also learn how the stage was set for an encore, whose final act is still being played out on the world stage.

Chapter 14

The Gambit: Iraq Invades Kuwait

In This Chapter

- ◆ The limited options open to Saddam at the end of the Iran-Iraq War
- ◆ Iraq and Kuwait: the history
- ◆ Persistently low oil prices
- ◆ Kuwait's relative weakness
- ◆ The détente with Iran
- ◆ The United States sends mixed signals

On August 2, 1990, the Iraqi army rolled into Kuwait and occupied the country. Seven days later, on August 9, 1990, Iraq formally annexed Kuwait, calling it the nineteenth province of Iraq.

Saddam's Big Bad Idea

Considering (with the benefit of hindsight, of course) that …

- ◆ The (first) Bush administration reacted immediately and forcefully, stating that the invasion "will not stand"

- Within weeks, an Arab-Western coalition had arrayed itself against Saddam

- The United Nations quickly instituted a series of biting sanctions that cut Saddam off from the revenue of Western oil markets

… Saddam's decision turns out to have been a very bad idea.

It's possible that Saddam Hussein completely misread the tea leaves on the question of Kuwait. By the same token, it's also possible that he knew precisely the kind of reactions his action would bring about. In either case, the big question—given the forceful reaction of the international community—was and is: "What was he thinking?"

A Method to the Madness?

As with many other wars, the causes of the Gulf War appear to be rooted deeply in the misunderstandings of key players. One can certainly make a convincing argument that Saddam misread the United States—and an equally convincing argument that the United States misread Saddam.

As we have seen, the aftermath of Saddam's last invasion attempt had not been good. He had just concluded a surrealistically costly war (in terms of people, resources, and lost oil revenues) with Iran. His country was badly damaged, domestic industrial production was down, and oil revenues were down. The price of oil was very low, and Iraq's wartime lenders were now lining up with their hands out. Saddam was forced to constantly reschedule his mounting debt payments, and he continued to delay much-needed domestic investments. His international stature, instead of growing, was diminishing, and the pending demise of the Soviet Union and the end of the Cold War had minimized U.S. attention—and the prospect of aid from the Americans.

To put it bluntly: The man needed money.

The Russians and the Iranians Make Life Even Tougher

Unfortunately for Saddam, world oil prices continued to stay well below their 1979 levels into the year 1990. Production was up, Russian oil was flooding the market, and Iran, too, was pumping as much as it could to rebuild its war-shattered economy.

The prospects at that time for driving oil prices higher seemed poor. Only a serious crisis in the region, where a significant portion of production was threatened, would drive up oil prices again. It's possible that Saddam's thinking may have proceeded along these lines: If he himself could not deliver the goods at home, then he had to find someone to blame. (Remember: Dictators need an enemy.)

From Saddam's perspective, there were few obvious options. What could he do to get more money from his own limited oil capacity? What could he do to increase the price or the amount of oil he controlled?

One thought that may have crossed Saddam's mind was that any kind of a military crisis in the Persian Gulf would cause oil prices to spike. By threatening Kuwait, and by moving troops in (even if only for a little while) he could force oil prices up from their historically low levels.

Target: Kuwait

Kuwait was right next door, and it appears to have seemed like the perfect target to Saddam Hussein. The country was much smaller than Iraq in terms of population (less than 1 million native Kuwaitis compared to the 16 million Iraqis) and geographical size. Kuwait's military was tiny when compared to the Iraqi military machine; Kuwait had only about 20,000 men under arms. At that time, the total size of the Iraqi army is estimated to have been one million men overall.

> ### Increase Your Iraq IQ
>
> Kuwait was founded on June 19, 1961, when the British withdrew and set up a sovereign state. In 1989, there were 826,586 Kuwaitis, and 1,316,014 foreign workers. Kuwait's economy is dependent on oil, and it is one of the richest oil producing nations in the world. The country is ruled by the ailing Sheik Jaber al-Ahmad al-Sabah and his royal family.

File Under "It Seemed Like a Good Idea at the Time"

Why take Kuwait? The main answer, of course, has to do with control of oil resources. Kuwait had fully functioning oil facilities, which would have allowed Iraq to get its oil to market. Kuwait also had enormous reserves of oil. If Saddam was to control Kuwait, he would control a larger share of the world's known oil reserves. Increased control of that much more oil would have had the twin effect of increasing the OPEC quota for an enlarged Iraq—meaning more oil revenues for Iraq—and more influence within OPEC and more leverage in dealing with the organization's heavyweight, Saudi Arabia. Furthermore, if Iraq controlled more oil, and had more influence in OPEC, Saddam would have had a greater opportunity to manipulate world oil prices.

Another reason for invading Kuwait, of course, was equally as pragmatic. Saddam owed Kuwait more than $13 billion, and he had little prospect of paying that money back any time soon. Saddam could wipe out a large portion of his debt by taking over Kuwait.

Of course, Kuwait was only one of many Arab countries that had lent Saddam money. Saddam needed those countries to temper their demands for repayment, to give him more time and more flexibility in making his payments. By showing that his military was powerful, and that he was not afraid to use it to get what he wanted, he may have felt he could (for instance) frighten the Saudis into backing off ... and perhaps then win territorial concessions from them in the *Neutral Zone* or elsewhere.

> **Desert Diction**
>
> When the British created the countries of the Middle East following the breakup of the Ottoman Empire at the end of World War I, they could not settle the border between Iraq and Saudi Arabia. Rather than worry about it, the country makers simply created a buffer zone between the two countries, called the **Neutral Zone.** Later, oil was found under the zone, and the two countries agreed to share the development costs and revenues from that region. During the Iran-Iraq War, Saudi oil donations to Iraq were pumped from oil fields in the Neutral Zone.

In the end, however, the move into Kuwait may simply have been a gambit ... a ploy that seemed to Saddam, for reasons that may not ever be completely clear to outside observers, well worth the risk involved.

A Deadly Housekeeping Agenda

Before Saddam could safely invade Kuwait, he needed to tend to some housekeeping chores at home. First, he had to make sure that the Kurds would stay in check in the north. Second, he needed to be sure the Iranians would not interfere. Third, he needed to be sure the United Sates would not object, and if they did, that they would not do anything to stop him.

Saddam appears not to have been particularly concerned about the potential reaction of the other Gulf Arab states; he may have concluded (correctly) that none of them had the military resources to stop him.

A Flip-Flop to End All Flip-Flops

To minimize the possibility of problems with the Kurds as he marched into Kuwait, Saddam needed to keep the Kurds militarily weak. To do that, he had to make sure that they would not be re-armed by the Iranians. (You'll recall that the Iranians were the traditional supporters of the Kurds.)

If he planned to keep the Kurds quiet as he made his move in Kuwait, Saddam would have to give the Iranians something. What he decided to give them was nothing short of mind-boggling.

The one thing that the Iranians really wanted from Saddam was equal control of the Shatt-al-Arab waterway. So despite eight years of bloody fighting to *keep* the Iranians from controlling this waterway, Saddam handed it over with a stroke of his pen. In 1990, Iraq agreed to the mid-channel boundary between the two countries, thus yielding something that hundreds of thousands of Iraqis had died to prevent.

You Might Well Ask ...

How could Saddam do this without incurring the wrath of his own people? The reaction of the Iraqi people was not his main concern. Saddam seems to have assumed that better living conditions were the public's main interest at that time, and that the people would have little objection to some form of foreign policy maneuvering that they had never had any say over, anyway. This, of course, is one of the by-products of a closed society. The dictator can (and often does) reverse policies almost overnight, without concern for public reaction.

The only reactions that Saddam appears to have concerned himself with were the Iranians, who were satisfied for now, and the Americans, whose attitude he now set about to discover.

Testing the Waters

Saddam began by making some extremely aggressive demands of Kuwait. He accused Kuwait and the UAE of producing too much oil and keeping market prices artificially low. Kuwait, of course, denied these accusations, and it is doubtful that Kuwait and the UAE together, even if they wanted to, could have produced enough oil to depress prices without the rest of OPEC knowing about it. Somehow, though, only Saddam was able to divine this supposed violation of OPEC solidarity.

Saddam also accused Kuwait of illegally pumping oil from the Iraqi half of the Rumalyah oil field—one of the largest proven oil deposits in the world—that both countries shared. During the Iran-Iraq War, Iraq had not been able to pump oil from their side, but the Kuwaitis had been able to continue pumping unabated. The Iraqis accused the Kuwaitis of having pumped from the Iraq half of the field by using *horizontal drilling* techniques. The Kuwaitis denied this charge, but Saddam continued to insist on it. There is no clear evidence that the Kuwaitis ever did as Saddam claimed.

Saddam also pressed old claims that significant portions of Kuwaiti territory actually belonged to Iraq. These included the entire Rumalyah oil field, a band of territory along the Iraq-Kuwait border, and the Persian Gulf islands of Bubiyan and War-bah, which bordered Iraq's Persian Gulf coast. Like the Iranians on the Strait of Hormuz, the Kuwaitis had the ability to interfere with Iraqi Gulf shipping if they really wanted to.

When the British created the borders between Iraq and Saudi Arabia and Kuwait and Saudi Arabia in 1922, they did not clearly delineate the exact location of the line between Iraq and Kuwait. The area was considered to be empty desert, even though local tribes did live there. Later, the British *did* define the border, in a memorandum written in 1923, and Iraq explicitly referred to this memo when applying for membership in the League of Nations. By referring to the memo, Iraq was acknowledging that the border with Kuwait was indeed defined. In 1990, however, Saddam insisted that the border was never formally identified and that no treaty between Iraq and Kuwait defined that border. Therefore, according to Saddam at least, a significant portion of Kuwait territory actually belonged to Iraq.

> **Desert Diction**
>
> **Horizontal drilling** is a technique by which an oil rig sends out drills to the side, instead of straight down. This technique allows a single well to extract much more oil than it might otherwise be able to.

Finally, Saddam invoked the age-old Iraqi claims that all of Kuwait was really a part of historic Iraq. The claim was tenuous, but persistent. The Iraqis claim that Kuwait was at one point a part of an Ottoman Empire district that was actually governed as a part of the administrative area that became part of Iraq. The reality was somewhat different, in that the Ottomans never formally included Kuwait in their Basra vilayet. In fact, the British had insisted on this last point (that Kuwait was *not* a part of the Basra vilayet) when they agreed to let the Ottomans take nominal control of the Kuwaiti region in the early 1900s. Still, the Iraqis used this argument repeatedly through the years. Various Iraqi rulers had raised the argument about Kuwait in 1961, 1973, and now in 1990.

Thus, with a combination of fact, fiction, and good old-fashioned bluster, Saddam began to lay the foundation for his case that Kuwait was actually the nineteenth province of Iraq. He made it clear that Iraq considered Kuwait's alleged oil-pumping intransigence a threat to Iraq, and that Iraq would eventually deal with the situation in an appropriate manner.

A Deafening Silence

The other Arab countries, as Saddam no doubt had anticipated, didn't rally to Kuwait's support during the OPEC meetings, or in other Arab forums. Kuwait was effectively isolated in these arenas.

With the Arab countries apparently willing to let Saddam do what he wanted, the Iraqi leader moved on to the task of gauging the American reaction to his attentions toward Kuwait. Many analysts now feel that a clear and forceful U.S. objection, or a U.S. warning not to proceed down the path he was beginning to follow, might well have dissuaded Saddam from outright invasion and annexation of Kuwait. This is not to say Saddam would have stopped bullying Kuwait or stopped demanding concessions from the country. However, it might have staved off an actual, troops-on-the ground invasion by the Iraqis. Whatever the case, that strong, clear U.S. warning was never made.

In fact, official statements from the Bush administration offered a very different impression. On July 31, 1990, Assistant Secretary of State for Near Eastern Affairs John Kelly testified before Congress on the situation with Iraq. By now, members of Congress were becoming concerned by Saddam's threats against Kuwait. (As it turned out, they were right, Saddam would invade Kuwait in about 48 hours.) Kelly testified that, "… the United States has no commitment to defend Kuwait and the U.S. has no intention of defending Kuwait if attacked by Iraq."

Back in Baghdad, a similar message had been conveyed directly to Saddam Hussein in a July 25 meeting between the U.S. representative in Iraq, April Glaspie, and Saddam. (This was a little over a week before Saddam invaded Kuwait.) Glaspie and Hussein met at Saddam's Presidential Palace in Baghdad. By this time, Glaspie and the U.S. government were well aware of Saddam's bluster and bullying toward the Kuwaitis. In fact, there was real concern about the recent tenor of Saddam's tirades. He had increasingly spoken about the Kuwait "situation" in terms of Iraq's survival. While most other people in the world did not make the connection between the continuation of the Iraqi state and the continued existence of an independent Kuwait, Saddam somehow did. (In a way, given his need to get money to prop up his position, if one substituted the word "Saddam" for the word "Iraq," the claims may have made more sense.) If Saddam was deliberately sending messages about his ultimate intentions in order to test the waters, he received no corresponding messages from the Americans to back off.

By the middle of August 1990, Iraq had massed more than 30,000 troops on the border with Kuwait. This move was one of the first real indications that Saddam was doing more than just rant in his Palace. Glaspie was dispatched to Saddam to find out what, precisely, he intended to do. After the war, the BBC obtained a transcript of the meeting, an excerpt of which is provided here:

> **GLASPIE:** I have direct instructions from President Bush to improve our relations with Iraq. We have considerable sympathy for your quest for higher oil prices, the immediate cause of your confrontation with Kuwait. (pause) As you know, I have lived here for years and admire your extraordinary efforts to rebuild your country. We know you need funds. We understand that, and our opinion is that you should have the opportunity to rebuild your country. (pause) We can see that you have deployed massive numbers of troops in the south. Normally that would be none of our business, but when this happens in the context of your other threats against Kuwait, then it would be reasonable for us to be concerned. For this reason, I have received an instruction to ask you, in the spirit of friendship—not confrontation—regarding your intentions: Why are your troops massed so very close to Kuwait's borders?

> **SADDAM:** As you know, for years now I have made every effort to reach a settlement on our dispute with Kuwait. There is to be a meeting in two days; I am prepared to give negotiations only this one more brief chance. (pause) When we [the Iraqis] meet [with the Kuwaitis] and we see there is hope, then nothing will happen. But if we are unable to find a solution, then it will be natural that Iraq will not accept death.

> **GLASPIE:** What solutions would be acceptable?

> **SADDAM:** If we could keep the whole of the Shatt-al-Arab—our strategic goal in our war with Iran—we will make concessions [to the Kuwaitis]. But, if we are forced to choose between keeping half of the Shatt and the whole of Iraq then we will give up all of the Shatt to defend our claims on Kuwait to keep the whole of Iraq in the shape we wish it to be. [Note from the author: Saddam's definition of Iraq obviously included Kuwait as its nineteenth province; he was arguing that he gave up full control of the Shatt-al-Arab in order to focus on Kuwait's "intransigence," unimpeded by Iran.] What is the United States' opinion on this?

> **GLASPIE:** We have no opinion on your Arab-Arab conflicts, such as your dispute with Kuwait. Secretary [of State James] Baker has directed me to emphasize the instruction, first given to Iraq in the 1960s that the Kuwait issue is not associated with America.

This transcript indicates that, at the very least the Bush administration's official representative in Iraq did not firmly communicate any U.S. intention to defend Kuwait if Iraq attacked. While the Bush administration's intention all along may have been to firmly defend Kuwait (as it ultimately did), that intention certainly was not communicated clearly to Saddam Hussein during this meeting.

All Systems "Go"

Perhaps to Saddam, the road now seemed free of obstacles, and the lights all seemed to be shining green. The Iranians had been bought off with the Shatt-al-Arab agreement. The Arab states were ambivalent about support for Kuwait and could not really do much to stop Iraq even if they really wanted to. To all appearances, the United States was—or at least seemed to be—aloof about the possibility of an Iraqi invasion. The Iraqi troops were in place, well armed, and in high spirits.

"Radical Saddam" Makes His Move

At 6 A.M. on August 2, 1990, George Bush sat in the Oval Office den and made the following entry in his diary:

> Brent [Scowcroft] came over at 5 confirming that Iraq had moved into Kuwait … they're trying to overthrow the Emir. Yesterday evening about 9 I met with Scowcroft and there were scattered reports that Iraq had moved …. I'm moving the fleet up early from [the Indian Ocean]. Saudis are concerned, and in my view all the [Gulf] countries must be quaking in their boots. This is radical Saddam Hussein moving …

"Radical Saddam" had indeed stepped to the center of the geopolitical stage. He would remain there for the next 13 years.

The Least You Need to Know

- ◆ Saddam felt increasingly boxed in as time went by after the Iran-Iraq War. He was running out of money to subsidize his position in Iraq.

- ◆ Saddam owed a tremendous amount of money to Kuwait, his weak next-door neighbor.

- ◆ Saddam began to bully Kuwait and make serious accusations about "provocative" Kuwaiti behavior.

- ◆ Saddam then bought off Iran to keep the Kurds from being armed and satisfied himself that the Arab countries would not step in to help Kuwait.

- ◆ U.S. diplomats failed to send a signal that an Iraqi invasion of Kuwait would be vigorously opposed.

15

The Reaction to the Invasion of Kuwait: Isolating Saddam

In This Chapter

- ◆ The U.S. reaction to Saddam's invasion of Kuwait
- ◆ The U.S.-Arab coalition
- ◆ Iraq's attempt to widen the Arab-Israeli war
- ◆ Diplomacy and bloodshed

On August 2, 1990, the world awoke and found Iraqi troops in Kuwait City—and heard the fading echoes of Kuwaiti military resistance to the invasion. In the face of the most massive army in the region, Kuwait had been overrun.

The Rebellion That Wasn't

Saddam claimed that Iraqi troops went into Kuwait in support of a rebellion against the Kuwaiti royal family. This claim was shown to be false when Iraq was unable to form even a puppet pro-Iraqi government to run Kuwait. Like the other Gulf states, Kuwait is ruled by a royal family. This family didn't indulge in democratic institutions, but at the same time, the

Kuwaiti royal family wasn't dealing with domestic dissent at any significant level. There are only about one million Kuwaitis, and they enjoy a fairly high standard of living.

Increase Your Iraq IQ

Apparently caring little for plausibility or his own international image, Saddam eventually shrugged off the initial pretext of supporting a (nonexistent) rebellion and formally annexed the entire country on August 9. The northern part of Kuwait was added to the Basra province, and the rest of Kuwait was pronounced the nineteenth province of Iraq. The Rumaylah oil field was now fully in Saddam's control.

A cynic might suggest that the Kuwaiti ruler "buys off" his population with oil revenues. However you look at it, there was no indigenous rebellion of the kind that Saddam was claiming in 1990.

The Iraqis had moved in after midnight on August 2 and caught the Kuwaitis off guard. About 120,000 soldiers and 2,000 tanks had reached Kuwait City within hours. The 20,000-man Kuwaiti military put up some resistance, but most units were taken by surprise and all were completely overwhelmed. Many Kuwaiti soldiers were killed or captured in the initial assault. Eventually about 7,000 Kuwaiti military personnel made it to Saudi Arabia with about 40 tanks. The Kuwaiti air force attacked the invading Iraqis and then retreated to Saudi Arabia as well. This remnant of the Kuwaiti military would regroup in Saudi Arabia and eventually would participate in the Alliance counteroffensive in Kuwait.

Increase Your Iraq IQ

The Republican Guard was made up of Sunni Arabs who swore loyalty to Saddam Hussein. Initially formed in the 1970s, the Guard was only open to men from Saddam's own Tikriti tribe. During the Iran-Iraq War, the Guard was opened to any college student in Iraq. The Guard was comprised of infantry, armored, and mechanized divisions, as well as special operations brigades. The Guard distinguished itself in the Faw Peninsula battles against Iran. The Guard received the best equipment and training and was considered to be the cream of the Iraqi army. Most of the rest of the Iraqi army was made up of Shiite conscripts, who did not receive the same attention and resources as the Republican Guard.

After consolidating their hold on Kuwait City, the Iraqi mechanized divisions of Saddam's elite Republican Guard pushed southward to the Saudi Arabian border.

Saddam did not press forward into Saudi Arabia, apparently content with his takeover of Kuwait and the oil resources there. He would be able to exert more pressure on Saudi Arabia and other Gulf states through his enlarged territory, increased oil control, and the mere fact that he had used his army to invade another nation.

American Reaction

On August 5, President George Bush made an important public statement: "This will not stand, this aggression against Kuwait." This commitment to reversing the Iraqi invasion was a clear statement of U.S. resolve. The Bush plan was to isolate Hussein completely, not only from the West, but from the Arabs and the rest of the world as well.

Saddam, the Arabs, and the West

Whether or not that resolve came as a surprise to Saddam Hussein is hard to say. He had no doubt expected objections, and even outrage, from other countries, including the United States. It seems likely, however, that he simply expected the crisis to blow over and Kuwait to remain in his hands. How likely was it, after all, that the Arab world would allow itself to be allied with countries like the United States and Great Britain?

Saddam may also have assumed that Western powers would not back the United States fully in any response to the Iraqi invasion. The French and Japanese had been conducting a large amount of business with Iraq, and Saddam seems to have counted on that fact, plus the historic lack of cohesion among the Western powers, to result in stern words but no real action in response to his invasion of Kuwait.

Finally, Saddam may have figured he could thwart any ultimate alliance by taking advantage of the ongoing Arab-Israeli conflict. Any Western-Arab alliance, if it were to form against him, could perhaps be ruptured by drawing Israel into the fight. The Arab countries would split from the Western powers (who would stand by Israel). Here was the reasoning: By escalating the conflict from a world vs. Iraq conflict to an Arab vs. Israel conflict, Saddam could hold on to his new conquest, because the vital element of the Arab country participation in any anti-Iraq coalition would be gone. And Saddam would emerge as the Arab-uniting leader of a long-sought conflict with the Israelis.

Such, at any rate, appeared to be the thinking in Baghdad: Divide the opposition and raise the stakes.

The West Stands with Bush

The Western powers, however, rallied behind the United States almost immediately; even France and Japan joined in. The next step for the Bush administration was to build an Arab-West coalition strong enough to isolate Saddam and push him out of Kuwait.

Saddam was correct if he thought that the Arab countries would have a difficult time falling in behind U.S. leadership. However, the fear that his military move had engendered with the other Arab states outweighed the Arab leaders' aversion to working with the West. On August 6, Bush received permission from Saudi Arabia's King Fahd to base U.S. troops in his country.

The Arab world had begun to join the Western powers against Saddam. The Saudi ruling family decided to work with Bush, and shortly thereafter, the other Gulf states came on board. Egypt, Syria, Saudi Arabia, and Kuwait all signed onto the Coalition. King Hussein (no relation) of Jordan decided not to join the coalition, but he did not come out in support of Iraq, either.

One Man Against the World

Turkey offered its full support to the anti-Iraq coalition, and Iran stayed on the sidelines. In an ominous turn of events for Saddam, the Soviet Union gave its tacit blessing to the anti-Iraq coalition. Ultimately, 38 countries joined the Coalition, and a total of 650,000 troops were arrayed against Iraq.

Saddam could not find any other allies to his cause. He was on his own.

Increase Your Iraq IQ

Turkey, a Muslim country, was and is a critical U.S. ally in the region. The people of Turkey are Muslim, but they are not Arab (they are Turkic). Like Iraq and Iran, the Turks also have a Kurd minority within their borders. Turkey is a member of NATO, and in general was a steadfast partner to the United States in its maneuvering against Saddam in the first Gulf War, though the same was not true in the second.

Action at the United Nations

The Bush administration then turned to the United Nations to generate a legal mandate to expel the Iraqi military from Kuwait. On August 2, the same day that Iraq was discovered in Kuwait, the *United Nations Security Council* passed a resolution calling for Iraq to leave Kuwait immediately and unconditionally.

> **Desert Diction** _____
>
> The **United Nations Security Council** includes five permanent members (the United States, the United Kingdom, France, China, and Russia) and 10 rotating members (made up of other nations in the United Nations) who are elected by the General Assembly to serve 2-year terms on the council. The chairmanship of the council rotates among all the members. Only the Security Council can mandate a UN-sponsored military intervention on behalf of a UN member country. All Security Council decisions must be approved by a vote among its members. The five permanent members can veto any measure under Security Council consideration.

Along with a series of resolutions calling for Iraq's withdrawal from Kuwait, the United States also led the United Nations in creating economic sanctions against Iraq as well. As a result of this diplomacy, the United Nations also passed an array of economic sanctions blocking the exports from Iraq, as well as any imports to Iraq. Now, Saddam's only revenue source—oil sales—was cut off. Rather than enrichment from the occupation of Kuwait, Saddam was even more impoverished.

Trying to Cut a Deal?

Facing a united coalition of Arab and Western states, forced to deal with a steady buildup of troops in Saudi Arabia, and cut off from making money, Saddam may have had second thoughts about the invasion. He tried to talk his way out of the problem, while holding on to the gains of the invasion of Kuwait.

On August 23, 1990, Saddam offered to withdraw from Kuwait in return for the UN sanctions being lifted, guaranteed access to the Gulf, and full control of the Rumalyah oil field. These conditions were rejected by the Bush-led coalition.

It's easy to understand why. To the West, rewarding unilateral military action against a sovereign state with diplomatic concessions smelled an awful lot like appeasement. Moreover, caving in on "guaranteed access to the Gulf," some analysts reasoned, could set the stage for future Iraqi aggression against Kuwait. The islands of Bubiyan and Warbah were located immediately off the Iraqi Gulf coast. Iraq could claim that control of those islands was part of the "guaranteed access" to the Gulf.

The Coalition Says "No, Thanks"

Instead of agreeing to the proposal, the Bush administration sent in 230,000 American troops to defend Saudi Arabia, in "Operation Desert Shield." Saddam responded to the American buildup by sending more Iraqi troops into Kuwait. Bush responded by sending in an additional 200,000 soldiers. The buildup was on for both sides.

The United States was sending a huge number of troops to Saudi Arabia—far more, it would seem, than were needed simply to defend that country.

Saddam Counters: The War of Words

Now that it had been made clear that he could not expect to withdraw and maintain control of at least part of Kuwait, Saddam tried to break the Arab-West coalition. If he could do that, then perhaps he could hold onto Kuwait.

Saddam may have sensed that the Coalition, while firm, was not long-lived. Eventually it would have to crack. His hope could have been to break that coalition apart before any military action took place.

In early September 1990, Saddam accused President Bush of being a criminal and demanded he stand trial in Baghdad. By making these accusations, Saddam was trying to pry the Arab states from the West. He charged President Bush with the crimes of …

- Sending U.S. troops into the areas of the holy Muslim shrines (remember that Saudi Arabia is the home of Mecca and Medina).

- Threatening to attack Iraq (there were 430,000 U.S. soldiers in or en route to Saudi Arabia).

- Imposing economic sanctions against Iraq. (Saddam was referring to the fact that the United States had led the approval of UN sanctions.)

- Ordering the CIA to plot against Iraq (an unproven, but seemingly obvious U.S. move considering the situation in the region).

By making these accusations, Saddam was trying to insert a wedge between the United States and the key Arab nations with which the Americans had established alliances after 1973: Egypt, Jordan, the other Gulf states, and Saudi Arabia.

Playing the Israel Card

Saddam also tried to draw Israel into the standoff, as he would again do during the actual fighting. Apparently in the hope of getting President Bush to make public statements in support of Israel—statements that would alienate the Arab coalition members—Saddam and his ministers, notably his foreign minister, Tariq Aziz, began to bluster about Israel.

Saddam threatened to launch missiles at Israel in the event of hostilities. By making these claims, Hussein was attempting to show himself to be an outspoken anti-Israel leader and trying to rally other Arab countries to that cause. He was attempting to remind the Arabs of what bound them all together against Israel and its ally, the United States.

Iraqi officials had been making bellicose statements about Israel in the months leading up to the Kuwait invasion. On April 2, 1990, Reuters news agency quoted Saddam as saying: "I swear to God we will let our fire eat half of Israel if it tries to wage anything against Iraq." Saddam went on to boast of the size of his chemical weapons arsenal, and promised to use those weapons on any country that would threaten Iraq with nuclear weapons. On June 18, 1990, the Baghdad Domestic News Services quoted Saddam, "We will strike at [the Israelis] with all the arms in our possession if they attack Iraq or the Arabs."

> **Iraq Fact**
>
> Tariq Mikhail Aziz was the deputy prime minister of Iraq. A long time ally of Saddam Hussein, Aziz was the primary spokesperson for the Iraqi government and the main point of contact between the United States and Iraq at senior government levels.

> **Increase Your Iraq IQ**
>
> In April 1990, British intelligence had discovered that an Iraqi chartered vessel was loaded with large tube sections. These sections were part of a "super gun" that could fire projectiles at Iran or Israel. The British thwarted the attempted delivery.

After the August 1990 invasion of Kuwait, Saddam stepped up the rhetoric. He threatened again to attack Israel if the Coalition attacked Iraq. According to Reuters, on December 26, 1990, Saddam said, "Tel Aviv will receive the next attack, whether or not Israel takes part" in a coalition attack on Iraq. Tariq Aziz went a step further when he had a meeting with Secretary of State James Baker on January 9, 1991 (just six days prior to the start of fighting). When asked if Iraq would attack Israel in the event of a coalition move against Iraq, Aziz responded, "Yes. Absolutely, yes."

(Later, during the actual fighting, Saddam would keep his promise, firing missiles at Israel in an attempt to draw the Israelis into the struggle.)

The Waiting Game

Finally, on November 29, 1990, the UN Security Council passed a resolution approving the Coalition to use force to get Iraq out of Kuwait. The 15-member Security Council voted 12 to 2 in favor of the resolution. China abstained, and Cuba and Yemen voted against the measure, known as Resolution 678.

Resolution 678 had a deadline of January 15, 1991. The clock was ticking on Saddam. As the year turned from 1990 to 1991 and the deadline approached, he stood fast in Kuwait, and played a waiting game.

The Least You Need to Know

- ◆ Saddam may have been surprised by the forceful and immediate response by the Bush administration following the August 2, 1990, occupation of Kuwait.

- ◆ Iraqi offers to withdraw, keeping some of the gains of taking Kuwait, were rejected by the Coalition.

- ◆ The United States responded by building an Arab-West coalition against Saddam, getting UN cover for sanctions against Iraq.

- ◆ Saddam attempted to break the Arab-Western coalition arrayed against him by means of divisive rhetoric, much of it designed to draw Israel into the conflict.

Chapter 16

The Assault: The Alliance Holds

In This Chapter

- A storm in the desert
- The air war
- The war on the ground
- Saddam stays in power

In the last chapter, we saw how the Bush administration had assembled an international coalition to isolate Saddam—a coalition that included Arab countries. It was vital that Arab states participate; failure to win their support could have made it easier for Saddam to transform his invasion into a wide-ranging conflict between the Arab and Western worlds—with destabilizing consequences for both sides.

The Bush administration's immediate response to Saddam's move was known as "Operation Desert Shield," a full-scale military buildup of troops, material, planes, armor, and bases. The coalition partners joined in, sending their share of troops and/or money to support the effort.

The coalition nations shared the Bush administration's goal of removing Iraq from Kuwait unconditionally. Despite the troops and resources arrayed against him, Saddam refused to leave Kuwait unconditionally. It became increasingly apparent that military force would be required.

The Coalition prepared for the attack; the Bush administration got the United Nations to approve the action, and even set a deadline for withdrawal. Saddam still did not budge, however; attack became inevitable.

When the assault on Iraqi troops in Kuwait began, Operation Desert Shield turned into "Operation Desert Storm." The storm that was unleashed on Saddam was formidable. The campaign used the planes and troops of 38 countries and had a war chest of more than $53 billion pledged by coalition and noncoalition countries alike.

What Was the Goal of the Campaign?

According to President Bush's National Security Directive 54, issued on January 15, 1991, the goal of Operation Desert Storm was to evict Iraq from Kuwait, period. The text of Section 2 of the directive reads as follows:

> Pursuant to my responsibilities and authority under the Constitution as President and Commander in Chief, and under the laws and treaties of the United States, and pursuant to H.J. Res. 77 (1991), and in accordance with the rights and obligations of the United States under international law, including UN Security Council Resolutions 660, 661, 662, 664, 665, 666, 667, 669, 670, 674, 677, and 678, and consistent with the inherent right of collective self-defense affirmed in Article 51 of the United Nations Charter, I hereby authorize military actions designed to bring about Iraq's withdrawal from Kuwait. These actions are to be conducted against Iraq and Iraqi forces in Kuwait by U.S. air, sea and land conventional military forces, in coordination with the forces of our coalition partners, at a date and time I shall determine and communicate through National Command Authority channels. This authorization is for the following purposes:
>
> a. to effect the immediate, complete and unconditional withdrawal of all Iraqi forces from Kuwait;
>
> b. to restore Kuwait's legitimate government;
>
> c. to protect the lives of American citizens abroad; and
>
> d. to promote the security and the stability of the Persian Gulf.

Increase Your Iraq IQ

The countries that formed the coalition to confront Iraq over its invasion of Kuwait included nine Arab states (Bahrain, Kuwait, Egypt, Morocco, Syria, Saudi Arabia, Oman, the United Arab Emirates, and Qatar) as well as Afghanistan, Argentina, Australia, Bangladesh, Belgium, Canada, Czechoslovakia, Denmark, France, Germany, Greece, Hungary, Honduras, Italy, Morocco, The Netherlands, New Zealand, Niger, Norway, Pakistan, Poland, Portugal, Senegal, South Korea, Spain, Syria, Turkey, the United Kingdom, and the United States. More than $53 billion was pledged in financial support by coalition and noncoalition nations; Switzerland (a noncombatant) contributed funding, and Saudi Arabia and Kuwait were the two largest financial donors.

Target: Saddam?

If the National Security Directive is read at face value, the Bush administration wasn't directly targeting Saddam as an individual. But make no mistake, the Bush administration did want Saddam gone. Although there was no formally stated objective to remove Saddam from power, the Bush administration appears to have hoped (or even assumed) that Hussein would be overthrown as a by-product of a military defeat in Kuwait.

If getting rid of Saddam was a goal of Desert Storm, why was it not explicitly stated as one? The most likely answer is that the coalition that the Bush administration assembled agreed only on the goal of getting Saddam out of Kuwait. The members did *not* agree on the difficult question of whether Saddam himself should be overthrown.

Kicking Iraq out of Kuwait was a clearly defined goal, with a clean ending everyone in the Coalition could endorse: the Iraqis moving back across the Kuwait-Iraq border. The end point was unambiguous, and the morality of the goal was generally acceptable to the international community. Iraq had unilaterally invaded an independent neighbor and taken away its

Iraq Fact

The debate that occurred between Western (mainly the Bush Sr. administration) and Arab states over what to do with Saddam in 1990 and 1991 was echoed by a similar debate in 2002. The Bush Jr. administration engaged in the same dialog, with the same Arab partners, over what to do about Saddam. The younger Bush was far less successful in convincing the erstwhile Arab allies to support the course he chose.

right to exist as a state. This type of naked aggression had to be stopped, no matter who did it, no matter where it was.

On the other hand, a commitment to overthrow Saddam could have meant more casualties, a protracted coalition occupation of Iraq, and a less certain outcome to that occupation. Also, the morality of overthrowing a sovereign ruler of an independent state, no matter how reprehensible, was much less clear as a universally moral goal of freeing an occupied state. Furthermore, the Arab states, while willing to participate in a coalition to defend one of their own (Kuwait), would be far less willing to partici-pate in a coalition to oust the leader of one of their own (Iraq).

> **Desert Diction** _____
>
> **Operation Desert Shield** was the name of the military buildup operation in Saudi Arabia. Its nominal purpose was to set up a deterrent military force, strong enough to defend the Arab Gulf states.
>
> **Operation Desert Storm** was the follow-up to Desert Shield. It was the name of the Coalition air-ground attack on Iraqi troops in Kuwait. (The original term for the very brief ground campaign portion was Operation Desert Sword, later changed to Operation Desert Sabre). Its purpose was to expel Iraq from Kuwait.

In short, getting an Arab-Western coalition to agree to getting Iraq out of Kuwait was one thing; getting them to agree what should happen to Iraq afterward was quite another.

The "Mother of All Battles"

The stage was set, and the pieces were in place. The UN Security Council set a dead-line of January 15, 1991, for a complete Iraqi withdrawal from Kuwait. When the deadline passed, and Saddam stayed put, President Bush ordered the action to begin on January 17, 1991.

This date was six and a half months after the August 2, 1990, UN Security Council Resolution demanding Saddam leave. Rather than leave, Saddam had dug in and exhorted his soldiers and his people to prepare for the "mother of all battles" that was soon to come.

The Air Assault Begins

On January 17, 1991, coalition forces began bombing targets in Kuwait and Iraq.

Attack helicopters, fixed-wing fighter and attack aircraft, bombers, and cruise missiles launched from both aircraft and ships were used over the next five weeks to destroy Iraqi military targets, from artillery and anti-aircraft positions, to troop concentrations, tanks and other ground vehicles, aircraft, and command and control centers in Iraqi cities like Basra and Baghdad. Despite some losses to Iraqi anti-aircraft batteries, coalition aircraft essentially controlled the skies and could fly their sorties at will.

The bombing campaign was carried out first against major targets; when these were obliterated, bombing proceeded against secondary targets; and the bombs were dropped on anything that *looked* like a target in a military zone.

> **CAUTION**
>
> **Oil Spill Ahead**
>
> Despite all of the intense bombing, a surprising number of Iraqi weapons facilities survived the bombing campaign, and continued to produce weapons. These facilities would soon become the focus of international weapons inspectors, and a source of international tension.

Civilians Suffer

Although overthrowing Saddam was not a stated goal of the air campaign, certain coalition bombing efforts were clearly aimed at doing just that. Coalition bombing targets also included parts of the Iraqi infrastructure, such as oil facilities and power plants. Granted, destroying these targets did impair Iraqi capabilities on the front lines (at least indirectly), but the immediate impact was economic disruption and physical suffering among the Iraqi people.

It's possible that coalition planners sought to foster domestic unrest against Saddam, by showing his weakness to his own people and by increasing their misery under his rule.

This raised a fateful question that continues to play out today: If the lights went out and the food ran low, would the Iraqi people eventually blame Saddam for the darkness and the hunger—or would they see the West (rather than Saddam) as the architect of their misery?

> **Increase Your Iraq IQ**
>
> After he invaded Kuwait, Saddam had prominently housed "guests" at strategic sites like power plants and munitions depots. These "guests" (read: hostages) were foreign nationals who were unlucky enough to be in Iraq after the Iraqi invasion of Kuwait. Eventually, these "guests" were released, probably because Saddam realized he was not winning the PR war by keeping them.

Saddam Hussein, Media Mastermind

Saddam's actions during the bombing period alternated between attempting to position the Iraqi people as the victim of a heartless Western-led military campaign and making unsubtle threats.

He tried to turn world public opinion against the Coalition by showing the effects of the bombing campaign on civilians, both Western and Iraqi. (Had he yielded to protracted appeals from all around the globe, including the Arab world, to withdraw from Kuwait, those casualties would, of course, never have occurred.)

Increase Your Iraq IQ

On February 13, 1991, Saddam's campaign to manipulate world opinion was aided by an errant strategic bombing strike on the Al Firdos bunker in Baghdad. More than 200 Iraqi civilians were killed in that attack. Saddam presented the bodies on TV for all the world to see. The public outcry induced the Coalition to reduce its strategic bombing in Baghdad. In a small way, Saddam had helped ensure his own survival by showing the effects of Coalition bombing on Iraqi civilians. He did this by causing the Coalition leadership to limit the strategic bombing, lessening the civilian suffering, and weakening support within the Bush administration for a (quiet) plan to oust or eliminate Saddam.

Saddam's war of words now included a war of reporters, as he used CNN for all it was worth. At one point, CNN ran Iraqi footage of a "Baby Milk" factory that had supposedly been destroyed by Coalition bombing. The CNN footage included a battered sign that read "Baby Milk" in English. Of course, it seems improbable that a factory that produced a product in the middle of Baghdad would have an English sign over it, or that a factory producing infant formula would call its product "Baby Milk." Granted, CNN did indicate that their footage was subject to Iraqi censorship, but the messages got through to the viewing audience nevertheless.

SCUDs over Israel

As he had threatened, Saddam responded to the bombing by attempting to split the Coalition. Shortly after Iraq came under attack, Iraq started bombing Israel.

On January 18, 1991, the day after the Coalition first struck, Iraq launched its first *SCUD missiles* at Israel. Saddam's goal was simple: induce the Israelis to strike at Iraq, which would make it increasingly difficult for the Arab countries to remain part of the Coalition. Saddam had made this intention clear in late 1990, and President Bush, in his National Security Directive 54, had acknowledged this threat openly: "The United States will discourage the government of Israel from participating in any military action. In particular, we will seek to discourage any preemptive actions by Israel. Should Israel be threatened with imminent attack or be attacked by Iraq, the United States will respond with force against Iraq and will discourage Israeli participation in hostilities."

The United States sent Patriot surface-to-air missile batteries to Israel, to shoot down the incoming SCUDs. The Patriots were very effective in this task, although Israel was hit by a number of SCUDs. Ultimately, Saddam's plan failed, as the combination of U.S. diplomacy, Israeli forbearance, and Patriot missiles restrained an Israeli military response. The Coalition continued to hold throughout the month of January and into early February 1991.

The diplomacy that the Bush team conducted in keeping Israel on the sidelines, while all the time they were being attacked, is impressive. The efforts of the diplomats were only surpassed by the patient courage of the Israeli people who absorbed the SCUD strikes without retaliating.

> **Desert Diction**
>
> The surface-to-surface **SCUD missiles** that Iraq launched at Israel were made by the Soviet Union in the 1980s. Iraq had bought them from the Soviets during the Iran-Iraq War, for use against targets in Iran. Fired from a mobile launcher, the SCUD was capable of reaching targets hundreds of miles away.

> **Oil Spill Ahead**
>
> Surprisingly, Saddam also fired SCUDs at Saudi Arabia. This practice seemed to fly in the face of his "draw in Israel" strategy, but launch them he did, to attack U.S. troops stationed there, and to punish the Saudis for allowing the U.S. to stage troops in the Kingdom.

While international attention was focused on Baghdad bunkers, "Baby Milk," and Israeli SCUD craters, the Coalition continued to rain tens of thousands of tons of munitions on unfortunate Iraqi soldiers along the front in Kuwait. The impact of B-52 bombings on Iraqi forces could be felt 20 miles away across the desert. Away from the spotlight, the Iraqi army was being pummeled into submission.

The Iraqis didn't sit completely still, however. On January 29, 1991, an Iraqi armored column moved into the Saudi town of Khafji on the Saudi Arabia-Kuwait border. Initial gains by the Iraqis were reversed, and two days later they were forced back out of Khafji. Although Saddam's intentions are not clear (as he didn't organize for a full-scale assault), the initial setback was a sort of wake-up call for coalition forces that Iraq's military would be a tough opponent in the coming fight. Of course, the opposite generally proved true, but that wasn't clear from the Khafji incident.

An Offer from Saddam

On February 15, with Soviet diplomat Yevgeni Primakov working the halls in Baghdad, Saddam offered to withdraw from Kuwait. President Bush called the offer a "cruel hoax" and refused to consider the offer.

Why did Bush refuse Saddam's offer? Saddam had once again put conditions on the withdrawal, conditions that could have meant noncompliance with the various UN resolutions. What's more, the Iraqi offer was for a gradual withdrawal, not an immediate one. Bush wasn't willing to grant Hussein any conditions, nor give him time on the ground in Kuwait. The president's reasoning was apparently based on pragmatic considerations as well as logistical ones: Once the initial offer was accepted, the Arab-West coalition would begin to dissolve.

The Bush administration feared that the longer Saddam delayed his withdrawal, the less likely coalition troops could ever be used to expel him from Kuwait. In the end, Saddam could simply hold on to some of the territory, or gain some concessions on the Rumalyah oil field, and be even stronger for his next move (whatever that might be).

Thus the U.S. position: The withdrawal had to be complete and unconditional, in accordance with UN Security Council Resolution 660. Saddam, at this point, was having none of it.

The ground war was set to begin.

Increase Your Iraq IQ

The UN Security Council eventually would pass 12 resolutions directed at Iraq. These resolutions demanded that Iraq leave Kuwait (UN Security Council Resolution 660), established a range of economic sanctions to isolate Iraq from world trade (UN Security Council Resolution 661), and finally, authorized that the Coalition could use force to expel Iraq from Kuwait (UN Security Council Resolution 678).

The Ground War

The ground war can be summarized in a quote by Lieutenant General Tom Kelly: "Iraq went from the fourth-largest army in the world to the second-largest army in Iraq in 100 hours."

General Kelly was referring to the fact that the Iraqi army basically surrendered without much of a fight. (In fact, Iraqi soldiers surrendered to TV camera crews when they couldn't find soldiers to surrender to.) The vaunted Iraqi army capitulated with stunning rapidity.

Command of the coalition forces was divided between the Americans and the Saudi Arabians, with the Americans calling the shots. General Norman Schwarzkopf commanded the Western countries, including the United States, British, and French forces, while Saudi Lieutenant General Khalid ibn Sultan ibn Abd al Aziz Al Saud commanded the 24 non-Western coalition countries, including Saudi Arabia, Syria, Kuwait, and Egypt. The non-Western troops included 20,000 Saudi Arabian troops, 7,000 Kuwaiti troops who had escaped the Iraqi invasion, and 3,000 troops from the other Gulf states.

The joint command structure was another acknowledgment of Arab sensibilities and had helped to keep the Arab states in the coalition. This command structure also recognized Saudi Arabia's status as the nation hosting the Coalition—and footing most of the bill for the staging and conduct of the operations.

The Sweeping Hook and the Body Blow

The ground attack started on February 24, 1991. The Arab troops were divided into two task forces: Joint Forces Command North, consisting of troops from Egypt, Saudi Arabia, Syria, and Kuwait; and Joint Forces Command East, consisting of forces from Saudi Arabia, Kuwait, Bahrain, and Qatar. The North group deployed on Kuwait's western border with Saudi Arabia, and the East group deployed along the Gulf coast below the Kuwaiti border. These troops set up the blocking forces that kept the Iraqi units from moving south when the main attack hit them.

The main attack came from U.S. Army 7th Corps, flanked by the U.S. 18th Airborne Corps and the U.S. 1st Marine Expeditionary Force. These attacking units were covered by a sweeping hook of U.S. and French forces. On the other side of the line, Saddam had deployed more than 100,000 troops along the Kuwaiti coast line, anticipating a Marine amphibious landing that never came. These troops were not in place to resist the Marines crossing the Saudi-Kuwait border.

The U.S. Army's 18th Airborne Corps and the 7th Corps were positioned along a stretch of the Saudi Arabian-Iraqi border (the allied extreme left flank and center). The 1st Marine Expeditionary Force (MEF), comprised of the 1st and 2nd Marine divisions and the detached Tiger Brigade of the U.S. Army's 2nd Armored Division, was on the extreme right flank. On either flank of the 1st MEF were Joint Force elements from Saudi Arabia, Syria, Egypt, Kuwait, Pakistan, Oman, and the United Arab Emirates.

The battle plan called for the two Army corps to launch an attack across the border deep into the Iraqi desert, then make a hard right turn. As the two Army corps attacked on the left and center, the 1st MEF and the Joint Force elements on the right were to drive into Kuwait. On the first day of the ground campaign the main elements of the 1st MEF punched through the Iraqi defenses and raced toward Kuwait City. They were temporarily slowed, not so much by resistance, but by thousands of physically and emotionally exhausted Iraqi soldiers who surrendered in droves. By day's end, the 1st MEF had advanced some 20 miles into the heart of Kuwait, far beyond pre-attack expectations.

As the Marines were moving into Kuwait, the Army's 18th Airborne Corps on the extreme left of the coalition line attacked into the Iraqi desert. In the vanguard of the 18th was the French 6th Light Armored Division, along with the 2nd Brigade of the U.S. 82nd Airborne Division, the 3rd Armored Cavalry Regiment and the 24th Infantry Division. As French tanks and American paratroopers and infantrymen advanced, their flank was covered by a helicopter-borne force of the U.S. 101st Airborne Division. By moving into the rear of the Iraq positions, they cut off Iraqi forces fleeing back toward Baghdad, and covered the left flank of the 7th Corps primary American attacking force. The 7th Corps was comprised of the 1st and 3rd Armored Divisions, the 1st Cavalry Division, the 1st Infantry Division, the 2nd Armored Cavalry Regiment, and the British 1st Armored Division. Destroying or receiving the surrender of all the Iraqi forces it met, the 7th Corps moved north 100 miles, turned east and drove straight toward the Basra Road.

The Iraqi Army Collapses

Hemmed in by 7th Corps armor and 1st MEF attacking forces, the Iraqi units fleeing Kuwait were pounded along the Basra Road (what became known as the "Highway of Death") by Coalition aircraft. The losses were staggering. As they left Kuwait, the Iraqi troops set fire to hundreds of oil wells in Kuwait, in a last vengeful attempt to fulfill one of Saddam's earlier objectives: Drive up the price of oil. With the Kuwaiti production off line, oil prices would have to rise.

Finally, on February 27, 1991, President Bush unilaterally declared a cease-fire, stating that, "Kuwait is liberated. Iraq's army is defeated. Our military objectives have been met." While the military goals of the Coalition were fulfilled, the political goals were not.

Under the smoking skies from burning Kuwaiti oil wells, Coalition and Iraqi military leaders agreed to a cease-fire, and over the next several days agreed to the terms of a lasting cease-fire. Saddam was out of Kuwait, but he was not out of power.

How Had the Iraqis Done So Poorly?

What happened to the Iraqi army? Why did it surrender so quickly? How was it overcome so decisively?

Only 148 U.S. troops were killed during the fighting, compared to tens of thousands (and some estimates of over 100,000) Iraqi soldiers. These Iraqis were battle-tested veterans of the Iran-Iraq War. Why didn't they put up a better fight?

It was a different kind of war than the Iraqi army was used to. In the Iran-Iraq War, it had become proficient in fighting a grinding, trench-warfare style of campaign. They had proven successful in digging in and staving off Iranian "human wave" attacks. The Iraqi high command prepared for a similar style of fighting in Kuwait. The troops were pushed to forward positions, where they dug in behind a line of fortifications and awaited a coalition frontal assault.

Increase Your Iraq IQ

Why didn't the Iraqi army fight better in face-to-face engagements? A contributing factor was that the allied air campaign had seriously weakened the Iraqi troops on the front line. The five weeks of heavy bombing had taken its toll. The Iraqi troops at the front had received little food, water, or even instructions from their commanders. Many units were effectively isolated from their own military structures. Further, their morale and effectiveness had been severely degraded by the incessant pounding of their positions.

Also, the Iraqi troops were no longer fighting for their homeland, and the foot soldier in the field didn't see the benefit of fighting for Kuwait. The majority of troops were Shiites, and their relationship with the Iraqi Sunni command structure was always distant. As that structure broke down, the Shiite soldiers were more willing to pack it in than their Sunni counterparts. However, even the Sunni Republican Guard units didn't fare well in the fighting—though they didn't surrender in the same numbers as the Shiite units.

However, the Coalition launched a mobile attack that was designed to cut off the Iraqi troops, encircle them, and then destroy them. The superior speed and mechanization of the Coalition forces made the difference almost immediately. The Iraqis were drawn out of their defensive positions and forced to fight on the move. Their tactics and equipment were not designed for this kind of fighting, and they could not match the Coalition firepower on the ground.

There was a frontal assault, but by the time it came, the Iraqi troops melted away almost immediately.

By the Numbers

The Iraqi army had about 540,000 troops in Kuwait. Of that number, roughly 100,000 were killed, 300,000 were wounded, and 60,000 were captured. The United States lost 148 troops in combat, 458 were wounded, and 121 were killed in non-combat situations. The Iraqis lost 4,000 tanks and 2,140 artillery pieces. The Coalition lost four tanks and one artillery piece. The Iraqi air force lost 240 aircraft; the Coalition lost 44 aircraft.

Victory over Saddam (or Was It?)

After President Bush's unilateral declaration of a cease-fire on February 27, the Coalition and Iraqi commanders met to hash out the details of the cease-fire on March 3. Iraq's leadership in the negotiations, representing Saddam Hussein, agreed to abide by all of the UN Security Council Resolutions passed against Iraq in relation to the invasion of Kuwait. The following day, coalition prisoners of war were released, and the end game was in play … or was it?

The Gulf War was over—the military objectives of the Coalition had been achieved. The Iraqi army in Kuwait had been decimated, and its effectiveness as a fighting force was drastically reduced. The coalition negotiators were at the table, setting the terms that would, they hoped, keep Iraq from ever mounting a threat to its neighbors again.

True enough, the Iraqi military had been beaten and was no longer a potent threat as a fighting force. However, its effectiveness as a police force was still very much intact.

In the next chapter, we'll see how Saddam would use that force in the months following his Gulf War defeat to preserve his own grip on power. The Gulf War was over, but the conflict between Saddam Hussein and the West was just beginning.

The Least You Need to Know

♦ Operation Desert Shield turned into Operation Desert Storm with the opening of the coalition bombing campaign.

♦ The bombing campaign was intended to degrade Iraqi military capabilities (which it did well) and effectively destabilize Saddam's grip on power (which it did not do well).

♦ The coalition troops launched the ground campaign on February 24, 1991. The main attacks went extremely well for the coalition troops, and extremely poorly for the Iraqis.

♦ The fighting ended 100 hours after it started, with a total Iraqi military defeat.

♦ Although the Iraqi military had been humbled as a fighting force, it retained its effectiveness as a police force.

Chapter 17

The Aftermath: Saddam Survives

In This Chapter

- ◆ The Coalition stops short of invasion
- ◆ A quick settlement
- ◆ Lingering loopholes
- ◆ The West waits for Saddam to fall

After 100 hours of ground war, the Iraqi army was fleeing from Kuwait in panicked disorder.

There was no way they could have stopped the Coalition forces from driving all the way to Baghdad, or, presumably, from capturing Saddam Hussein. Already, thousands of Coalition troops were in Iraq proper and many more were heading that way. Their commanders, however, ordered them to stop.

The Coalition wasn't going on to Baghdad. Its mission had been accomplished: Iraq had been expelled from Kuwait. Rather then moving on to Baghdad, the Coalition military commanders sat down to negotiate a hastily defined cease-fire with their Iraqi counterparts. As soon as the firing stopped, the chances for the Coalition to resume military operations grew fainter, and the chances for Saddam to survive the overwhelming defeat grew stronger.

With each passing day, Saddam showed how well developed his survival skills had become.

Mission Accomplished?

Clearly, the Bush administration's stated goal had been met: Kuwait had been liberated and the Iraqi military had been weakened so that it could not be used against other countries.

The unstated goal of the Bush administration, however, was to overthrow Saddam Hussein. The Bush administration had determined by Saddam's invasion of Kuwait that Saddam was a serious threat to stability in the region, and a threat to U.S. interests (including the free flow of reasonably priced oil).

CAUTION

Oil Spill Ahead

The likelihood of the Iraqi army invading a neighbor was dramatically reduced after the Gulf War, but the likelihood of Iraq supporting international terrorists—and of that country becoming a base-of-operations for global terrorism—was not lessened.

However, as we have seen, this could not be a formal coalition objective, because the Arab states in the region were not willing to fight to overthrow one of their own. At the same time, it was quietly assumed—by both the Bush administration and its coalition allies—that Saddam would fall if his army was defeated.

That, as it turned out, was wishful thinking.

The Coalition Does Not Invade Iraq

The door was wide open, but the Coalition forces did not invade Iraq at the end of the first Gulf War. The Bush (Sr.) administration stopped, as it was faced with the following hard geopolitical realities in 1991:

♦ The Bush administration did not want to go into Iraq alone, and the rest of Coalition, particularly the Arab states, were not willing to support a continuation of the war on Iraqi territory.

♦ The Bush administration decided it was better to stop and let a militarily weakened Saddam hang onto power.

◆ The Bush administration assumed, like almost everyone else at that time, that the Iraqi people would finish the job the Coalition had started by overthrowing Saddam.

Looking at the first possibility: The American military would have had to enter Baghdad and get Saddam on its own. Such a unilateral move could have almost immediately alienated the Arab allies and could have reversed all the gains made up to that point. The United States could well have found itself dealing with Iraq on its own, which the aftermath of the U.S. invasion after the second Gulf War shows to be a difficult and very unpopular task.

Looking at the second possibility: While this option seems to run against all the rhetoric, it's important to bear in mind that there was (and still is) considerable uncertainty regarding the kind of government likely to emerge in Iraq after Saddam Hussein. At the beginning of the Gulf War, Saddam was regarded as a regional threat to U.S. interests, but not necessarily a threat to U.S. domestic security. This view changed considerably at the end of the war, but the maxim about it being "better to live with the devil you know than the devil you don't" applied.

The most likely reason the Coalition ultimately decided to stop short of Baghdad is a combination of the first possibility and the third one—the assumption that the Iraqi people would finish off Saddam on their own. During the bombing campaign, the Bush administration had tried to oust Saddam indirectly through the strategic bombing of Baghdad, Basra, and other inland Iraqi targets. This bombing was intended both to weaken Iraqi military capabilities and to weaken Saddam's governing capabilities, and perhaps to finish off Saddam himself.

On the last day of the air campaign, the U.S. Air Force pounded a Ba'th headquarters building in the hopes of killing a significant portion of the country's leadership, and possibly even Saddam. Even if the United States couldn't kill Saddam with bombs, its leaders must have hoped that its bombs would end up getting rid of him anyway. If the Iraqi people were made to suffer and see what destruction Saddam had wrought on them, they would rise up and throw him out. Or more likely, a rival clique of army officers would stage yet another coup.

A coup that would oust Saddam and install a more Western-friendly leadership in Iraq was, realistically speaking, about the best that the first Bush administration could hope for at the end of the Gulf War.

Flames in Kuwait

As we saw in Chapter 16, the Iraqis had set fire to more than 500 Kuwaiti oil wells and effectively put Kuwaiti oil production off-line for months. The tactic resembled the scorched earth policies of the Red Army retreating across Russia in front of the Nazis in World War II, or Union General Philip Sheridan's systematic devastation of the Shenandoah Valley during the American Civil War. The environmental impact of 500 flaming oil wells, spewing burning oil across the landscape, was catastrophic. The oil fields were suggestive of what the pit of Hell might look like, with no sun overhead, searing heat all around, and flames at one's feet.

> **Oil Spill Ahead**
>
> Despite predictions that they would last for years, the last oil well fires in Kuwait were extinguished in November 1991. Thanks to the efforts of professional oil well fire fighters from the United States and other oil-producing nations, the fires were out only nine months after the end of hostilities.

The Bush administration had also left the door open for a U.S.-led operation to overthrow Saddam at the end of the Gulf War. The National Security Directive 54, Section 10 warns:

> Should Iraq resort to using chemical, biological, or nuclear weapons, be found supporting terrorist acts against U.S. or Coalition partners anywhere in the world, *or destroy Kuwait's oil fields*, it shall become an explicit objective of the United States to replace the current leadership of Iraq. [emphasis added]

One of the conditions President Bush pre-defined for overthrowing Saddam (destruction of Kuwaiti oil fields) was certainly met in February 1991. Nonetheless, the Bush administration did not go into Baghdad. Events simply had unfolded too fast, and the need to wrap up the conflict was accelerated by the unforeseen rapidity of the Iraqi military collapse.

What Bush Didn't Want

No matter how much the Bush administration wanted Saddam out of power, it still wanted Iraq to remain intact. The administration did not want a Shiite-dominated state emerging in Iraq in 1991. The other Arab states, all Sunni-controlled, would not have tolerated a Shiite-controlled state allied to Iran. (Remember that Iran was and still is controlled by a Shiite theocracy.) Also, the administration wanted a return to stability, and the resumption of predictable oil deliveries. (U.S. gasoline prices had shot up during the Gulf War.)

The Bush administration also didn't want to see an independent Kurd state. As noted previously, NATO ally Turkey, whose cooperation had been vitally important to the success of Operation Desert Storm, had interests in this regard; the ever-potential antagonist Iran was similarly opposed to an independent Kurdish state on its border. With a collapse of military authority, and a power vacuum at the center, the emergence of a breakaway Kurd state was a real possibility.

So it was that the Coalition stopped short of demanding the overthrow of Saddam Hussein, or even of occupying Baghdad. They simply stepped back, waited for Humpty Dumpty to have his great fall, and hoped someone better would come along.

> **Increase Your Iraq IQ**
>
> I was convinced, as were all our Arab friends and allies, that Hussein would be overthrown once the war ended.
>
> —George H. W. Bush, in *All the Best, George Bush*

Meanwhile, Back at Home ...

As the smoke rose from 500 burning Kuwaiti oil wells, the Kurds in the north and Shiites in the south rose with it. The war ended abruptly, and Saddam was faced with uprisings at home that threatened his supremacy in Iraq. However, these rebellions didn't threaten his power base. In fact, they strengthened it.

Remember that Saddam represented the Sunni minority, and that his power base came from Sunni army officers and ruling elites—not from the Kurds or Shiites. These Sunni elites rallied around Saddam. They appear to have done so in order to preserve their own positions, as much as out of any personal loyalty to him.

> **Iraq Fact**
>
> The Bush administration wasn't looking to destroy the state of Iraq or carve new independent entities out of it. In fact, National Security Directive 54 stated clearly in Section 9: "The United States recognizes the territorial integrity of Iraq and will not support efforts to change current boundaries."

Threat from Within?

A far more potent threat to Saddam would have come from a military coup led by disaffected Sunni generals in his own circle. However, that coup never materialized. Saddam kept tight control over his generals, and they were soon occupied with the battles against the Kurds and Shiites.

The Sunni ruling elite was, as always, completely opposed to Kurdish or Shiite power-sharing, and so the Sunni-run, Shiite-manned army was quickly dispatched to the Kurd areas to battle those insurgents. Meanwhile, the Sunni Republican Guard remnants were sent into Shiite areas to quell the uprisings there. Amid savage reprisals, including helicopter gunship attacks and rumors of biological weapons being used, the rebellions were put down by the end of the year. In fact, the most significant military campaigns against the Kurds were wrapped up before May 1991.

As usual, Saddam moved fast at home to cut off the dissent before it could spread.

Iraq Fact

Saddam was able to suppress the domestic rebellions that followed the Gulf War for two reasons:

♦ He still had the firepower to do it, and

♦ No one stopped him.

Remember that Saddam began the Gulf War with one of the largest armies in the world. Saddam didn't send all of his troops into Kuwait. He held some back to keep an eye on the Iranians, Syrians, and Turks, and for domestic security. So, even after his armies in Kuwait were smashed, Saddam still had enough troops on hand for domestic control. As for the second reason: Saddam was obviously willing to bet that the Coalition didn't have the political will or unanimity to commit ground troops on behalf of the Kurds or the Shiites. He bet right.

No-Fly Zones: Too Little, Too Late

In response to Iraqi brutality against the Kurds and, later, the Shiites, the United States, Britain, and France established no-fly zones in the north and south, marking areas where Iraqi airplanes were forbidden to fly. The *northern no-fly zone* was established in April 1991; it essentially provided an American air umbrella over the Kurds. Prior to the creation of the northern no-fly zone, however, the Iraqis used helicopter gun ships with terrible effect, and they were able to batter the Kurds into submission.

Oil Spill Ahead

France withdrew from enforcement activities in December 1996, stating that the no-fly zone's humanitarian mission had been satisfied. The United States and Britain continued to enforce the no-fly zones up to the invasion of Iraq in 2003.

Saddam was able to do the same to the Shiites in the south prior to the establishment of a *southern no-fly zone* in August of 1992.

After the launch of the no-fly zones, the Shiites and Kurds enjoyed the protection of the U.S. and UK fighter cover. However, the no-fly zones became as much source of conflict as of protection.

Desert Diction

The **northern no-fly zone,** called Operation Provide Comfort, was established to protect the Kurds from Iraqi helicopter gun ships. The no-fly zone area is bounded by the thirty-sixth parallel.

The **southern no-fly zone** was established to protect the Shiite rebels from Iraqi aircraft. Called Operation Southern Watch, the southern zone was first bounded at the thirty-second parallel (to protect the Shiites in the marsh regions) and later extended to the thirty-third parallel.

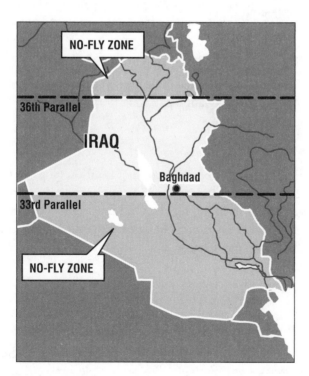

No-fly zones in Iraq.

Hasty Negotiations

It's safe to say that the coalition leaders who negotiated the cease-fire with Iraq did not make the most of the opportunity they were given to permanently diminish

Saddam's military power. Certainly, the battlefield victory did not ensure that the Bush administration's political objectives would be automatically fulfilled.

Why was Saddam so unbowed, despite his battlefield losses? One answer may have to do with the relative brevity of the Gulf War. Saddam's defeat did not have the psychological impact on him or his people that a longer, protracted struggle (like the Iran-Iraq War) might have had. Furthermore, since the Coalition wasn't coming to get him, Saddam could afford to be as aggressive as he wanted, as long as he stayed in his own yard. The Coalition had shown him that while they would not let him add to Iraq, they were not going to subtract from it, either—or physically remove him from power.

In order to survive, Saddam needed to act as if he had not lost, which is precisely what he did. He set about suppressing opposition at home and fought vigorously at the negotiating table to get whatever he could from the cease-fire agreement.

It worked. The anticipated popular revolt against Saddam never took hold.

> ![CAUTION]
> **Oil Spill Ahead** _____
>
> Prussian military theorist Carl von Clauswitz once wrote: "The ultimate outcome of war is not always to be regarded as final. The defeated state often considers the outcome merely as a transitory evil, for which a remedy may still be found in political conditions at some later date." Saddam probably looked at the Gulf War defeat in much the same way.

Blowing the Endgame

The speed at which the ground war ended, and the Coalition's lopsided military victory, caught everyone off guard, including the U.S. senior military commanders. Much time had been spent on planning for the Gulf campaign's beginning and its middle, but little time had been spent on planning for the campaign's end. However, as noted military theorist Carl von Clauswitz has observed, every war has a beginning, a middle, and an end. The "end" is the negotiations that conclude the fighting and secure the political objectives.

The Bush administration was not adequately prepared for the end game. Saddam, on the other hand, seemed more than ready for that part of the contest.

In fact, in April 1991, General Norman Schwarzkopf, commander of the Western Coalition forces in the region during the Gulf War (and de facto commander of all Coalition forces in the region), admitted in his report on the battle, "The rapid success of the ground campaign and our subsequent occupation of Iraq were not fully anticipated. Thus, some of the necessary follow-on actions were not ready .... Documents for war termination need to be drafted and coordinated early." And a

U.S. Central Command foreign-policy expert was even more explicit when he said, "We never did have a plan to terminate the war."

The Cease-Fire Conditions, as stipulated by UN Security Council Resolution 687 were …

- Iraq must acknowledge Kuwait sovereignty.

- Iraq must destroy all of its ballistic missile systems (SCUDs) with a range of more than 150 kilometers.

- Iraq must repatriate all Kuwaiti and other nationals, and support the International Red Cross and Red Crescent Societies in this area.

- Iraq must finance a compensation fund to meet its liabilities for damages it inflicted during its occupation of Kuwait.

Nowhere in Resolution 687 is there any requirement that threatens Saddam's domestic grip on power. So as long as Saddam didn't have to negotiate on his own survival, he could accept the cease-fire terms and tend to his business at home. With his own survival covered, he could start over again, building his military, enhancing his prestige, and tightening his grip on power.

The Least You Need to Know

- The Bush administration did not overthrow Saddam at the end of the Gulf War because its allies would not have supported it.

- The Coalition stopped short of intervening to stop Saddam from suppressing Kurd or Shiite rebellions at the end of the Gulf War. The Coalition objective was simply to expel Iraq from Kuwait.

- The Coalition military leaders were not prepared to negotiate effectively when the fighting ended.

- The no-fly zones that were unilaterally set up by the United States, Britain, and France shortly after the war ended came too late to save Shiite and Kurd rebels from brutal reprisals by Saddam's forces, but they later protected those groups from Saddam's air attacks.

- The Coalition underestimated Saddam's grip on power inside Iraq.

Of Sanctions and Inspections

In This Chapter

- ◆ Iraq's increasingly bold defiance of UN weapons inspectors
- ◆ World opinion turns against economic sanctions
- ◆ Internal repression
- ◆ Rumblings against Kuwait (again)
- ◆ Saddam's definition of success

Throughout the 10 years following the Gulf War, from 1991 to 2001, Saddam was a very busy man. By the end of that decade, the Iraqi dictator had gone a long way toward wiping away the results of his overwhelming military defeat in the first Gulf War.

A Busy Decade

During the 1990s, Saddam worked steadily on ...

- ◆ Shoring up his position at home by portraying himself as the victor in the Gulf War.
- ◆ Squirming out from under the weapons inspectors, through defiance and guile.

- Shrugging off the economic sanctions by waging an effective PR campaign in the United Nations and the world press, and relying on international disinterest.

- Trying to assert his leadership in the Arab world by bullying Kuwait and vilifying Israel and the United States.

We'll look more closely at Saddam's post-war activities in this chapter.

An Independent Kuwait

One thing appeared certain from the Gulf War experience: Saddam would never, ever invade Kuwait again.

Or would he?

How could he after the disastrous defeat Iraq suffered in 1991? At the end of the Gulf War, Iraqi Foreign Minister Tariq Aziz, representing the government of Iraq, agreed to UN Security Council Resolution 687, which specified that Iraq recognized Kuwait's right to exist as an independent nation. With the dramatic defeat of the Iraqi army, and the presence of U.S. troops in Saudi Arabia and pre-positioned equipment in Kuwait, Saddam's ability to bully Kuwait and Saudi Arabia was in fact significantly decreased.

Nevertheless, Saddam resorted, from time to time, to threatening Kuwait as a means of attempting to change the price of oil and, just perhaps, to destabilize his smaller neighbor. At the end of the war, the UN declared a demilitarized zone, where Iraqi and Kuwaiti military activities were forbidden. However, in January 1993, just two years after their last move south, the Iraqi military sent its first patrols into the demilitarized border zone. These patrols prompted a series of sharp warnings to Iraq from the United States (led by the Clinton administration), Britain, and France. When Saddam continued to send patrols into the demilitarized zone along the border between Iraq and Kuwait, these three countries responded by bombing military targets in southern Iraq. Saddam pulled back in the wake of the bombing.

Saddam tried to integrate his actions toward Kuwait with the UN inspectors' actions toward Iraq. In other words, Saddam was trying to leverage whatever he could to resist UN weapons inspections. One of the only credible threats he had was that of (re)invading Kuwait. So Saddam continued to "play the Kuwait card"; his belligerence appeared to be a tactic to undercut UN sanctions or inspections. For example, in October 1994, Saddam aimed to lessen the impact and access that UN weapons inspectors and the IAEA (International Atomic Energy Agency) had in Iraq at that time (more on this later). Saddam massed troops on the Kuwaiti border on October

4, 1994. The UN and U.S. reaction was firm and unmistakable, however, and Saddam pulled the troops back by October 16.

Later, in March 2001, Saddam played the same game. In the midst of an argument with the UN over whether Iraq could retain some of its oil revenues to invest in a pipeline across Syria, Saddam's oil minister began to grumble that Kuwait was drawing too much oil from the al-Ratga oilfield that the two countries share. Tariq Aziz demanded—you guessed it—compensation from Kuwait for the oil that had supposedly been pilfered. Kuwait denied the charges and refused compensation. Iraq again made threatening moves toward Kuwait, but pulled back again after being allowed to invest the needed resources in the Syrian pipeline.

Why did Saddam threaten to invade Kuwait every few years? Leverage. Iraq raised the Kuwait threat in order to try to get an adjustment on some other issue, like economic sanctions or weapons inspections. Over time, these kinds of threats contributed to the complex factors that helped reduce UN oversight and involvement in Iraq. Saddam used the threat of force and resistance to UN actions to get some relaxation of the constraints that would otherwise have bound his options.

> **Iraq Fact**
>
> The UN Security Council responded to Iraqi troop movements in 1994 with Resolution 949, which condemned the massing of Saddam's forces near Kuwait, demanded their withdrawal from the Kuwaiti border, and expressly forbade Iraq from massing troops in the southern part of its territory. The resolution also insisted that Iraq cooperate with weapons inspectors.

New Threats, Different Neighbors

By using the Kuwait card, some extremely effective PR, and growing international indifference, Saddam steadily managed to work his way out from under some very strict limitations on his military power. Maintaining the second U.S. policy objective—eliminating the potential for Iraq to threaten its neighbors militarily—became increasingly difficult in decade following Operation Desert Storm.

Revamping the Iraqi Military Machine

The Coalition had devastated Iraq's conventional military power by the end of the Gulf War, leaving Saddam no choice but to accept the conditions laid down by the Coalition and reinforced by the UN Security Council. Of the 42 Iraqi divisions in place at the start of the Gulf War, 40 were determined to be noncombat ready by the end of the 100-hour war. Although Saddam regrouped fairly quickly, the ability of the Iraqi military to mount a credible conventional threat to Kuwait, let alone Iran, Saudi Arabia, or Turkey, was dramatically reduced in the immediate aftermath of the war.

After such losses, it would take Saddam a long time to rebuild his conventional arsenal, and reorganize his military. Instead, Saddam began to focus on developing *weapons of mass destruction,* such as biological and chemical weapons, to replace conventional firepower.

It had long been suspected (and is now beyond dispute) that Saddam had used chemical weapons against Iran and also against the Kurds. At the end of the Gulf War, the Bush administration was wary of these weapons and wanted to be sure Saddam could not continue to develop them. The United States was also interested in curtailing Saddam's ability to deliver weapons over longer distances using ballistic missiles. The two targets for these missiles would have been Israel and/or U.S. troops that were stationed in Saudi Arabia at the time.

Desert Diction

Weapons of mass destruction can kill thousands of people at one time, and, in some cases, wipe out everything in a given area. Generally, biological, chemical, and nuclear weapons are classified as weapons of mass destruction. These weapons tend to be managed by international conventions that prohibit or restrict their use.

UN Security Council Resolution 687, which specified the provisions of the cease-fire, included the instruction that Iraq was required to identify and then destroy all ballistic missiles with a range greater then 150 kilometers. This enabled Saddam to retain a missile threat against its neighbor Iran, but kept it from reaching strategic targets in Saudi Arabia or Israel.

Anticipating (correctly) that Saddam would not willingly allow the destruction of these weapons or the missiles that would deliver them, the cease-fire requirements included provisions for UN-managed weapons inspections. Rather than allow the coalition military leaders to establish all the terms of these inspections, the Iraqis negotiated for some limitations on the inspections—limitations that they later leveraged to the hilt.

Presidential Palaces Sprout Up Throughout Iraq

For example, Saddam's Presidential Palaces were excluded from the otherwise universal access that would be granted to the weapons inspectors. The argument put forth by the Iraqi government was that Saddam's personal homes should be off limits, as they were obviously not places where weapons of mass destruction would be stored.

This argument sounded rational during the negotiating process, and the cease-fire agreement included this exception to the weapons inspectors' access. Almost immediately, however, Iraq decreed tens, and eventually hundreds, of buildings as "Presidential Palaces." Several of these buildings were suspected weapons manufacturing or storage facilities. However, according to the hastily negotiated inspection agreement, the inspection teams were not allowed to search Presidential Palaces. In hindsight, granting this exclusion was a diplomatic fiasco for the Bush (Sr.) administration. The haste of negotiations certainly contributed to the oversight in the inspection agreement.

The Inspection Two-Step: War by Other Means

Whatever they couldn't legally maneuver around, the Iraqis steadily resisted through simple intransigence. This intransigence grew more and more bold as former Coalition partners began to leave the Gulf War alliance and the UN became increasingly disinterested in weapons inspections and more concerned about hardships imposed by UN mandated, but U.S. enforced, economic sanctions. Let's start at the beginning of the inspection process, and see how Saddam got away with making a mockery of it, and finally rejected it all together.

Hostilities Resume

On June 17, 1991, the UN Special Commission (*UNSCOM*) was created. Its mission was to monitor disarmament in Iraq, along with the International Atomic Energy Agency (IAEA). Just one week later, Iraq defied the UNSCOM and IAEA inspectors. Iraqi military personnel opened fire on UNSCOM inspectors who were trying to stop a truck loaded with equipment for use in making nuclear weapons. The equipment was eventually located and destroyed, but Saddam had shown he was going to do his best to undercut the UNSCOM/IAEA inspectors.

Desert Diction

The United Nations Special Commission was called **UNSCOM**. Created on June 17, 1991, in the wake of the Gulf War, UNSCOM's mission was to inspect Iraqi weapons facilities, and destroy any weapons of mass destruction and the production facilities to make them, that could be found in Iraq.

Biological Weapons Found

On August 2, 1991, one year after the Iraqi army invaded Kuwait, UNSCOM inspectors uncovered evidence of a large-scale biological weapons program in Iraq. The inspectors found materials that are used to make biological weapons. Faced with UNSCOM successes, which now included finding his biological weapons, Saddam disallowed UNSCOM access to its own helicopters to carry out their inspections on September 18, 1991.

The United States responded by threatening to shoot anyone who got in the way of the UNSCOM helicopters. Saddam backed down on September 24, 1991, but he had gained a week of time to avoid further weapons discoveries. The United Nations Security Council responded on October 11, 1991, with Resolution 715, which mandated continuous monitoring of Iraqi weapons programs and demanded that Iraq cooperate fully with the UNSCOM and IAEA weapons inspection teams.

"Yes, We Have Biological Weapons"

By May 1992, UNSCOM inspectors uncovered equipment and weapons hardware to go along with the biological agents that were found in August 1991. Faced with the mounting evidence, Iraq finally admitted that it had been developing biological weapons capability. Saddam insisted, though, that the weapons were purely defensive in nature.

Weapons of mass destruction do just that: destroy massively. It is hard to differentiate a "defensive" weapon of mass destruction from an "offensive" one, but somehow Saddam could make this distinction, as if notions of "offense" or "defense" mattered.

"Yes, We Have Chemical Weapons"

The UNSCOM inspectors also uncovered stockpiles of chemical weapons in Iraq as well as their production facilities during this time. UNSCOM began destroying the chemical weapons in July 1992. Caught red handed, Saddam admitted that he had chemical weapons and insisted on his right to use them.

Saddam again tested UNSCOM's resolve in January 1993, when Iraq refused to allow UNSCOM to use its own aircraft to move around inside Iraq. (At this time, Saddam also sent his first patrols into the demilitarized zone.) In response to both moves, the United States, United Kingdom, and France launched the air strikes mentioned previously in this chapter. On January 19, 1991, Saddam relented and allowed UNSCOM flights to resume.

A Dangerous Game of Cat and Mouse

With his biological and chemical weapons systems being sniffed out, Saddam dug in his heels on the delivery systems—his missiles. In June 1993, Saddam rejected an

UNSCOM attempt to place surveillance cameras at his missile test sites. Again, there were dire threats from the United Nations, and Saddam backed off by July.

A year or so later, Saddam was up to his old tricks again. On October 6, 1994, he stated that he would not assist UNSCOM, which prompted the UN Security Council to pass yet another resolution—Resolution 949—on October 15, insisting that Saddam allow inspections.

UNSCOM continued to pry into Saddam's weapons programs, and on July 1, 1995, Iraq acknowledged that its defensive biological weapons program was really offensive, but insisted it was not ready for use. It was only after Saddam's own son-in-law, Lt. General Hussein Kamel Hassan al-Majid, who was in charge of the program, defected and told the world that Iraq's various weapons programs were much further along than Saddam had claimed, that Iraq ponied up the details of the program. (Iraq did this rather than face a strengthening of UN economic sanctions, which Saddam was making great progress on getting lifted.)

> **Iraq Fact** _____
>
> On August 8, 1995, two of Saddam's sons-in-law and their families fled Iraq and ended up in Jordan. The Jordanians granted them asylum. They were Lt. General Hussein Kamel Hassan al-Majid, who was in charge of Iraq's weapons programs, and his brother, Lt. Colonel Saddam Kamel Hassan al-Majid, who was in charge of presidential security. These two men told a great deal about what they knew, which prompted Iraq to come clean on more details of its mass-destruction weapons programs. Amazingly, the brothers returned to Iraq in February 1996, under Saddam's guarantees that he would not harm them. Both brothers were shot three days after they got back.

Iraq disclosed on August 20, 1995, that it had a stockpile of the deadly nerve agent VX, which is among the most lethal chemical weapon agents known. On top of that cheerful news, Saddam also disclosed that he was on the way to developing crude nuclear weapons, but that the facilities had been destroyed during the Gulf War. Whether true or not, UNSCOM had not confirmed the existence of Iraqi nuclear weapons facilities or weapons themselves.

In May 1996, UNSCOM destroyed Saddam's main biological weapons facility at Al-Hakem.

The World Sleeps

As 1996 rolled on, the weapons inspectors were becoming increasingly frustrated in their work. It was clear to them that Saddam was hiding more than he was showing.

Any information they uncovered, or forced Saddam to disclose, only pointed them toward even more weapons that the inspection teams suspected were beyond their reach. Instead of throwing in the towel, Saddam continued to do his best to thwart the inspectors. He only opened the doors, or the books, when absolutely forced to do so.

Without clear evidence of current weapons capabilities (despite the recent disclosures), Saddam was counting on international indifference to do much of his work for him. He was banking on the fact that the only way the UNSCOM and IAEA inspections could be enforced was through a military strike. As the years rolled on, only the United States and the United Kingdom were willing to make those strikes. And every time the United States or United Kingdom dropped a bomb, they raised murmurs of protest from Arab and Western European countries, who began to see the inspections (and the dire effects of the economic sanctions) as heavy-handed Western bullying. Saddam bet that he could take a hard line without bringing about a major military response.

The Game Gets Serious

The deadly dance continued, but now Saddam began to lead rather than follow. In March 1996, Saddam openly blocked UNSCOM inspectors from visiting five sites for 17 hours. The Security Council voiced its concern, and passed another Resolution (number 1060) on June 12, 1996, but no military response was taken. As Saddam continued to block inspectors during 1997, the UN Security Council passed Resolution 1134 on October 23, 1997, which condemned the actions but did not do much more. Even this mild slap on the back of Saddam's hand only passed 10 to 0, with 5 members abstaining. Saddam was gradually winning the inspections war.

Emboldened by Resolution 1134's soft-pedal approach and lukewarm support, Saddam had the Revolutionary Command Council (the decision-making body in Iraq) declare that Iraq would no longer allow U.S. inspectors or U.S. aircraft to be part of the UNSCOM teams. The Security Council, true to form, condemned the RCC statement with Resolution 1137 on November 12, 1997. This time, the Security Council imposed a travel ban on Iraqi officials in response.

The Russians, looking to get more involved in Iraq's oil industry, brokered a deal that allowed the UNSCOM teams to continue their work in November 1997. However, it quickly became clear that the inspectors were still being blocked from visiting the sites they wanted to see.

During the first few months of 1998, General Secretary Kofi Annan brokered an agreement that would allow UNSCOM inspectors full access, including Presidential Palaces. The agreement, specified in Resolution 1154, did not mandate military response if Iraq did not comply. By May 1998, the travel ban was lifted as Iraq appeared to accept Annan's deal. But, just as things appeared to be calming down, on August 5, 1998, Saddam unilaterally cut off inspection access and stated that inspections would only be resumed when the economic sanctions on Iraq were lifted.

Finally, in the face of this move, the Clinton administration threatened to bomb Iraq. On November 14, Saddam backed down and the attack was called off. Saddam promised complete cooperation. By mid-December, however, he was back to his old tricks and blocking inspectors.

This time, the Clinton administration, with British support, launched *Operation Desert Fox*, on December 16, 1998.

However, even with this military action, the tide was shifting at the UN. On December 17, 1998, as Desert Fox was winding down, the Security Council passed Resolution 1248, stating that if Saddam complied with inspections for nine months, economic sanctions could be lifted. The new inspection teams would be called UNMOVIC (UN Monitoring, Verification, and Inspection Commission). UNSCOM was gone.

Desert Diction

Operation Desert Fox was a coordinated bombing attack on Iraqi weapons targets by U.S. and UK aircraft and missiles. It was launched in response to Saddam Hussein's unilateral refusal to comply with UNSCOM weapons inspections.

This was a crucial change of direction. For the first time, economic sanctions and weapons inspections were linked, and Saddam could bargain one limitation on him against the other one. Saddam rejected the offer, and continued to bar the inspections. The standoff continued.

On August 24, 2001, Tariq Aziz insisted that Iraq would not cooperate with UNMOVIC in anyway. After Desert Fox, however, no further military assaults were launched on Iraq for the purpose of gaining Iraqi compliance with weapons inspections.

In 2002, the second Bush administration reiterated the call to open the doors to inspections, but Saddam again refused and said that inspectors would only be allowed in when sanctions were lifted. Saddam reinforced the new Iraqi position: sanctions or inspections, but not both.

Iraqi Vice President Taha Yasin Ramadan made this statement February 13, 2002, confirming Saddam's position on inspections: "There is no need for the spies of the inspection teams to return to Iraq since Iraq is free of weapons of mass destruction."

At the time, the statement seemed preposterous to most Western observers.

The Sanctions: A Close-Up Look

The economic sanctions that the United Nations imposed on Iraq in August 1990, immediately following Iraq's annexation of Kuwait, were intended to persuade Iraq to withdraw from Kuwait. After the war ended, the sanctions were continued in order to repay Kuwait for economic damages for the war and to limit Saddam's ability to finance the rebuilding of his army or weapons programs.

On paper, the sanctions were intended to cut Iraq off from international trade and only allow imports that were approved by the United Nations. The sanctions started out with the full support of coalition members in 1991, but over the ensuing 10 years, support for the sanctions steadily eroded.

There were three reasons for the waning support for the sanctions: human suffering, greed, and indifference. The sanctions are blamed for the deaths of thousands of Iraqis, mainly children. Also, Iraq has a lot of oil, and trading that oil for products and services means big money for countries like Russia, France, Saudi Arabia, Syria, and Turkey. Finally, many UN members were simply too far removed from the Gulf War to see the need for the sanctions. They viewed the sanctions as an anachronism whose time had passed.

The Greed Factor

You'll recall from previous chapters that Iraq makes very little of what it consumes. The only real method for Iraq to get the things it needs (food, medicine, oil equipment, or weapons) is to sell oil and buy them.

By 1995, it was becoming apparent that Iraqi civilians, particularly Kurds and Shiites, were suffering and dying because Iraq was cut off from needed food and medical supplies. The sanctions, aimed at containing Iraqi military might, had actually helped Saddam retain his grip on power in the years immediately following the Gulf War. Why? Well, even though the United States, United Kingdom, and France set up the no-fly zones that effectively limited Saddam's ability to attack the Kurdish and Shiite insurgents militarily, the sanctions gave him the excuse to deny them food and medicine. Since the sanctions forbade imports of those items, there were none to be had for the Kurds or Shiites.

In 1995, responding to reports that the Iraqi people were suffering terribly under the UN sanctions, the UN Security Council proposed a food-for-oil plan. The plan would be reviewed every 60 days, and the limits could be adjusted as conditions warranted. Under the plan, Iraq would be allowed to sell limited amounts of oil, if the

United Nations could oversee how the revenues were allocated inside Iraq, including a guarantee that a portion would be allocated to the Kurds. The Iraqis objected to this last point, and negotiations over the amounts allowed, the types of materials that could be purchased, how much would be allocated to the Kurds, and who would distribute the humanitarian materials, stretched into mid-1996.

Finally, a deal was reached in August 1996 in which the Iraqis agreed to allocate a portion of the humanitarian aid to the Kurds, with the proviso that the Iraqi government would be responsible for the distribution itself. The United States had objected to this last provision, until it was alone in its objections. Finally, the United States gave in on that point, and the *oil-for-food* deal went forward.

After the UN Security Council created the oil-for-food program in 1996, foreign oil companies lined up to invest in Iraqi oil. Over the years, the United Nations gradually increased the allowed export amount, and Iraq's neighbors, including Turkey, Syria, Jordan, and Saudi Arabia, all worked with Iraq to repair oil transmission facilities in their countries.

As these transmission facilities were improved, more oil could be passed through them. More oil meant more transshipment royalties for the host country. Other countries, like Russia, saw opportunities to exert their influence in the region and increase their trade with Iraq by helping to develop Iraqi oil fields.

> **Desert Diction**
>
> The **oil-for-food program** allowed Iraq to export a set amount of oil and use the proceeds to buy food, medicine, and other humanitarian items. That program became a major source of kickbacks and graft for many of the UN officials involved. A special UN commission has been created, as of this writing, to investigate the charges.

> **Increase Your Iraq IQ**
>
> One way Saddam tried to keep more oil money, and sidestep UN controls, was by requiring a 50-cents-per-barrel surcharge from anyone moving oil out of Iraq. This surcharge, decreed in December of 2000, was supposed to be paid to a separate account, outside of UN oversight. It is unclear how many shippers paid this fee to Iraq, though payments were made.

Oil and Blood

For Saddam and the Sunnis, the oil-for-food program was a good deal. For the Kurds and Shiites, the program was only partially successful. Remember, Saddam got to allocate the humanitarian items purchased under the oil-for-food program. Thus, the man who openly attacked the Kurds and Shiites in the aftermath of the Gulf War was now responsible for delivering their food and medical supplies. The lion's share of aid stayed in the major Sunni cities, like Baghdad and Tikrit. Much less aid made its way to the Shiite areas in the south, and cities like Basra, or the Kurd areas in the north, and their cities like Kirkuk.

Oil Spill Ahead

According to a UN Security Council report on the oil-for-food program, in the first half of 2000, Saddam only spent about half of the money ($4.2 billion) Iraq received from the legal exports of oil ($8 billion). The other half was horded for future use. Of the half that was spent, about 33 percent went to buying food, and only about 2 percent went to buying medicines. Also, it is estimated that Saddam made almost $2 billion in smuggled oil sales during that period, and apparently none of that money was used to by food or medicine. Of the food and medicine that was purchased, most of that remained in Sunni areas. The Shiites and Kurds were denied most of the goods that were purchased. Some food and medicine did make it to the Kurds and Shiites, but at Saddam's pleasure, and nowhere near enough to meet the needs of the people there.

The result of the five years of sanctions after the Gulf War, and the ensuing years of limited oil-for-food trade was an unmitigated human disaster in the Shiite and Kurd areas in Iraq. Tens if not hundreds of thousands of Iraqi people, most of them children, died due to poor nutrition and lack of medicine. Even as the United Nations gradually increased the amount of oil Iraq can export each year, most of the aid did not reach those who needed it most. Some was allocated, with UN permission, to oil equipment investments, most was allocated to the Sunnis, and the rest went to the Kurds and Shiites.

The Sanctions Become a Fiasco

In the face of this human suffering, the United States maintained that the sanctions were essential to (1) containing Saddam's weapons of mass destruction programs, and (2) countering his conventional military buildup. However, the majority of the world community saw the situation differently. They saw the suffering of the Iraqi people as inordinate punishment for the crimes Saddam had committed. Each time the United States spoke out in favor of keeping the sanctions, and Saddam showed evidence of dying Iraqi children, world opinion shifted further away from the U.S. position, and toward the Iraqi one.

> ⚠️ **Oil Spill Ahead** _____
>
> The United States intercepted a Russian tanker shipping illegal Iraqi oil in April of 1995, and fined Royal Dutch Shell over $2 million for its role in the smuggling. The Iranians tended to look the other way while Saddam shipped his oil out illegally via the Gulf, which allowed him to move it down the Gulf unmolested. Also, Saddam has shipped oil out of a supposedly closed pipeline through Syria. In January 2002, it was apparent that Syria was exporting a great deal more oil than it had in previous years. Experts suspected that Syria was transshipping Iraqi oil, in defiance of UN sanctions. Turkey announced it was going to import over 80,000 barrels per day of Iraqi oil in 2002. These imports were not covered by the UN oil-for-food program, showing the limits to sanctions enforcement among Iraq's trade partners.

Sanctions: How Tough?

Since the initiation of the oil-for-food program in 1996, Iraq steadily lobbied to sell more and more oil, and also worked to get control of more money from its exports outside of UN control. Saddam consistently pushed to get more of the oil revenues gained from exports allocated to oil equipment, in order to repair and rebuild oil extracting and transmission facilities. Over time, these limits were raised to the point where the limit was more than the amount Iraq could actually export—due to the poor state of its domestic infrastructure.

American Isolation ... and a Big Question

So, as the years moved on, time appeared to be on Saddam's side. He had managed to win the peace after losing the war.

Iraq was no longer the isolated pariah it once was. Although not universally embraced, Iraq gained the sympathy of a broader base of Arab and non-Arab countries that were drawn to Iraq for humanitarian and economic motives. On the other hand, by insisting on defending an increasingly untenable position on the issues of sanctions and inspections, the United States was increasingly isolated and was blamed by the international community for the desperate state of the Iraqi people.

The Least You Need to Know

♦ Saddam steadily turned defeat into victory after the Gulf War.

♦ Iraq threatened to invade Kuwait even after its 1991 defeat.

♦ Iraq managed to block all weapons inspections in its territory.

♦ Iraq portrayed the suffering of its people under UN sanctions as the fault of the United States, rather than due to Saddam's allocation methods.

♦ Saddam managed to export increasing amounts of oil through legal and illegal means, to the point where the sanctions lost much of their effectiveness.

Part 5

The Gulf War, Part 2

After the first Gulf War, Saddam showed his ability to survive, despite all the odds. In the aftermath of a decade's worth of Saddam defying the United States, the terror attacks of September 11, and an assassination attempt on his father, George W. Bush stubbornly pushes Hussein out of the limelight, only to find himself in the harsh glare of those same lights.

19

America's Countdown to Invasion in Iraq

In This Chapter

- ◆ The Bush Doctrine: Iraq in the axis of evil
- ◆ The fascination with Saddam Hussein
- ◆ "Enforcing" the UN resolutions and the search for WMD
- ◆ Run up to the invasion: old friends alienated
- ◆ Timeline: January 2001 through March 2003

In January 2001, George W. Bush took the oath of office as President of the United States.

In March 2003, he pieced together a narrow military coalition to overthrow the government of Iraq—over the objections of America's closest allies and a large portion of the rest of the world.

In between those two events, America's global defense and diplomatic strategy, indeed its sense of its role and mission in the world, changed profoundly, and Iraq was one of the first places where the change played out.

Basically, the new Bush Doctrine (more on that in a moment) collided with an apparent obsession with Saddam Hussein. The result was the overthrow of Hussein regime, and the dramatic reordering of post World War II alliances. In this chapter, we follow this change over three distinct periods ... and perhaps begin to get a sense of the motivations at work during each one.

Period #1: January–September 2001: A New President

During his first eight months in office, George W. Bush appears to have downplayed the immediate security risk presented by Iraq in particular and the Middle East in general. Iraq as a foreign policy issue was depicted as being on the periphery. However, some former Cabinet members and media analysts present a different picture. Whether out of spite or truth, these people presented the image of an administration that was keenly aware of Saddam Hussein, and considering ways to remove him from power. (We will examine the motivations for this attitude in the next chapter.) The following timeline highlights some key events from the first days of the George W. Bush administration, up through the September 11, 2001 attacks upon the United States.

Iraq Fact

Saddam does not control the northern part of the country. We are able to keep his arms from him. His military forces have not been rebuilt.

—Condoleeza Rice, July 2001.

And

... we're not all that worried about Saddam.

—attributed to Secretary of State Colin Powell during this same period.

January 20, 2001. George W. Bush is inaugurated in Washington after a controversial presidential election, complete with hanging chads in Florida.

Early 2001. According to former Treasury Secretary Paul O'Neill (who resigned his position in protest over his apparent lack of autonomy within the Cabinet), several discussions about invading Iraq took place in the very early phases of the Bush administration, even though the administration publicly downplayed the threat posed by Saddam's regime in its early months.

February 16, 2001. American and British Air Forces launch new attacks against Iraqi installations near Baghdad, in response to Iraqi military moves that were in violation of the UN imposed regulations on Iraq.

March 28 2001. An Arab Summit in Jordan concludes; but there is no consensus on the group's position with regard to Saddam Hussein. Ambivalence over Saddam is tempered by anger over U.S. support for Israel and the dire effects of U.S.-imposed UN sanctions on Iraq.

May 31, 2001. Led by the United States, the existing oil-for-food initiative is maintained by the UN Security Council, rather than a new "smart sanctions" initiative that would have effectively removed most of the controls over Iraqi use of the program proceeds. (The oil-for-food program became clouded in controversy, with UN officials and Saddam Hussein apparently colluding to siphon off billions of dollars from the proceeds that were supposed to go to procuring food and medicine for Iraqis).

June 3, 2001. Iraq pledges to stop exporting crude oil as a result of the UN's decision to extend the oil-for-food program by single months, instead of the six-month term to which Baghdad had grown accustomed. The United States was pushing for the tighter restrictions in an attempt to rein in Saddam's abuses of the program, and the one-month extensions were a way to do that.

July 11, 2001. Iraq resumes oil exports, ending its five-week protest.

August 10, 2001. Reacting to reports of misappropriations of funds from the oil-for-food program, U.S. and British diplomats oppose a UN proposal to allow Hussein to use one billion dollars annually to supposedly improve Iraqi infrastructure and increase oil production, given the lack of guarantees over how that money would actually be spent.

August 30, 2001. Iraq announces that it has downed an American "spy aircraft"; the United States maintains the plane was on a legal and normal patrol, and the United States attacks Iraqi military targets in retaliation. Analysts surmised that Iraq may have upgraded its surface-to-air missile capability.

Tragedy, and the Reaction

September 11, 2001. Terrorist attacks on the United States destroy the World Trade Center, damage the Pentagon, and result in the downing of an airplane in rural Pennsylvania.

Approximately 3,000 lives are lost. It is the most deadly foreign attack on the United States in American history.

Within six hours of the attacks, Secretary of Defense Donald Rumsfeld tells his aides to begin work on possible military strike against potential perpetrators of the attacks, including the Taliban in Afghanistan and the regime of Saddam Hussein.

Iraq Fact

CBS News eventually reports the contents of notes taken by one of Secretary Rumsfeld's aides during a critical meeting following the attacks of September 11th. They read as follows:

> [I want the] best info fast. Judge whether good enough. Hit S.H. at same time. Not only UBL .... Sweep it all up. Things related and not.

(SH refers to Saddam Hussein. UBL refers to Osama (Usama) bin Laden.)

According to retired General Wesley Clark, there was a "concerted effort" to assign blame for the September 11 attack specifically, and the terror threat to the United States in general, on Iraq. Clark (who later campaigned for the Presidency himself and so his criticism may be politically motivated) also claimed that the administration tried to use the attacks as a justification for attacking the Iraqi leader. Clark later told NBC *Today Show* host Ken Russert that he received a call on September 11 at his home from a "Middle Eastern think tank" insisting that he say publicly that September 11 was an example of state-sponsored terrorism, and that it was connected to Saddam Hussein. However, this is no evidence that the "think tank" was acting on Bush administration orders, or was even involved in official policy making. (Clark also never named the organization.) Rather, the call (if it did happen) shows the general tenor of outrage in the wake of the horrible events that occurred. People were looking for answers, and applying blame even when facts did not support the accusations. People in official and unofficial roles were unprepared for what had happened, and were wrestling with the results.

Period #2: September 2001–September 2002: A New Strategy

The idea of invading Iraq may not have been new for the Bush Administration, but public justification for the invasion was new. How did it happen, despite the fact that years later unequivocal evidence linking Hussein to the terrorist attacks still does not exist? The year following the terrorist attacks on America culminated in a new National Security Strategy, which was formulated as a direct consequence of the September 11 attacks.

This strategy became known as the "Bush Doctrine." The doctrine acknowledges the United States is in a position of unprecedented pre-eminence, and that it will act to preserve and extend that pre-eminence against a newly perceived threat of terrorism. The doctrine is built on five elements.

Increase Your Iraq IQ

Today the United States enjoys a position of unparalleled military strength and great economic and political influence ... We will defend the peace by fighting terrorists and tyrants. We will preserve the peace by building good relations among the great powers. We will extend the peace by encouraging free and open societies on every continent.

Defending our nation against its enemies is the first and fundamental commitment of the federal government. Today that task has changed dramatically. Enemies in the past needed great armies and great industrial capabilities to endanger America. Now shadowy networks of individuals can bring great chaos and suffering to our shores for less than it costs to purchase a single tank. Terrorists are organized to penetrate open societies and to turn the power of modern technologies against us.

To defeat this threat, we must make use of every tool in our arsenal—military power, better homeland defenses, law enforcement, intelligence, and vigorous efforts to cut of terrorist financing. The war against terrorists of global reach is a global enterprise of uncertain duration. America will help nations that need our assistance in combating terror. And America will hold to account nations that are compromised by terror, including those who harbor terrorists—because the allies of terror are the enemies of civilization. The United States and countries cooperating with us must not allow the terrorists to develop new home bases. Together we will seek to deny them sanctuary at every turn.

—Commonly known as the Bush Doctrine, from the National Security Strategy for the United States, the White House.

Focus on Terror

One of the tenets of the Bush Doctrine is a focus on combating terrorism. The doctrine specifies that the United States will focus its domestic and foreign policy and military resources on defeating terrorism—specifically, terrorism that threatens the United States and its interests. The Bush administration made it clear that the United States simply will not accept the inevitability of another September 11. This is not to suggest that no other major terrorist attacks will occur on U.S. soil—only that the United States will not wait and hope that one does not occur.

Pre-Emptive Intervention

Another tenet of the new Bush Doctrine is that the United States will not wait to react to an attack on itself or its interests, but rather it will move against a threat before it occurs. This policy is new, in that it publicly claims the United States' intention to seek out threats and eliminate them before they harm the United States. What is more, the Bush Doctrine does not limit pre-emptive action to sanctions and diplomacy. Rather, the Bush Doctrine keeps military action (including surprise attack) as a tool of strategy. As we shall see in Chapter 21, this strategy was employed in Operation Iraqi Freedom.

Unilateral Action

Along with the willingness and claimed right to act preemptively, the Bush Doctrine declares that the United States may act alone, if it is in its best interests. The Bush Doctrine cites the urgency of protecting the United States before a threat materializes that could harm it. Under the Bush Doctrine, Uncle Sam will go it alone, if need be. Again, we shall see how the Bush administration followed this strategy when approaching Iraq.

Urgency

The Bush Doctrine assumes a sense of urgency that the United States must act *now* because terrorists are actively working against the United States and its interests, constantly. The Bush Doctrine suggests that there is a race of preparedness: U.S. prevention preparedness against terrorist attack preparedness, or the creation of threats like weapons of mass destruction.

Fostering Democracy

The Bush Doctrine also promotes the U.S. goal of fostering democratic, civil societies around the world. These types of societies are considered allied to U.S. interests, and not threatening or fostering of terrorism against the United States and its allies. We shall see later in the book how this goal of democracy building also was an initial driver in post-Saddam Iraq.

International Organizations: Obsolete or Revitalized?

In the run-up to the invasion of Iraq, the United States clearly signaled its willingness to go it alone (unilateralism), use force first (pre-emption), topple a dictatorship (foster democracy), and do it soon (urgency). The only missing piece was the clear Iraqi support of terrorism (try as they might, the Bush administration never was able to prove a direct connection between al Qaeda and Saddam Hussein).

The doctrine also called into question the ability of existing multilateral institutions like the United Nations to participate in global order as defined by the Bush Doctrine (and the reality of U.S. pre-eminence). As we shall see, the Bush Doctrine alienated old allies, and marginalized the role of established institutions when those bodies did not adhere to the U.S. strategy.

As we shall see, old standbys such as NATO and allies like Canada and Germany refused to support the U.S. actions against Saddam Hussein. These countries did support the U.S.-led Coalition against the Taliban in Afghanistan in the immediate aftermath of the September 11 terror attacks. However, these same countries could not support the U.S. strategy as it was applied to Iraq.

The difference was that the Coalition attack on the Taliban was in response to an attack on the United States, whereas the attack on Iraq was in *anticipation* of an attack on the United States (as claimed by the stated goal of disarming the Hussein regime of weapons of mass destruction). The lack of agreement on the threat made it impossible for these old allies to support the new U.S. actions.

Fateful Exchanges

The Bush Doctrine required a fundamental revision to U.S. military strategy. At this critical time, the U.S. intelligence community faced the challenge of needing to provide detailed information on developments inside Iraq, while suffering from a lack human intelligence (spies) on the ground. The turmoil caused by the rapid shift in policy and strategy created an atmosphere where sketchy data could be turned into bad intelligence, and that intelligence could be used to promote controversial decisions.

Here are some key events from the period:

September 12, 2001. President Bush tells his counterterrorism expert, Richard Clarke, "Go back over everything, everything. See if Saddam did this." According to Clarke, he responded to the President by saying, "But Mr. President, al Qaeda did this." The response from the President: "I know, I know, but ... See if Saddam was involved. Just look. I want to know any shred."

Clarke would later maintain that immediately after the September 11 attacks the U.S. intelligence community had already concluded that no operational connection existed between al Qaeda and Saddam Hussein.

According to a March 22, 2004, *Washington Post* article, as Clarke was leaving the Oval Office on September 12, he was reminded by the President to "Look into Iraq, Saddam."

In a later interview on *60 Minutes*, Clarke stated that his instructions from the President were "very intimidating," and led him to believe that he "should come back with that answer." This last statement by Clarke, if true, can be interpreted in two ways. Critics of President Bush will cite this as evidence that he was spoiling for a fight with Iraq, and that he was seeing the September 11 attacks as more "proof" of Saddam's threat. Supporters of President Bush will argue that the President was simply following all the possible causes of the attack. (The immediate military move, remember, was a multinational armed invasion of Afghanistan, since it was determined that the Taliban had been fostering al Qaeda in the years prior to the attacks.)

September 15, 2001. Paul Wolfowitz, Undersecretary of Defense under Secretary Donald Rumsfeld, advocates a military strike against Saddam Hussein. Wolfowitz estimated that the likelihood that Saddam was involved in the September 11 attacks is between 10 and 50 percent. However, this analysis is not shared by all the intelligence agencies. (In fact, it becomes clear in the coming months that the U.S. intelligence community was caught off guard by the attacks, and intelligence assets focused on al Qaeda were woefully inadequate).

September 17, 2001. The President signs a classified document outlining his plan to launch a military campaign against the Taliban regime in Afghanistan. The document, according to the *Washington Post*, also contains an instruction to begin the planning necessary to invade Iraq.

> **Iraq Fact**
>
> Ahmed Chalabi was the leader of the Iraqi National Congress, an exile group of Iraqis based in London. Chalabi was a controversial figure and was not universally respected by the Bush Cabinet. Chalabi became a member of the interim authority in Iraq, but was also the target of a U.S. investigation into his apparent ties to Iran in 2004.

September 18, 2001. The first stories appear in U.S. media about an alleged meeting in April 2001 between an Iraqi diplomat and Mohammed Atta, ringleader of the September 11 attacks.

The meeting was initially seen as a "link" between Saddam's government and the Al Qaeda terrorists. However, the report was never leveraged by the Administration to prove that Saddam was to blame for the September 11 attacks, probably because the further evidence for the link could not be proven.

September 19 and 20, 2001. Ahmed Chalabi, President of the Iraqi National Congress, insists that Hussein's regime is harboring weapons of mass destruction. Chalabi's claims are given great weight in decision-making regarding the upcoming invasion.

Fall 2001. A CIA analyst offers his opinion to Greg Theilmann, Head of Nuclear Proliferation Monitoring at the State Department's Bureau of Intelligence Research, that a recently intercepted shipment of aluminum tubes headed for Iraq are meant for a major weapons development program. Theilmann is unconvinced, but the allegation is interpreted by the Bush Administration as a further indication of Saddam's continued effort to develop weapons of mass destruction.

Fall 2001. The *USA Today* reports in 2004 that in the fall of 2001 President Bush made his final decision to invade Iraq. The decision, if it did come about at this point in time, was reached without a Cabinet consensus, or the consent of Congress. (Congress gave its consent a year later, in October 2002). Those who support the President's viewpoint are able to upstage those who opposed it. The same jockeying for position probably took place within the Intelligence community, with evidence that supports the case for invasion being overemphasized, and evidence refuting the case being deemphasized. Not an uncommon occurrence in bureaucratic competition, but in this case, one with far-reaching consequences.

October 28, 2001. President Bush's public statements begin to define the new strategy on dealing with Iraq. "Either the UN will do its duty to disarm Saddam Hussein," he says, "or Saddam Hussein will disarm himself. In either case, if they refuse to act … the U.S. will lead a coalition and disarm Saddam Hussein."

November 27, 2001. Hussein's government rejects a U.S. appeal to let UN weapons inspectors back into Iraq. Iraqi government officials call for the UN to lift sanctions and for the removal of the "no fly zones" in the northern and southern tiers of the country. This continued intransigence by Hussein is seen as further evidence that Iraq poses an imminent threat to the United States.

November 21, 2001. President Bush asks Secretary Rumsfeld about the Defense Department's plans for invading Iraq. Rumsfeld replies that his current plan is out of date, and the President orders him to develop a more viable plan. According to investigative reporter Bob Woodward, when General Tommy Franks, then serving in Afghanistan, got word that the Bush administration was preparing plans to invade Iraq, he let loose with a "string of obscenities." If Bob Woodward is to be believed, General Franks was not convinced that attacking Iraq was the proper move for the United States at that time.

December 2001. An expatriate Iraqi informs U.S. intelligence that he was, while in Iraq during 2001, deeply involved in the reconstruction of Iraqi facilities that could be engaged in the production of weapons of mass destruction. The expatriate, Adnanih Ihsan Saeed al-Haiberi, tells American intelligence officials of a series of biological facilities secreted away beneath the ground. Al-Haiberi's claim that he has personal knowledge of at least 20 facilities connected to Iraq's chemical or biological weapons development receives wide media coverage. After the invasion, however, his allegations were proved to be wrong, and no facilities were found where he claimed them to be.

December 17, 2001. Czech officials stated that there was no evidence supporting the contention that Mohammed Atta met with Iraqi intelligence agents in April, or indeed that Atta visited Prague at all in 2001. Not convinced of the accuracy of the Czech claims, U.S. intelligence officials still believe that the meeting had in fact taken place.

The "Axis of Evil"

January 29, 2002. During a speech before Congress, President Bush identifies Iraq, Iran, and North Korea as an "axis of evil," and states that "The United States of America will not permit the world's most dangerous regimes to threaten us with the world's most destructive weapons." President Bush also states that countries of the world must be "with us or against us" in the fight against terror. The remarks are controversial, and the President's new unilateral stance (remember the Bush Doctrine) alienates many allies, including those fighting alongside the United States in Afghanistan.

February 6, 2002. *The New York Times* reports that the CIA has found no evidence to support the argument that Saddam Hussein has played any role in terrorists operations against the United States over the past 10 years. The *Times* report also indicates that senior CIA officials have concluded that Hussein is not a source of chemical or biological weapons to terrorists groups.

February 13, 2002. The Iraqi government again announces that it will refuse to permit UN arms inspectors to come back to Iraq. This continued refusal to obey UN sanctions, and the UN's continued reluctance to enforce its own orders, is cited by the Bush administration as further reason for the United States to go it alone against what it claims (and many would say it truly believed) to be a threat to the United States and its interests in the region.

March 21, 2002. In the UN, Russia blocks plans to remove middlemen from Iraqi oil transactions. Russian firms have benefited from oil sales since the beginning of the UN's "oil for food" program.

April 8, 2002. Iraq issues a statement that it will suspend its oil-for-food exports for one month as a "gesture of support" to Palestinians.

May 3, 2002. Iraq concludes three days of heated discussions with representatives of the UN on disarmament and the role of weapons inspections—without reaching any conclusion about when inspectors might return.

May 14, 2002. The United Nations Security Council formally revises the "oil for food" program, implementing a list of "dual-use" goods that have military and civilian applications. Under the new arrangement, Iraq can use the proceeds from oil sales, which are to be deposited in an escrow account, to obtain goods that do not appear on the UN "dual-use goods" list.

August 29, 2002. Vice President Cheney says publicly that another series of UN weapons inspections would be no guarantee that Iraq has closed down its programs to produce weapons of mass destruction. Cheney is referring to the apparent lack of ability of the inspectors to find weapons, even though no WMD have been found as of this writing, two years later.

A New Security Strategy Is Born

September 12, 2002. Citing the new Bush Doctrine, President Bush describes the Iraqi government as a "grave and gathering danger," and predicts that compliance with UN resolutions on disarmament must be carried out, or "action will be inevitable."

September 19, 2002. Iraq's Prime Minister declares that his government has no nuclear, biological, or chemical weapons, and announces that the weapons inspectors who were kicked out of the country in 1998 may return, but on specific terms.

Period #3: On the Road to War: The Alienation of the Allies

The determination of the Bush administration to attack Iraq, based upon the Bush Doctrine and an obsession with Saddam Hussein's apparent threat to the United States, eventually alienated most of America's traditional allies. The unilateralism of the Bush Doctrine became a major factor in U.S. diplomacy.

2002 and early 2003. Vice President Cheney visits CIA headquarters in Virginia a number of times and questions analysts about their work relating to Saddam Hussein and Iraq. Some analysts say that they feel pressured by the Vice President's visits; others report a feeling of engagement and support. Critics of the administration's policies will see Cheney's actions as stressing to these analysts that he wished to see intelligence that would support the administration's decision to wage war against Saddam.

October 16, 2002. President Bush signs a resolution passed by Congress that gives him the authority to use military force against Hussein's regime if the administration's diplomatic initiatives fail.

November 8, 2002. The UN Security Council adopts yet another resolution confirming that UN inspectors have the right to inspect all territories of Iraq for weapons. The resolution further requires the Iraqi government to render an "accurate, full, and complete" assessment of its weapons programs within the next 30 days.

December 7, 2002. Saddam delivers a formal denial that he has weapons of mass destruction; Saddam probably does not believe, even at this late date, that the United States would ever really invade on its own.

December 19, 2002. American Secretary of State Colin Powell argues that the Iraqi government is in "material breach" of UN resolutions related to weapons programs. The term "material breach" is critical, since military action is allowed under the UN sanctions when a "material breach" of the sanctions occurs.

January 28, 2003. President Bush announces that "the British government has learned that Saddam Hussein recently sought significant quantities of uranium from Africa. Saddam Hussein has not credibly explained these activities …. He clearly has much to hide." The British intelligence data on which the President's statement relies is controversial, first being claimed to be false in the aftermath of the invasion of Iraq, and then later, during the summer of 2004, being shown to have some evidence in fact.

February 28, 2003. According to the Russian Foreign Minister, his nation "does not support any resolution (before the United Nations) which could directly or indirectly open the way to an armed resolution of the Iraq problem. Naturally, Russia has the right of veto. If the interested international stability demands it, Russia, of course will exercise its right."

March 7, 2003. British Foreign Minister Jack Straw introduces a resolution to the UN Security Council authorizing military action against Iraq in the event it does not transfer weapons, delivery systems, and technical facilities banned by UN resolutions, to UN inspectors, by March 17. The United States, Britain, and Spain issues a demand that Saddam must turn over the banned weapons by March 17 or face military action.

March 10, 2003. French diplomats join the Russians in vowing to veto any resolution authorizing military force in Iraq. Germany and China also oppose military action. The unilateralism of the Bush Doctrine creates a rift among U.S. allies and between the United States and UN.

March 17, 2003. The United States, Great Britain, and Spain declared that diplomatic efforts are no longer effective in resolving the "material breach" of the sanctions. President Bush gives Saddam Hussein 48 hours to leave Iraq.

The End of the Road

The Bush administration pushed for the invasion of Iraq, by claiming that Saddam Hussein represented an imminent danger because he possessed weapons of mass destruction. Prior to the first Gulf War, Saddam had used weapons of mass destruction, on Iranian troops during the Iran-Iraq War and later on the Kurds inside Iraq. However, in the years following the Gulf War, Saddam claimed that all the weapons had been destroyed.

The problem was complicated by Saddam's continued defiance of UN sanctions, the ineffectiveness of the "oil for food" program to limit Saddam's ability to spend the proceeds on nonsanctioned items, and lack of will in the UN to enforce its own resolutions.

Iraq Fact

The "Coalition of the Willing" included a large number of countries in principle, but a relatively small number of traditional U.S. allies.

Coalition partners that committed troops or personnel in noncombat roles included: Albania, Australia, Bulgaria, Czech Republic, Denmark, Marshall Islands, Netherlands, Palau, Poland, Romania, Slovakia, Spain, Ukraine, United States, and the United Kingdom.

Other Coalition members, that did not send troops, included Afghanistan, Angola, Azerbaijan, Colombia, Costa Rica, Croatia, Dominican Republic, El Salvador, Eritrea, Estonia, Ethiopia, Georgia, Honduras, Hungary, Iceland, Italy, Japan, Kuwait, Latvia, Lithuania, Macedonia, Micronesia, Mongolia, Nicaragua, Philippines, Portugal, Rwanda, Singapore, Slovenia, Solomon Islands, South Korea, Tonga, Turkey, Uganda, and Uzbekistan.

France, Germany, Saudi Arabia, Canada, and Mexico were not members of the Coalition.

The situation came to head when the George W. Bush administration took office. The administration seemed preoccupied with Saddam, and some insiders claim now that plans were being made almost immediately to remove him from power.

After the terrible attacks of September 11, the new Bush Doctrine of pre-emptive, unilateral action to defend U.S. interests created severe disruptions in the U.S. intelligence community, and the resulting scramble for power and position promoted faulty intelligence reaching policy makers.

The unilateralism of the Bush Doctrine, while providing a path for U.S. action, alienated traditional U.S. allies and marginalized the UN.

As a result, the United States found itself standing alone, except for Great Britain, Spain, Poland, Ukraine, Australia, and a large number of smaller nations, on the eve of a massive invasion of Iraq. In this chapter, we looked at the effect the Bush Doctrine had on U.S. policy and diplomacy. In the next chapter, we will look more deeply at the causes of the Bush administration's apparent preoccupation with Saddam Hussein.

The Least You Need to Know

- The Bush administration was focused on Saddam Hussein, from its earliest days.

- The September 11 attacks caused turmoil in U.S. policy and intelligence circles, and a link between Saddam and the terrorist was searched for, but not found.

- The Bush Doctrine, resulting from the September 11 attacks, redefined the U.S. foreign policy and put Saddam squarely in its crosshairs.

- The Bush Administration claimed that Iraq possessed weapons of mass destruction, and the administration became increasingly alarmed by the UN's inability to find them and by Saddam's refusal to allow inspections.

- The collision of the Bush Doctrine, an apparent preoccupation with Saddam, and a belief that he possessed WMD resulted in a unilateral invasion of Iraq.

Why the United States Invaded

In This Chapter

- ◆ The Bush administration claims of WMD in Iraq
- ◆ The U.S. intelligence community's failure to present accurate information
- ◆ The Bush administration's selective interpretation of sketchy data
- ◆ The real reason for the invasion?

In the months and weeks prior to the U.S.-led invasion of Iraq, the Bush administration offered a range of reasons for invading the country. The reasons shifted over time, but the continued insistence on the need to invade Iraq indicated that the administration was focused on attacking no matter what.

In this chapter, we will consider what was truly motivating the Bush administration to invade Iraq, even to the point of shifting its stated reasons for invading as time wore on.

The Stated Reasons for the Invasion

The Bush administration had three main arguments for the invasion of the Iraq:

1. Saddam had weapons of mass destruction or at least was actively seeking to acquire them, and he could very easily share or sell them to enemies of the United States

2. Saddam was supporting terrorists, possibly including al Qaeda

3. Saddam was openly defiant of clear and repeated UN resolutions imposed after the first Gulf War, to control his aggressive military weapons programs

We'll take a look at these reasons, as well as a few more, in this chapter.

The Bush administration claimed—or, as appears more clearly after the fact, strongly implied—that it had clear and exceptionally urgent intelligence information about the Iraqi regime. This information pointed to a threat to the American people and to global peace and stability and it would be irresponsible to ignore this in the aftermath of the September 11 terror attacks.

The fact that so many respected senior officials painted this dire picture was, in and of itself, persuasive for many Americans, including this author.

Even critics of President Bush concluded that the foreign policy team with which the president had surrounded himself, unanimous as they were in their statements, must certainly have identified *something* of grave importance in the intelligence data. The reason the American people supported the invasion was that that *something*, whatever it was, was sufficient to alarm the Bush administration, and so was probably worthy of taking very seriously.

The prospect put forth by the administration was sobering: Saddam Hussein, a tyrant who had used weapons of mass destruction before, was bent on securing chemical, biological, and/or nuclear weapons. With those weapons, Saddam could threaten the region and its vital oil, and perhaps even attack America.

The argument went more or less as follows: "If Hussein is on the brink of obtaining such weapons, he needs to be taken out, because all that is necessary to achieve his aims and secure revenge for his humiliating defeat of the first Gulf War, is to share these devastating weapons with the enemies of the United States, and specifically with members of terrorist

Iraq Fact

Facing clear evidence of peril, we cannot wait for the final proof—the smoking gun—that could come in the form of a mushroom cloud.

—George W. Bush, Cincinnati, Ohio, October 7, 2002

movements." As President Bush put it in October 2002, "… A terrible line would be crossed … Saddam Hussein would be in a position to pass nuclear technology to terrorists." The administration was arguing that the United States needed to get Saddam before he got us.

America Goes Along

Eventually, Congress authorized the president to use force, apparently for the same reasons that the majority of Americans decided to support the Bush administration initiative: a firm belief that if the administration was even close to being right about the dangers it predicted from Saddam Hussein, then it was time to act and act decisively (remember the element of pre-emption that is part of the Bush Doctrine—see Chapter 19).

During the run-up to the invasion, the UN weapons inspectors did not find evidence of the weapons the Bush administration claimed were there. However, Saddam's continued resistance to allowing the inspectors to go into his many "palaces" (many of which were palaces only in name), and his eventual refusal to even allow inspectors into the country, enabled the Bush administration to continue its claims that Saddam had the weapons (depending on how you look at it, Saddam's intransigence enabled the Bush administration to *believe* that Saddam had the weapons).

The Intelligence Picture: How Clear?

In July 2004, the Senate Select Committee on Intelligence released a report blaming the U.S. intelligence community for critical failures in the run-up to the invasion of Iraq. One of the key findings of the report was that there really was no evidence supporting the claim that Saddam had the much sought after weapons of mass destruction.

Increase Your Iraq IQ

Although we think the judgments were not unreasonable when they were made nearly two years ago, we understand with all that we have learned since then that we could have done better. Some of our judgments have held up. Some have been called into serious question. One significant error was in allowing the key judgments in our [National Intelligence] Estimate on Iraq, that's the short summary at the front of the Estimate, to be published without sufficient caveats and disclaimers where our knowledge was incomplete. This is particularly unfortunate since the full text of that document, which apparently was not reviewed by all the readers, spells out the uncertainties and dissents much more fully.

—Deputy Director of Central Intelligence John McLaughlin, July 9, 2004

Among the troubling questions raised by the report was just how aggressively did CIA Director George Tenet and other senior intelligence officials work to ensure that intelligence cited by the administration as justification for a war with Iraq was both accurate and presented in the proper context?

As we saw in Chapter 19, President George W. Bush had placed Iraq in general, and the removal of Saddam Hussein in particular, at a high level of priority in the very first days of his administration—long before the September 11, 2001, attacks on America. After the attacks and the resultant U.S. invasion of Afghanistan, the Bush administration renewed its focus on Iraq.

Increase Your Iraq IQ

Getting Hussein was now the administration's focus. From the start, we were building the case against Hussein and looking at how we could take him out and change Iraq into a new country. And, if we did that, it would solve everything. It was all about finding a way to do it. That was the tone of it—the president saying, "Go find me a way to do this."

—Former Treasury Secretary Paul O'Neill, quoted in Senator Edward Kennedy's speech to the Council of Foreign Relations, February 5, 2004.

Did the Bush administration "cherry-pick" intelligence, sometimes from dubious sources, in pursuit of the goal of removing Saddam Hussein from power? Were Tenet and his colleagues lax in their duty to ensure that the President's intelligence analyses—and, by extension, the administration's public assessments of that intelligence—accurately reflected the realities America faced in making the decision to go to war? These are important questions. The answers either support the administration's stated rationale for removing Hussein or contradict that rationale.

The 2004 Senate Select Committee report found that the evidence was in fact contradictory to the original claims, and members of the bi-partisan commission behind the report have since stated that the congress would not have voted to support the invasion if they had this intelligence at that time. Truly a damning statement, and someone is to blame. As of this writing, the blame has been placed on CIA Director Tenet and the U.S. intelligence community. Tenet clearly became the fall guy, when he resigned in advance of the report's release in July 2004.

The unanswered question is what role the Bush administration played in using the data it was given. Was the Bush administration simply misled by bad intelligence, or did the administration deliberately misrepresent the intelligence to further its predetermined goal of toppling Saddam Hussein? As of this writing, the Senate committee has not released that portion of their report.

Former CIA director George Tenet.

(Public Affairs Office, U.S. Office Pristina, Kosovo)

Motivations for Invasion

There are several potential motivations that could have caused the Bush administration to decide to invade Iraq. Let's look at some of the big ones in more detail.

The WMD Threat

Vice President Cheney made a speech on August 6, 2002, to the Veterans of Foreign Wars in which he claimed: "… we now know that Saddam has resumed his efforts to acquire nuclear weapons … many of us are convinced that Saddam will acquire nuclear weapons fairly soon." This was a point on which the intelligence community was not united, but Cheney's rhetoric made it appear that the evidence was persuasive.

On September 8, 2002, the claims continued when Cheney said that "(We) do know, with absolute certainty, that he (Saddam) is using his procurement system to acquire the equipment he needs in order to enrich uranium to buy nuclear weapons." It turns out that there was no confirmed intelligence to support this claim, but many Americans were forced to conclude that Cheney had good reason for his certainty.

Shortly before Congress voted to authorize military action, President Bush continued this thread and said: "Iraq has attempted to purchase high-strength aluminum tubes … which are used to enrich uranium for nuclear weapons. If the Iraqi regime is able to produce, buy, or steal an amount of highly enriched uranium a little larger than a single softball, it could have a nuclear weapon in less than a year."

In his State of the Union Address, President Bush cited a report that Iraq had been seeking uranium ore from Somalia and the Democratic Republic of the Congo. This information turned out later to be false. The question of whether or not the President or his staff knew that this information was false at the time they appealed to it has yet to be resolved.

Similar overemphasis of sketchy intelligence is evident with regard to the question of whether Iraq was funding a chemical weapons program. A September 2002 report from the Defense Intelligence Agency stated that, "There is no reliable information on whether Iraq is producing or stockpiling chemical weapons, or where Iraq has—or will—establish its chemical warfare agent production facilities."

Yet for some reason, in the same month, Secretary of Defense Rumsfeld was able to tell the Senate Armed Services Committee that "We do know that the Iraqi regime has chemical and biological weapons of mass destruction," and that the Iraqi leader had, "amassed large, clandestine stocks of chemical weapons." The reality proved otherwise after the invasion, but the fact that the intelligence community had grave doubts about such statements somehow never made it through the administration's public assessments.

The Bush administration implied repeatedly that they knew something the rest of the world did not, and what they knew pointed toward not just a threat, but an imminent threat:

> Some have argued that the nuclear threat from Iraq is not imminent—that Saddam is at least 5–7 years away from having nuclear weapons. I would not be so certain.
>
> —Secretary of Defense Donald Rumsfeld, September 18, 2003
>
> We know where they are. They're in the area around Tikrit and Baghdad in the east, west, south and north somewhat.
>
> —Secretary of Defense Donald Rumsfeld, March 20, 2003, when asked during an interview about Saddam Hussein's weapons of mass destruction.
>
> This is about an imminent threat.
>
> —Deputy Press Secretary Scott McClellan, February 2003
>
> A threat of unique urgency.
>
> —President George W. Bush, October 2, 2002

While it is easy to disagree, there always is the chance that the Bush administration truly believed Saddam had weapons of mass destruction. While the evidence to the contrary seems overwhelming, there were many experts who felt Iraq was up to something. Remember the infamous aluminum tubes that supposedly could have been used in a centrifuge to process uranium? The Department of Energy (DOE) refuted the CIA estimates that the tubes were immediately ready for use in a centrifuge. However, even the DOE agreed that the tubes could have been used, with modifications, in a centrifuge. In addition, the UN weapons inspectors themselves generally agreed that the Iraqis were pursuing a nuclear program. This may be a fine point, but a critical one. Saddam did *not* have the nukes in 2002, but there were strong indications that he was working hard to get them. Of course, we can look back from our vantage point today and argue that the contemporary view was wrong, but it was shared by many at the time.

Oil Spill Ahead

... there are 40 or 50 pages in this report dedicated to aluminum tubes and whether they were for centrifuges or not, but I must always remind people that the National Intelligence Estimate, the Intelligence Community, said he did not have nuclear weapons yet, said he would not have them for another five to seven years. Said that he wasn't yet enriching uranium. Said he didn't have fissile material. These tubes were detected as part of the things that could have contributed eventually to an enrichment program. In fact, there's a success story buried in this that very few people know about. That is working with our partners overseas we kept, if my memory serves, close to 100,000 of these tubes from ever getting into Iraq. I believe the tubes that were found in Iraq were not of the high tolerances as the ones going in, and all of the agencies who looked at these tubes thought they could be adapted. Even the Department of Energy, which had a very strong view on these particular things, agreed with the overall assessment in the Estimate that he was reconstituting his nuclear program.

—Deputy Director of Central Intelligence John McLaughlin, July 9, 2004

A Link Between Saddam and al Qaeda?

One of the administration's most important claims in support of the invasion of Iraq was the notion of some kind of linkage between Saddam Hussein and al Qaeda. The argument was that Saddam would provide weapons of mass destruction to Al Qaeda.

On September 25, 2002, President Bush stated: "You can't distinguish between al Qaeda and Saddam when you talk about the war on terror."

In his State of the Union Address he gave in January 2003, the President said, "Evidence from intelligent sources, secret communications, statements by people now in custody reveal that Saddam aids and protects terrorists including members of al Qaeda." Bush went on to claim that Hussein could provide "lethal viruses to a shadowy terrorist network."

In early 2003, President Bush gave a radio address in which he claimed that "Saddam Hussein has longstanding, direct, and continuing-type terrorist networks ..." He continued, "Senior members of Iraqi intelligence and al Qaeda have met at least eight times since the early 1990s. Iraq has sent bomb making and document forgery experts to work with al Qaeda. Iraq has also provided al Qaeda with chemical and biological weapons training. An al Qaeda operative was sent to Iraq several times in the late 1990s for help in acquiring poison gasses. We also know that Iraq is harboring a terrorist network planner. This network runs a poison and explosive training camp in northeast Iraq. And many of its leaders are known to be in Baghdad."

According to the Senate Select Committee on Intelligence findings, there was no operational connection and no clear pattern of connections between al Qaeda and Saddam Hussein. Look at this way: Saddam Hussein was a secular dictator, and Osama Bin Laden a radical fundamentalist. Their worldviews in many ways were very different. Still, history makes strange bedfellows, and these two did share one common powerful motivation: hatred for the United States.

Increase Your Iraq IQ

They surveyed the data, and picked out what they liked. The whole thing was bizarre. The Secretary of Defense had this huge Defense Intelligence Agency, and he went around it .... This administration has had a faith-based intelligence attitude, its top-down use of intelligence: we know the answers; give us the intelligence to support those answers .... Going down the list of administration deficiencies, or distortions, one has to talk about, first and foremost, the nuclear threat being hyped.

—Greg Thielmann, former director of the State Department's Bureau of Intelligence and Research, quoted in Senator Edward Kennedy's speech to the Council of Foreign Relations, February 5, 2004

Faith-Based Intelligence

The Bush administration appears to have made a calculated decision to emphasize only the most alarming elements of the intelligence available to it, and to pluck other intelligence out of its context. In the case of the reports of actual locations for the weapons of mass destruction, it appears now that the administration listened more attentively than it should have to the Iraqi exile community, and less attentively than it should have to the more seasoned analysts within its own intelligence apparatus.

Much of the data that came from the Iraqi exiles was "raw information" (unanalyzed and non-corroborated from other sources) rather than "finished intelligence" (corroborated, tested, and reasonably confirmed by other sources and analysts). However, senior officials were provided with pieces of this raw information in their briefing documents, and they ignored the caveats and reservations offered in the documents.

One side of the argument is that the administration officials picked out only the intelligence that supported their arguments, and discarded the intelligence that refuted it. The other side could be that group think was in play, and people simply did not delve into the details once the generalities seemed to support the prevailing opinion.

Increase Your Iraq IQ

I think it was an error to say them [claims of WMD in Iraq] with that degree of certainty in the summary of this Estimate. If you look at the body of the Estimate, there are many caveats and many qualifiers. This is a kind of art form in this business which frankly we will now change. The art form has always been that when you get to the summary of a National Estimate, you stand back from all of the evidence you put on the record, and all of the qualifiers, and say, "Here's what I really think." And that's what we did in this case. We assessed that they had chemical and biological weapons.

Frankly, we won't do that again. In the future, our summaries of Estimates will mirror exactly what we're saying in the body of the Estimate. If you look at the body of this Estimate, you will see that the differences within the [Intelligence] Community are absolutely laid out in great detail, the qualifiers are there.

—Deputy Director of Central Intelligence John McLaughlin, July 9, 2004

So ... What Was the Real Reason to Invade Iraq?

If the Senate Select Committee report is accurate, and the truth of the matter is that the administration did *not* have concrete evidence of Iraqi weapons of mass destruction, there must have been some other reason for launching the invasion. There are a number of possibilities, and we will examine some of them here.

The Real Reason: The Continuous, Dependable Supply of Oil to the United States

Remember that Iraq is in the top three countries in terms of proven reserves of oil. When rebuilt, Iraq's daily production will have a significant impact on the global supply of oil, and thus the price of oil in the West. A friendly Iraqi regime, perhaps not even a member of OPEC, producing oil in quantities to keep the prices down, would be in the vital interests of the United States. Also, a bulwark of U.S. support in the Middle East, to counter balance a hostile Iran and increasingly unreliable Saudi Arabia, is a critical U.S. need. Saddam Hussein posed a constant threat to secure, dependable oil flows from the region. He sat on top of, and next to, more than 40 percent of the world's oil. His conventional army was large enough to pose a major challenge to every other country in the region, and that threat had to be dealt with.

This constant concern for the free flow of affordable oil may be the real reason for the pre-occupation with Saddam, and the Bush administration's single-minded determination to remove him from power. It may also be the reason the United States remains involved so heavily in the region, even at the cost of thousands of lives in and out of uniform. The simple fact is that the oil the United States needs is located over there, and the United States cannot afford to imperil its access to that oil. Even if administration officials do not openly state that, the reason Iraq mattered so much in the first place is because of its oil.

Unfinished Business

Yet another theory holds that the younger Bush entered office with a predetermined view to conclude the conflict initiated, but not finally resolved, by the first Bush administration. In this scenario, President Bush took it upon himself to settle the score with the man who had committed crimes and was going unpunished in the national arena, crimes that included an assassination attempt against his own father. It may seem far-fetched, but there certainly was no love lost between George W. Bush and Saddam Hussein, and the personal history between the two men did nothing to lessen the tensions.

Freedom for the Iraqi People

The administration never promoted freeing the Iraqi people as the primary objective for the invasion. In the aftermath of the invasion, administration officials increasingly began to cite this as the reason for the invasion. It looks like an attempt to move to Plan B (freedom), since Plan A (WMD) was not playing out. If liberating oppressed people is America's driving objective in Iraq, there remains a long list of tyrants to be deposed around the world.

The very question of what "freedom" means in the Middle East, and what it means in an Islamic society, need to be understood before we simply state that the U.S. model will work there. The undeniable history of Iraq shows that real, stable, democracy has never taken hold there before, and that democracy in the Arab Muslim countries of the Middle East is nonexistent. Democracy is always possible, but it will take an unprecedented set of circumstances to work.

This is not to say that oppressive regimes are good things, but they are tolerated around the globe, and have been for centuries. If we look at the Arab Muslim nations in the Middle East, the closest U.S. allies are not democratic. Ironically enough, a totalitarian regime may be the solution for Iraq that the United States (and indeed the rest of the world) will accept in the end. It won't be what the United States, or the Iraqi people want, but it may end up being that way even so, particularly if the United States tires in the face of the rising U.S. death toll.

Remaking the Region

Many earnest people within the Bush administration honestly believe that overcoming Saddam Hussein was the key to remaking the Middle East and to securing long-term economic and political reforms there. The theory here is that democracy is America's true security, and that the totalitarian regimes throughout the Middle East (remember there are no true democracies in the Muslim Arab Middle East) need to be changed to foster security for the United States. The theory holds that the terrorists who attacked the United States on September 11 came from these totalitarian Middle Eastern states (many came from Saudi Arabia), and these young men might have had a different motivation if they had more opportunities that would come with a democratic state. In addition, democracy begets civil society and personal freedoms that improve the lot of the average citizen.

On a less idealistic level, a stable democracy in Iraq would dramatically alter the balance of power in the region. Right now, political and economic power is concentrated into the hands of small ruling elites rather than larger masses of people. Islamic clerics also wield a great deal of power, particularly on the educational and social fronts. A broad-based, secular, popular democracy would dramatically lessen the influence of those two groups, who have proven to be less than ideal allies of the United States.

This making a democracy theory dovetails with the "free flow of oil" theory and the "freeing the Iraqi people" theory, and it raises many philosophical questions about the role and obligations of the United States under the Bush Doctrine.

Mix and Match?

It's likely that more than one, and perhaps all, of the above theories contributed to the Bush administration's decision to topple Saddam Hussein.

It is just as clear that the notions that Saddam Hussein presented an imminent threat to the United States' interests, that he had links to al Qaeda, and that he possessed weapons of mass destruction, were exaggerated. The failure of the U.S. intelligence community is to blame to a large extent. The big question—did the Bush administration react to the bad information, or did they have their minds made up to invade already—will continue to be debated for years to come.

The Least You Need to Know

♦ The Bush administration's insistence that Iraq posed an imminent and clear threat to the United States because of weapons of mass destruction have still not been found in Iraq.

♦ The Senate Select Committee on Intelligence report in July 2004 cites the United States intelligence community's failing to manage the information they did, and did not have.

♦ A critical question is whether the Bush administration was misled by bad intelligence work, or actively worked to mold the intelligence to suit its needs.

♦ As it became clear that Saddam's weapons did not exist, the Bush administration pointed to other reasons for the invasion, including the fact that Saddam was a tyrant and the Iraqis deserved better.

♦ The need to guarantee a secure, free flow of oil from the Middle East, and the desire to alter the balance of power in the region, may be the real reasons for the invasion of Iraq.

Chapter 21

The Invasion

In This Chapter

- ◆ The swift and decisive victory for the U.S. coalition
- ◆ The dissolution of the Hussein regime
- ◆ The changing face of the war
- ◆ Chaos follows victory
- ◆ The start of an uneasy occupation

In this chapter, you'll find out what happened on the ground between the first missile strike and the end of "major combat operations" in Iraq. You'll see the swift victory of a well-executed battle plan, but the first signs of a poorly planned occupation.

Prelude to War: Positioning the Pieces

In the weeks preceding the invasion, the United States and its coalition partners (notably the United Kingdom, Spain, Australia, and Poland) made the final preparations for the invasion. As the force buildup reached its peak in the final days prior to the assault, rifts between the United

States and its traditional allies widened. Already, France, Germany, and Russia had signaled their unwillingness to go along with the United States and United Kingdom. Canada, too, backed out of the U.S.-led Coalition. Arab and Muslim allies also refused to support the Bush administration's goal of toppling Hussein.

Saudi Arabia and Turkey Say No

The initial war plan called for a two-pronged assault on Iraq: north from Saudi Arabia and south from Turkey. However, these two Muslim nations were not willing to support the United States in its attack on Iraq. Early in the preparation phase, the Saudis made it clear that the United States would not be allowed to launch ground forces from Saudi territory, although air strikes could continue from airbases in the Kingdom.

Then on the eve of the invasion, Turkey's parliament voted to not allow the United States to stage troops on Turkish soil. The Turkish vote rejected a U.S. offer of billions of dollars in aid in return for the use of Turkish soil. These two Muslim allies joined France, Germany, Canada, and a host of other nations who would not support the U.S.-led Coalition. These nations simply were not convinced of the Bush administration's claims of Saddam's threat and were willing to tolerate Saddam's continued flaunting of UN resolutions. These nations were not willing to go to war to maintain the authority of the UN, and were not convinced that Saddam posed an imminent threat to anyone, even though some of them bordered Iraq itself.

U.S. troops arriving in Kuwait, preparing to go in to Iraq.

Iraq Fact

The Coalition that gathered to invade Iraq in 2003 was significantly different from the one that evicted Iraq from Kuwait in 1990. Many of the European and Arab nations that had supported the United States during Operation Desert Storm did not support the United States during Operation Iraqi Freedom.

The Quick Collapse

The campaign to defeat the Hussein regime's civil authority and military capability took roughly three weeks. The war was characterized by several elements:

Rapid Advance on the Ground and Overwhelming Air Power: As we will see, the Coalition forces were vastly superior to the Iraqi forces and achieved another stunning victory of arms.

"Bullet by Bullet" Coverage from Embedded Media: Journalists traveling with the Coalition units sent back intimate reports of the fighting. Public opinion in the United States was affected by detailed accounts of downed Apache helicopters, captured and subsequently rescued female soldiers, and ambushed convoys. During the middle of the war, the real progress and overwhelming success of the Coalition military was overshadowed by impatient expectations of immediate victory. (Remember that the Iraqis had crumbled in a matter of days during Operation Desert Storm.)

Stark Differences in Western and Arab Media Coverage and Impressions of the War: While CNN, Fox, and the other U.S. networks showed battle scenes, the Arab *Al-Jazeera* network showed the civilian destruction and graphic images of dead Coalition soldiers. Americans saw the war through CNN, while the Arabs saw it through Al-Jazeera.

The Transition from Armed Conflict between Uniformed Combatants, to Guerilla War: The rapid collapse of the Iraqi army led to guerilla fighting. Some of these fighters spontaneously took up arms, but others appeared to be regular army soldiers, who were simply fighting out of uniform.

Desert Diction

Al-Jazeera is the main Arab news network. Based in Qatar, Al-Jazeera focuses on the news from the Arab point of view. Founded in 1996, Al-Jazeera has become a major force guiding the perceptions of the Arab people to world events.

The Difference Between Military Campaigning and Occupation: As looting and riots erupted after Saddam's fall, the Coalition forces (certainly adequate for the military mission) appears inadequate to maintain stability.

Swift Coalition Victory On the Ground

As the ground war moved to a quick close, there was a good deal of surprise among western analysts at the speed with which Iraqi military forces surrendered, or simply vanished. The Saddam Hussein regime and its army broke apart completely under the hammer blow of the Coalition assault. Lacking broad popular support, senior decision makers within the Iraqi government fled, went into hiding, or gave up.

Timeline: The Ground War

March 19, 2003. "Operation Iraqi Freedom" begins with a series of cruise missile and bomber strikes at high-level Iraqi "targets of opportunity." The goal of these "decapitation strikes" is to kill Saddam Hussein, his sons, and other key Iraqi leaders on the first day of hostilities. The attacks fail to kill Saddam, but the tenor of the campaign was clear: Saddam and his regime were the targets.

March 20, 2003. The U.S. 3rd Armored Division begins its drive to Baghdad, while the British sweep toward Basra, and the 1st Marine Expeditionary Force attacks Umm Qasr. The campaign is characterized by embedded journalists, who provide intensely intimate and immediate reports of the fighting. On the other hand, Al-Jazeera also covers the fighting, and shows a vastly different picture of the suffering of Iraqi civilians and destruction of infrastructure. The duality of the media coverage underscores the basic ambivalence of the Arab world about the invasion, and their perception of Western attitudes about the war.

March 21, 2003. Major air operations begin. The Department of Defense publicizes the intense bombardment of aerial assault on Baghdad and other targets as a campaign of "shock and awe" intended to overwhelm the Iraqi command structure, and dishearten Iraqi soldiers. The goal is to minimize battle casualties by breaking the morale of Iraqi units, and encouraging mass defections of troops. Although some troops do defect, the massive immediate surrender doesn't happen.

March 22, 2003. Coalition troops continue to drive into Iraq. The oil fields and infrastructure on the Gulf coast and around Basra are secured. Iraqi troops set fire to some oil wells during their retreat. Protecting oil assets is a critical strategic goal of the campaign (remember the main reason for the invasion mentioned in Chapter 20). Oil would be the sole method for the Iraqis to finance their reconstruction, and that meant the oil infrastructure had to be saved. Also, as mentioned in Chapter 20, the free flow of affordable oil is a constant strategic requirement for any U.S. presidential administration.

March 23, 2003. Turkey grants the United States permission to fly troops over Turkish soil. U.S. Airborne troops will soon land in northern Iraq. They will cooperate with Kurdish fighters who are assaulting Iraqi army troops in the north. The U.S. troops are also there to discourage Turkey from sending in a large number of Turkish troops. Turkey was alarmed by the armed Kurdish forces just beyond its borders.

March 24, 2003. Coalition control over most of the oil fields in the south is established, and damage from fires is relatively light. Third Infantry Division troops reach a point within 60 miles of Baghdad and face the first serious resistance of the campaign. At the same time, U.S. Marines suffer casualties in fierce fighting at Nasiriya. Guerilla fighters, some former army troops, and some Saddam loyalists, emerge in place of the disintegrating Iraqi uniformed troops.

March 26, 2003. The U.S. 173rd Airborne Brigade parachutes into northern Iraq. These troops are the spearhead for the northern front that was envisioned in the original battle plan. U.S. troops will cooperate with Kurdish forces to seize critical cities and oil fields in northern Iraq.

March 28, 2003. The U.N. Security Council grants a 45-day renewal of the oil-for-food program, which had been suspended before military action began on March 19. Iraq launches SCUD missiles at Kuwait, and will continue SCUD attacks on Saudi and Kuwaiti targets for several days. Interestingly, these SCUDS *are* allowed under the weapons ban in place after the first Gulf War.

March 29, 2003. The Coalition begins to see a shift in the fighting, from combat between organized forces to guerilla warfare and paramilitary attacks. In fighting around Basra, Iraqi paramilitary forces fire on Iraqi civilians who attempt to flee the city. The paramilitaries are Saddam loyalists, who have no difficulties in shooting Shiite noncombatants.

April 3, 2003. Saddam Hussein International Airport is captured by U.S. forces, spearheaded by the 3rd Infantry Division. The airport has since been renamed "Baghdad International Airport."

April 4, 2003: As U.S. troops encircle Baghdad, confusion regarding Saddam's status and whereabouts continues; a videotape appears to show him walking a street in Baghdad. Reports in the Western news media raise the possibility that a double may have taken his place.

April 5, 2003: American forces cross the city limits and enter Baghdad. Iraqi troops continue to surrender in large numbers.

April 7, 2003: In the hunt for weapons of mass destruction, *The Washington Post* reports that U.S. troops have found the "smoking gun" or the much sought after evidence of an Iraqi WMD program. The supposed evidence is a large hoard of "chemical weapons" and a series of subterranean "bioweapons labs." The weapons and labs turn out to be nonmilitary in nature. The episode underscores the anticipation that large quantities of WMDs will soon be uncovered.

April 9, 2003. Baghdad falls. U.S. Marines help Iraqi citizens topple a 40-foot-tall statue of Saddam. American forces assume operational positions in the center of the city. Images of joyous Iraqi citizens suggest that the American military occupation has won popular broad popular support. The joy of liberated Iraqis is quickly tempered by scenes of looting and anarchy that soon follow. Coalition forces, too few in number to adequately control the situation, cannot stop all the looting or rioting.

April 10, 2003. Kurdish and Coalition forces wrest control of the critical northern city of Kirkuk from Iraqi troops. Kirkuk is a controlling point for the oil fields in the north of Iraq.

April 11, 2003. Coalition leaders announce that Saddam Hussein is no longer in control of Iraq, and that he has gone into hiding. Coalition forces prepare for an assault on Tikrit, the last ditch of the Saddam regime. Conventional wisdom holds that as long as Saddam may be alive and at large, his loyalists will fight in the hope that he would return to power.

April 12, 2003. The Associated Press reports that Hussein's science adviser, Lieutenant General Amer al-Saadi, is in the custody of Coalition troops. He maintains that Iraq has no WMD.

Iraq Fact

In April 2003, the Coalition introduces a list of 55 fugitive former Iraqi government officials in the form of a deck of playing cards. The cards become icons of the occupation, as one by one, the "cards" are captured or killed.

April 14, 2003: Tikrit falls after "surprisingly light resistance" to the Marines, according to a U.S. Marine commander.

April 15, 2003. Secretary of Defense Rumsfeld announces the coalition forces have shut down an unauthorized oil pipeline between Iraq and Syria.

April 18, 2003. Coalition forces battle Iranian People's Mujahadeen paramilitaries in eastern Iraq. The People's Mujahadeen incursion is the start of a pattern of Iranian activities in post-Saddam Iraq.

April 20, 2003. A 1,000-man special unit begins a systematic search for weapons of mass destruction in Iraq. As of this writing, over one year later, no WMD have been found.

April 23, 2003 American military forces report that the southern oil fields have begun production again, enabling the "oil-for-food" program to generate revenues for Iraqi reconstruction. Iranian-backed Badr Brigade agents appear in Shiite areas including Karbala, Najaf, and Basra. The Badr Brigade operatives are part of an Iranian effort to influence Shiite Iraqis and assert some control over internal developments in post-Saddam Iraq.

April 24, 2003. The UN Security Council votes another extension of the "oil-for-food" program. Oil export revenues are the only source of income Iraq can generate for the Iraqi rebuilding program. All other aid will come from the United States and its allies.

April 27, 2003. President Bush states that weapons of mass destruction may never be discovered in Iraq.

May 1, 2003. Standing aboard the aircraft carrier USS *Abraham Lincoln*, beneath a banner that reads "Mission Accomplished," President Bush announces the end of major combat operations in Iraq.

Increase Your Iraq IQ

Major combat operations in Iraq have ended. In the battle of Iraq, the United States and our allies have prevailed. And now our coalition is engaged in securing and reconstructing that country. In this battle, we have fought for the cause of liberty, and for the peace of the world … Operation Iraqi Freedom was carried out with a combination of precision, speed, and boldness the enemy did not expect, and the world had not seen before ….

We have begun the search for hidden chemical and biological weapons, and already know of hundreds of sites that will be investigated …

The Battle of Iraq is one victory in a war on terror that began on 11 September 2001, and still goes on …. Any outlaw regime that has ties to terrorist groups, and seeks or possesses weapons of mass destruction, is a grave danger to the civilized world, and will be confronted …. In the words of the prophet Isaiah: "To the captives, "Come out," and to those in darkness, "Be free."

—President George W. Bush, May 1, 2003.

Why Had the Iraqi Army Performed So Poorly (Again)?

Reminiscent of their defeat in 1991, the Iraqi army was thoroughly beaten the U.S.-led Coalition in less than a month. Why had the Iraqis performed so poorly? The answers come from several elements:

◆ Highly trained, capably led professional soldiers battling, in many instances, poorly trained conscripts.

◆ Superior Coalition training, equipment, and tactics to defeat even the elite Iraqi army units like the Republican Guard.

◆ A relatively shallow support for the Saddam Hussein regime on the part of most of the Iraqi army soldiers. The Shiite conscripts were not loyal to Saddam, and would not fight fiercely to prop up his dictatorship. On the other hand, those troops that were (and still are) fiercely loyal to Saddam did fight more stubbornly, and they form the core of the Sunni insurgency that has plagued Iraq since the collapse of the Hussein regime.

The Victory Opens Up Questions

The sweeping victory of Coalition forces during April 2003 soon gave way to the physical, political, and public relations challenges of rebuilding and reconstituting Iraq. This extraordinarily difficult task was complicated by the fact that, while major combat operations were over, the fighting was not. Iraqi paramilitary units like the *Fedayeen Saddam* were being subdued, but other guerilla fighters were appearing. Soon, Coalition forces would be facing suicide bombers and terrorist attacks from al Qaeda and other Islamic terror groups.

Desert Diction

The **Fedayeen Saddam** (meaning "Saddam's Men of Sacrifice" were paramilitary fighter fiercely loyal to Saddam Hussein. Using guerilla tactics, these fighters first appeared during Operation Iraqi Freedom. They fought Coalition troops and in some cases, Iraqi civilians, in their battles to preserve the Hussein regime. Iraqi regular army troops were almost as afraid of the Fedayeen Saddam as they were of the Coalition forces. Surrendering Iraqis feared that if the roving bands of Fedayeen saw them retreating in the face of Coalition forces, the Fedayeen would execute them for cowardice.

Transition from Military to Civilian Authority

As the military campaign turned into a nation-building campaign, the situation inside Iraq was already shifting from enthusiasm (on the part of the vast majority of Iraqis who did not support Saddam Hussein) to frustration over the reality of the chaos and damage that confronted the people.

On May 12, 2003, veteran State Department official Paul Bremer was instated as the new head of the Coalition Provisional Authority in Iraq. He replaced Lieutenant General Jay Garner, who was unpopular with the Iraqi civil authorities in place after Saddam's ouster.. Bremer was seen as a moderating, civilian influence on what to that point had been a military affair. As we will see in the next chapter, Bremer's job would be far from easy.

 Iraq Fact

The **Coalition Provisional Authority (CPA)** was created on April 2004 to oversee Iraq after Saddam Hussein's regime collapsed. It was headed by Paul Bremer, a veteran State Department administrator. The CPA turned governing authority over to the interim Iraqi government on June 28, 2004. The interim government would run Iraq until formal elections were held (originally planned for January 2005) to create a new Iraqi government.

Hearts and Minds?

In the very early phase of the invasion, there had been a hint of the difficulties that lay ahead.

In the turmoil after the collapse of Saddam Hussein's regime, the Iraqi National Museum was attacked by a mob and appeared to have been thoroughly ransacked. Priceless artifacts spanning 8,000 years of Mesopotamian history were lost. Almost immediately, U.S. troops were blamed for not protecting the museum from the mob. There were not enough U.S. troops available to protect the museum, and those who were on hand had been tasked to secure other strategically important sites, including the Ministries of Oil and the Interior.

The looting at the museum and the security problems at hospitals and power facilities made headlines around the world, and led many to ask what, precisely, the occupation plan had been. Of course, the situation is not always as it is portrayed, but that did not help Iraqi and outside perceptions of the Coalition troops who manned the occupation. For example, many Iraqi hospitals had been denied supplies by Saddam Hussein, who kept the supplies purchased through the "oil-for-food" program for his own supporters.

Many areas of Iraq, particularly outside Baghdad, had been without adequate electric power for years. Ironically, electrical production soon exceeded pre-war levels, but the distribution plan, which allocated the power equally across the country (meaning long deprived Shiite and Kurd areas received their share of electricity at the expense of Sunni areas that had traditionally enjoyed adequate electricity). As a result, bitter complaints about lack of electricity (and the attendant condemnation of Coalition forces) made headlines around the world. But the fact was that it was Sunnis doing the complaining rather than Shiites, many of whom were seeing their first dependable electric power in over a decade. The mistake made by the Coalition Provisional Authority was distributing the power equally, which meant highly visible Baghdad didn't have full electrical power, which in turn suggested that electricity was severely lacking throughout the country.

Increase Your Iraq IQ

It is known as one of the worst episodes of the war in Iraq: one of the world's greatest archaeological collections ransacked while American troops stood by, unable or unwilling to act. But now a different picture is emerging of the looting of the National Museum in Baghdad. Only a few dozen significant pieces, not thousands as originally reported, were stolen. And many, a new investigation has found, may have gone missing long before the Americans arrived in the Iraqi capital.

US officials revealed yesterday that several of the most important pieces that were thought to have been stolen have now turned up safe. The world-famous treasure of Nimrud, an extraordinary series of priceless 4,500-year-old gold artifacts, has been found in a flooded vault under the Iraqi National Bank. Other key parts of the museum's collection, including tens of thousands of Greek and Roman gold and silver coins, have been found in strongrooms in the Baghdad museum itself. Staff there now say that only 33 major items and around 2,000 minor works have gone.

"The treasure was never lost," Salman Faleh, the governor of the central bank, said yesterday. "We knew all along that they were there. It just took a bit of time to get at them because of the flooding ...."

There are also suspicions that some of the best artifacts that are missing had been stolen and sold several years ago. Senior figures in the Baath Party regime, such as Saddam's eldest son Uday, are known to have made millions from the international trade in antiquities. Some American and European specialists believe that most of the 33 missing items were taken in the first few hours of the collapse of Saddam's regime and were stolen "to order."

Professor McGuire Gibson, an Oriental specialist from Chicago University and a member of the UNESCO team investigating the thefts, said he had received reports that the "top five" items among the 33 had been smuggled to Tehran and Paris within days of their removal.

—Jason Burke, *The Guardian*, June 8, 2003

The museum incident is another instructive lesson on the complexities of postwar Iraq, and the problems of perception the Coalition nations face as occupying powers, rather than military victors. Lack of progress is considered a failing, even when the problems were not the fault of the troops on the ground.

The reality in the museum case is that most of the artifacts that were originally in the National Museum were *not* looted. Instead, they had been hidden by museum staff prior to the start of the fighting. When all was said and done, and the secreted pieces returned, some 33 major pieces and some 2,000 minor pieces ended up missing from the museum. A tragedy, to be sure, but still less tragic than the 170,000 pieces initially claimed to be taken. In fact, a global effort led by the United States and several universities and antiquities experts, has resulted in the recovery and restoration of many objects thought to be lost. Moreover, many of the missing pieces were actually believed to have been stolen by Uday Hussein, prior to the war, and sold by him on the black market.

This apparent lack of protection of Iraqi infrastructure and assets was the first big public relations and operational mistake of the occupation and it cost the invading forces a high price in terms of good will with the Iraqis, and the failings were duly noted in most of the international press, already highly critical of the U.S.-led invasion.

The Coalition troops seemed caught off guard by the extent of the looting, and unable to determine the real extent of the damages.

(Oval) Office Politics

Why were the Coalition forces unable to keep the peace? Simply put, there were not enough troops in country to do the job. The size of the invading force had been a major internal controversy within the Bush administration.

American forces for this invasion had been scaled back on the orders of Secretary Rumsfeld, who refuted the doctrine associated with current Secretary of Defense Colin Powell (who was the Commanding General in the first Gulf War) that military action must have overwhelming force both on the ground and in the air.

In an apparent effort to prove his strategy of a leaner, more efficient military, Rumsfeld had authorized a considerably smaller force than some of his generals had thought was necessary to adequately topple the Hussein regime and maintain order in its wake. However, the forces on the ground proved more than adequate to defeat Saddam's military, which led to the conclusion that the manpower levels were adequate for post-war occupation. As a result, no more troops were sent initially, and the Coalition was short critical manpower when the violence first started.

Who Has the Initiative?

The museum episode—which infuriated many Iraqis no matter what the reality of the situation—was a harbinger of things to come. American forces had overthrown Saddam, but as it turned out, they were not numerous enough to control turbulent events on the ground in Iraq, or to guarantee its security. Moreover, as occupier, the United States was in the unhappy position of needing to maintain the initiative in the face of several competitors.

Once Saddam's iron fist was crushed, old antagonists set out to pursue long-term agendas, and new players also entered the scene. The following groups were among those that began to exert their initiative:

◆ Saddam loyalists, seeking to preserve their power positions

◆ Militant Shiites, seeking to take control of post-Saddam Iraq

◆ Vengeful Kurds, seeking to redress decades of abuse from Sunnis who had enjoyed Saddam's protection

◆ Intriguing Iranians, who were executing a considered strategy to exert influence over developments inside Iraq

◆ Opportunistic al Qaeda operatives, who sought to pursue their ongoing goal of killing Americans and their allies, and ultimately destroying the United States

We shall look at this situation in more depth in Chapter 25.

The lack of adequate forces would become increasingly impossible to ignore in the months that followed. In the United States, there was a sense of relief that the war was over. On the streets of Baghdad and Fallujah and Karbala, however, a fair number of Iraqis were under the impression that it had just begun.

The Least You Need to Know

◆ The Coalition defeated the Saddam Hussein regime in just three weeks, in one of the most stunning and one-sided victories in military history.

◆ The rapid victory of the Coalition troops was broadcast in vivid detail to Western and Arab households, but the coverage was vastly different depending on who did the filming.

◆ The Coalition troops appeared ill-prepared and undermanned to maintain security after the war ended.

◆ The guerilla forces that emerged during the war continued their resistance in the weeks and months following the formal end of major combat operations.

◆ Public perceptions of the Coalition Provisional Authority rapidly changed from initial optimism over the fall of Hussein, to frustration and criticism over the slow recovery process.

◆ Several groups began to appear in post-Saddam Iraq, all of whom would contribute in their own way to the strife that still gripped the nation even one year later.

Part 6

Aftermath and Prelude

Saddam is gone, but the troubles for the United States seem to be just beginning. Turn the page to find out what is happening in Iraq today, and what might happen tomorrow.

Chapter 22

The Uneasy Occupation

In This Chapter

◆ The Coalition forces are faced with the difficulties of occupation

◆ The many faces of the insurgency

◆ Potential troubles in Kurdistan

◆ The torture at Abu Ghraib Prison, and its effects around the world

In the previous chapter, we saw how the stunning victory of Coalition arms began to turn into a difficult occupation.

Occupation Troubles

The Coalition forces were faced with a rapidly changing domestic situation inside Iraq in the months following the collapse of the Hussein regime. As we saw in Chapter 21, the Coalition seemed unable to control the widespread looting that went on for days after the fall of Baghdad. Gradually, the looting subsided, but peace was not restored.

A Strategic Surprise: The Resistance in Iraq

Four groups are capable of creating violence in Iraq in the post-Saddam era. These groups could sidetrack the rebuilding process. Each of these groups has created problems for the occupying Coalition forces, and threatens the stability of the new Iraqi governments. These groups include …

♦ The Sunni Arabs, whose minority position would be perilous with Saddam's protection gone

♦ The Shiites, the majority in Iraq, who would experience some Iranian influences

♦ The Kurds, traditionally restive under previous regimes, and eager to gain some real autonomy

♦ Outside terror groups, who would see the instability in post-Saddam Iraq as an opportunity to attack the United States and its interests

Prior to Operation Iraqi Freedom, the Coalition strategists conceivably viewed possible resistance in postwar Iraq like this:

♦ Any Sunni resistance would crumble along with the Iraqi army.

♦ The Shiites could be a problem, given the temptation from Iran to stir up trouble and keep the United States off balance, though there was the chance the Shiites would be grateful for the Coalition getting rid of Saddam.

♦ The Kurds could be counted on to support U.S. rebuilding efforts, as long as the United States provided some measure of security for them against the Turks and the Iraqi Sunnis.

♦ Terrorists (namely members of al Qaeda) could become a problem if security was not quickly re-established. The longer internal chaos and insurgency lasted, the more opportunities for foreign fighters to enter Iraq and pursue their agendas there. (We will look at the terrorist question in the next chapter.)

Instead, the United States found itself faced with trouble on all four fronts, but two developments were the most surprising:

♦ The Sunni resistance, focusing in the so-called *Sunni Triangle*, proved to be a resilient and organized guerilla fighting force, often operating in a seemingly coordinate manner across that region.

♦ The Shiites were ready to run affairs in their territory almost immediately, signaling a sophisticated support network already in place.

Desert Diction _____

The **Sunni Triangle** is the region in central Iraq, defined loosely as a 100-mile wide stretch of territory between Baghdad and Tikrit. This is the heartland of the Sunnis who were most loyal to Saddam Hussein. The tribes in this area benefited most from Saddam's patronage, and had the most to lose in his defeat. The majority of the resistance (80 percent of all guerilla attacks in 2003 and 2004, according to the *Christian Science Monitor*) against the Coalition forces has been centered in this region.

The situation called for exceptional diplomacy and care, particularly in the earliest days of the occupation, when every U.S. military move had the potential to be a flash point for violence. Not only would military action generate an armed response in many places, but other enforcement and rebuilding tactics would cause outrage and show the tremendous risks and difficulties facing an occupying force in this region.

The Evolving Face of the Insurgency

The U.S.-led Coalition forces have been on a constant war footing ever since the "end of major combat operations." In fact, by July 2004, Coalition deaths after the end of major combat operations surpassed those incurred during the three-week campaign. Across Iraq, unrest has persisted. It sometimes seems to the U.S. observer that *IEDs* (improvised explosive devices) are going off at random. However, we'll try to organize the chaos to better understand the various forces at work.

The Sunni Resistance

In the days immediately following the fall of Saddam, the Sunni resistance was mainly in the hands of die-hard Fedayeen Saddam fighters and other Ba'th loyalists. The resistance was scattered, and the U.S. forces appeared on the verge of mopping up the last pockets. However, the U.S. occupying commanders made a series of crucial errors that led to a crystallizing of Sunni resistance, and a deepening of the violence.

Desert Diction _____

IEDs, or **improvised explosive devices**, are crude bombs that are used to attack convoys and civilians in Iraq. These bombs are pieced together from various components, but are made by hand one-by-one, for use by insurgents and terrorists.

First, the Coalition disbanded the Iraqi army, sending thousands of men home with no jobs, and nothing to do except consider their recent defeat. Second, the Coalition Provisional Authority (CPA) removed all the Ba'th officials from positions of responsibility, providing more potential recruits for the Saddam loyalists. So, rather than dealing with a dwindling core of Saddam loyalists, the U.S. occupation forces found themselves facing a steady supply of insurgents, drawn from a large pool of potential recruits. Third, the Coalition leadership did not include the local tribal and village leaders, or *mukhtars*, in local peacekeeping decisions. As a result, occupation troops began to alienate the people, and their leaders from occupation forces and Coalition Provisional Authority.

> **Increase Your Iraq IQ**
>
> Ladies and Gentlemen ... we got him.
> —CPA Administrator Paul Bremer, announcing the capture of Saddam Hussein

In the vacuum that was left, the tribal leaders still exerted their traditional authority, and they began to work against the occupying troops, rather than cooperate with them. In the months following the fall of Saddam, the U.S.-led Coalition troops found themselves playing dual roles of battling insurgents in increasingly violent battles while continuing to protect (and participate) in the rebuilding of the country. The interim Iraqi government does include members who represent several of the leading tribes in Iraq. However, the tribes that dominate in the Sunni Triangle, including the powerful Delaimi tribe from the Anbar province, where Fallujah is located, were not included. Some experts believe that if the interim government included tribes from the Sunni Triangle, despite their previous allegiance to Saddam Hussein, the ability for insurgents to operate in these territories would be severely diminished. As it stands, the Sunni tribes that occupy the Sunni Triangle are on the outside looking in, and it is precisely in the Sunni Triangle where much of the Sunni insurgent attacks are taking place.

Even the death or capture of Saddam's henchmen did not rein in the insurgents. It was believed that as the people represented by the deck of cards were captured or killed, the Sunni insurgency would lose steam. If anything, the opposite was true. First, Uday and Qusay Hussein were killed in a gun battle with U.S. troops, and then on December 13, 2003, Saddam Hussein was captured in a hole in the ground in a farmyard in Tikrit. News of his capture, and subsequent photos of a bedraggled Saddam being examined by a U.S. medical corpsman, signaled that any hope of Saddam re-emerging in power was over. Still, the insurgency grinds on.

> **Desert Diction**
>
> Iraqi villages all have a **mukhtar**, the traditional leader in the village. The mukhtars are the focal point of local decision-making. Their involvement is vital for local cooperation to succeed.

Trouble in Fallujah

Fallujah, a city of 285,000 west of Baghdad, is known as the "city of mosques." There are more than 200 houses of worship in the city and in the villages nearby. Fallujah has for many years been an important center for Sunni Muslims in Iraq.

Located in the notorious "Sunni Triangle," Fallujah was not always a "hot spot." In fact, immediately following the overthrow of Saddam, the city of Fallujah was relatively peaceful. Looting was almost non-existent. But, in April 2003 the U.S. Army entered the city and set up their headquarters in the former Ba'th Party headquarters. The choice of the Ba'th headquarters rankled many of the people, and relations between the coalition forces and residents went downhill from there.

The trouble in Fallujah came to a head on April 28, 2003. Coalition forces opened fire on a large group of demonstrators protesting the American occupation. U.S. soldiers claimed they were firing in self-defense, but the insurgents said the firing was unprovoked. Fifteen Iraqis died, and a number of others were wounded. Following this event, Fallujah became a magnet for foreign terrorists, a rallying point for the Sunni insurgency, and a major threat to stability in Iraq.

The already tense situation began to unravel when four American contractors were killed in Fallujah on March 31, 2004 (an Iraqi journalist, reflecting the opinions of some Iraqis, referred to the victims as "mercenaries.") The contractors were beheaded and cheering mobs mutilated their bodies and then hung them from a bridge. The brutal murder of the American civilians indicated several new realities:

- The insurgency was now targeting those people who would rebuild Iraq, not just the soldiers in the occupying armies.

- The insurgency had widespread support in the Sunni Triangle, and resentment of occupying troops extended to U.S. companies that were seen as profiting from the misery, and keeping the lion-share of the contracts for themselves.

- Foreign terrorists were entering the picture. While it is not clear whether al Qaeda terrorists (led by Abu Musab Al-Zarqawi) perpetrated the brutal murders or if it was Sunni insurgents, Al-Zarqawi's followers claimed responsibility for the attack.

Iraq Fact

Abu Musab al-Zarqawi is a Jordanian-born Al Qaeda leader, who operated out of Fallujah in late 2003 and 2004. Al-Zarqawi is considered to be the mastermind behind many of the attacks in 2003 and 2004 on U.S. troops and Iraqi security forces and government figures.

At this point, the U.S. response deepened the spiral of violence. Vowing to capture those responsible, the U.S. Marines (who had replaced U.S. Army units in Fallujah in March 2004) initiated an attack on suspected perpetrators. The loss of civilian life was heavy, giving the insurgency new fuel for the fire.

In the months following the murders of the contractors, the situation in Fallujah has continued to deteriorate. As we shall see later in this chapter, the lawlessness in the city has created an opportunity for terrorist groups and has served as continuing inspiration for Iraqi insurgents.

Whither Fallujah?

Western reporters who visited Fallujah during the occupation reported that, far from taking its place as a stable component of the "new Iraq," the city had instead emerged as a fundamentalist Islamic substate. Embattled extremists there enforce Sharia (holy) law and swear allegiance not to the central authority in Baghdad, but to local clerics or their tribal leaders, while the remaining Ba'thists continue to fight because they have nothing left to lose.

Damaged military transport, probably by an IED along the road.

Power Plants, Pipelines, and Police Stations: New Targets for the Insurgents

The situation in Fallujah is representative of the situation throughout the Sunni Triangle. U.S. troops conduct counter insurgency strikes, while their patrols and convoys suffer from ambushes and IEDs (improvised explosive devices) that take a steady toll of casualties.

Increase Your Iraq IQ

Nothing could have been easier than gaining the good-will of the people of Fallujah had the Americans not been so brutal in their dealings. Tribal peoples like these have been the most easily duped by imperialists for centuries now. But now a tipping point has been reached. To Americans, "Fallujah" may still mean four mercenaries killed, with their corpses then mutilated and abused; to Iraqis, "Fallujah" means the savage collective punishment for that attack, in which over 600 Iraqis have been killed, with an estimated 200 women and over 100 children … A Special Forces colonel in the Vietnam War said of the town, Ben Tre, "We had to destroy the town in order to save it." That statement encapsulated the Vietnam War. The same is true in Iraq today—Fallujah cannot be "saved" from its mujaheddin unless it is destroyed."

—Iraqi journalist Rahul Mahajan

In addition to attacking U.S. troops, the insurgency is also targeting interim government figures, Iraqi police, and critical infrastructure. By attacking the government and the police, the insurgents hope to discourage fellow Iraqis from participating in the rebuilding of the country. By attacking power plants, pipelines, and police stations, the insurgents hope to continue the misery of the country, destabilizing the situation in order to bring down the fledgling government.

U.S. military convoy somewhere in Iraq.

The Shiite Resistance: Militants and Moderates

While the Sunni insurgents have been fighting in the Sunni Triangle, Shiites in the south have been resisting the Coalition occupation for different reasons. The end result is the same—violence against Coalition troops and civilian contractors engaged in rebuilding—but the motives are different.

> **Iraq Fact**
>
> Moqtada al-Sadr is a radical Shiite cleric, whose supporters are called the Mehdi Army, and who has opposed U.S.-led occupation forces. The son of revered Shiite cleric Mohammed Sadiq Sadr, who was killed by Saddam Hussein's regime, al-Sadr and his followers represent the more militant elements of Shiite Muslims in Iraq.

Staking a Claim to the Future

Shiite resistance in the south is characterized by militant fighters, mainly followers of radical cleric Moqtada al-Sadr, who want the U.S.-led occupation troops out of Iraq so they can create an Iran-like Islamic Republic in Iraq.

The other Shiite view is embodied by Grand Ayatollah Ali Sistani, the prime religious leader of the Shiites. Ayatollah Sistani is openly critical of the U.S.-led occupation, but has given his acceptance to the interim Iraqi government (led by the Shiite Prime Minister Allawi; for more on the new leadership in Iraq, see Chapter 24).

> **Iraq Fact**
>
> Grand Ayatollah Ali Sistani is the most senior Shiite cleric in Iraq, and one of five living grand ayatollahs. Sistani is considered the prime marja, or spiritual leader, of the Shiites. After maintaining a relatively low profile during the Saddam Hussein regime, Sistani has emerged as a powerful figure in post-Saddam Iraq. Sistani has been critical of the U.S. led occupation of Iraq, but has called for Shiites to support the interim Iraqi government. Sistani, as prime marja, plays a critical role in molding Shiite attitudes toward the new Iraqi government.

The Shiites in Iraq are not as cohesive as the Sunnis, perhaps owing to their majority status. In the immediate aftermath of Saddam's fall, followers of Sistani have clashed with more militant followers of al-Sadr. At one point in mid-2003, al-Sadr's followers surrounded Sistani's house demanding he leave the country. They probably felt that Sistani was too soft on the occupation. Sistani went into hiding, but remained in Iraq. In the months since that time, Sistani has maintained his primary leadership position, but the followers of al-Sadr are still a radicalized force to be reckoned with.

Ready to Rule

Even though there are divisions among the Shiites, when British troops occupied Basra and the surrounding Shiite areas, they quickly discovered that the local Shiite clerics and tribal leaders had already set up a functional provisional government. The British were willing to let these authorities handle local affairs, but the CPA refused to acknowledge their authority. Over time, that policy proved to be a mistake, as a potential ally or at least a cooperative leadership structure was ignored, and even made hostile.

Fighting in Najaf

On August 29, 2003, a car bomb at the Imam Ali Shrine in Najaf, one of the most holy Shia sites, killed more than 80 people, including a critically important Shia leader, Ayatollah Muhammad Baker Al-Haqim. At his funeral services, the mourners turn into a mob, shouting slogans against the U.S.-led occupation.

In the early part of 2004, followers of al-Sadr clashed with U.S. occupation troops in Najaf and Sadr City (formerly called Saddam City), a poor Shiite neighborhood in Baghdad. In another move that infuriated many Shiites, CPA Administrator Paul Bremer ordered an al-Sadr newspaper shut down, due to its open calls for attacks on American soldiers. The move was regarded as heavy handed from a nation with the First Amendment protecting free speech, and it only served to further galvanize al-Sadr's followers. (Interestingly, Interim Prime Minister Allawi, himself a Shiite, ordered the newspaper reopened in July 2004, stating that such censorship was inconsistent with the new Iraq.)

By April, U.S. troops had surrounded Najaf and were beginning to close in on al-Sadr and his followers. Battles and casualties mounted on both sides, and the tighter the U.S. army pulled its ring around Najaf, the more violent the fighting became.

In an effort to stave off a bloody battle in this holiest of Shiite places, the Iraqi President Ghaze al-Yawar negotiated a cease-fire, and the U.S. commander agreed to stand down. In return, al-Sadr ordered his followers to leave Najaf and to honor the cease-fire. Actual military authority was passed over to an Iraqi commander, and many of the troops under his command were former insurgents. No matter how it really played out, the cease-fire was regarded by many Iraqis as a victory for al-Sadr's forces, underscoring the unpopularity of the occupation to many Iraqis. The uneasy truce broke down in August, and Coalition and Iraqi Government forces are mounting a new attack on al-Sadr's militia.

With the interim Iraqi government taking a more prominent role in the daily life of Iraq, including police activities, the Shiite insurgency has diminished somewhat but still threatens to erupt. Even if al-Sadr backs down, or is killed, another leader will no doubt take his place. Radical Shiism will persist in the post-Saddam environment, unless put down by a strong central authority, or moderated by a larger majority who do not espouse the radical viewpoint. In the end, Ayatollah Sistani may hold the trump card as far as what kind of government emerges in Iraq. If Sistani calls for a *jihad* against the new government, it could lead to the dissolution of Iraq as we know it, and the creation of a Shiite theocracy on the Iranian model in the southern parts of Iraq. If Sistani calls for cooperation with the new regime, the new government will have a chance. Either way, Sistani will be sure that the new state is more palatable to Islamic law than the Hussein regime.

> **Desert Diction**
>
> A *jihad* is a holy struggle waged on behalf of Islam. It is considered a religious duty. Militant Muslims use the term to refer to war waged against the enemies of Islam (whomever that may be at the time).

The Kurd Question: Still Unanswered

Although most of the media attention has been centered on Iraqi insurgents in Fallujah and Najaf, and on the terror attacks of al-Zarqawi's followers, the Kurds have been gradually asserting themselves in the northern parts of Iraq.

Crisis Averted

The Kurds threatened to bolt from the interim government in March 2004, but a compromise worked out by Prime Minister Allawi maintained the government. The Kurds are seeking, as they always have, a level of autonomy inside the new Iraq. The Kurds will elect their own assembly in January 2005, which will have direct local control over the Kurdish areas, and Kurds are represented on the interim government and have an allocated number of seats in the upcoming parliament.

Revenge in Kurdistan

The Kurds have also been exacting their own sort of revenge for decades of Sunni Arab abuse under the Hussein regime. In the spring of 2004, Kurdish fighters evicted thousands of Iraqi Arabs from traditional Kurdish villages in the northern parts of Iraq in Erbil province. Again, clumsy CPA policy implementation has contributed to the problems. The CPA proposed a claims procedure, whereby dispossessed Kurds could appeal for reparations or a return of their homes and lands. However, the CPA was unable to implement the program quickly enough, so the Kurds took matters into their own hands, and began to retake the seized villages by force.

Kirkuk: Melting Pot or Flash Point?

The Kurds, Arabs, and Turkmen are colliding in Kirkuk. All three groups live in the city, but the Arabs were able to seize properties from the Kurds and Turkmen during the Saddam regime. Now, all three groups are vying for control of Kirkuk proper, and the surrounding oil fields. As of this writing, the situation is still unresolved, but if it is not careful, Coalition forces could find themselves being attacked by Kurds or Turkmen if Kirkuk erupts in fighting.

Torture at Abu Ghraib

In early January 2004, pictures surfaced that show terrible acts of cruelty being inflicted upon Iraqi prisoners at Abu Ghraib prison. The first issue is to settle what these acts of cruelty were. In Western media, these acts were and are referred to often as "prisoner abuse" while in Arab media they are called "torture." (Remember the phenomenon of vastly different coverage of the same events when U.S. media and Al-Jazeera are compared).

Oil Spill Ahead

Who would prefer that Saddam's torture chambers still be open?

—George W. Bush, March 19, 2004, in a speech prior to the publicizing of prisoner abuses at Abu Ghraib prison

On the road to Abu Ghraib.

So What Happened?

According to soldiers who were at Abu Ghraib, and as shown in several graphic photos, here is what happened:

Male detainees at Abu Ghraib were ...

◆ Beaten.

◆ Burned.

◆ Bitten by attack dogs.

◆ Stripped of their clothing and stacked in piles.

◆ Forced to do calisthenics in the nude.

◆ Led around on dog leashes.

◆ Subjected to sexual humiliation (naked detainees had to simulate sex acts with other detainees, masturbate publicly, and stand naked in the presence of family members, who were also stripped, and some were forced to wear women's underwear).

◆ Left naked in their cells for days on end.

More than that, it appears that some were left to die under circumstances suspicious enough to launch an official investigation by the U.S. Army.

To this author, it looks like torture, and not simple "abuse." Not every item on the list is equally repugnant, and some seem almost bizarre (like wearing women's underwear), but the beating, burning, dog attacks, and sexual humiliation are acts of torture in my book. Certainly, murder must be considered the ultimate torture act, if the investigations underway at the time of this writing prove the deaths were caused by these acts.

> **Iraq Fact**
>
> The U.S. Army launched formal investigations of 37 deaths at the Abu Ghraib prison, categorized 8 of them as "suspicious," and has authorized formal inquiry in those cases, with the potential for future criminal charges.

> **Oil Spill Ahead**
>
> The International Red Cross designated the military intelligence wing of the Abu Ghraib facility as practicing "systematic" mistreatment of prisoners, and described U.S. interrogation tactics there as "tantamount to torture."

Why Did It Happen?

The torture at Abu Ghraib is probably best described as a misapplication of practices used by the United States at the prison at Guantanamo Bay. In dealing with Taliban and al Qaeda combatants captured in Afghanistan, U.S. military interrogators at Guantanamo Bay in Cuba operated under a different set of rules. The Taliban and al Qaeda members that were sent to Guantanamo were not the typical prisoner. These were terrorists (or those who aided them) who wanted to destroy the United States. These were people who slammed jetliners into U.S. buildings, and wanted to do it again. To these people, the United States would not offer the protections of international law. Accordingly, the logic of the "enemy combatants" designation was designed to give the U.S. interrogators more latitude to extract information from people suspected to be al Qaeda terrorists, whose goal is the death of Americans in and out of uniform, and the destruction and murder of U.S. citizens at home and abroad.

In the post-September 11 world, the notion that the interrogation environment in place at Guantanamo is justified may be difficult for many Americans to challenge, and may even be approved by many in the abstract. But the same conviction that many Americans hold regarding the treatment of real and supposed al Qaeda members may not be as solid where Iraqi prisoners in Abu Ghraib are concerned.

Did the strategy of prisoner mistreatment in Guantanamo, outside the Geneva Convention framework, eventually foster a willingness to employ the same set of rules to Iraq?

Guantanamo East

Interrogators who had conducted interviews with suspects in Cuba ended up playing what *The New York Times* referred to as a "central role" in many of the interrogations at Abu Ghraib. Units who had conducted interrogations in Afghanistan, which was, like the Guantanamo interrogation unit, operating under the new set of post-September 11 rules that ignored the Geneva Conventions, also held responsibility for interrogations at Abu Ghraib. These interrogation teams assumed authority in highly sensitive areas of the prison. Severe abuses of Iraqi detainees took place during these teams' assignments there.

In Iraq, the prisoners were *not* designated as "enemy combatants" by the Bush administration, and so were entitled to the international protections due to prisoners of war under the Geneva Conventions. This fact is critical to understanding that even the Bush administration did not see the Iraqi prisoners as being on

> **Oil Spill Ahead**
>
> Military doctors working at the Bagram Air Base in Afghanistan determined in December 2002 that two Afghanis perished as the result of "blunt force injuries" they suffered while in American custody. Although no charges were filed, the same unit responsible for interrogation when the deaths occurred was later reassigned to Abu Ghraib.

the same level as the terrorist detainees in Afghanistan and Guantanamo. The rationalization that the treatment of Iraqi prisoners is acceptable in the same way many Americans may feel harsh treatment of al Qaeda members (or suspected members) may be acceptable, breaks down. The basic problem is that the Iraqi prisoners are not members of al Qaeda. In truth, these prisoners were captured during and after battles with U.S. troops.

Crossing the Line

The line was crossed. These Iraqi prisoners were subjected to forms of abuse and torture that generally are not applied to captured enemy soldiers. What is more, American soldiers and citizens alike generally believe that America operates on a higher moral plain than one that would support the torture of non-terrorists.

The fact that these events have served the purposes of those eager to produce and circulate anti-American propaganda does not detract from what actually happened within the walls of the prison. It angers, saddens, and frustrates Americans to watch al Qaeda operatives use the torture of Iraqi captives in Abu Ghraib as a justification for beheading Americans and their allies and posting the gruesome video on the Internet. I believe the al Qaeda terrorists would, and will, kill Americans no matter what happens elsewhere, but the torture at Abu Ghraib certainly provided fuel for the fire. (We will look at the terrorism factor in Iraq in Chapter 23.)

Increase Your Iraq IQ

Protection of the Iraqi people from the cruelty of Saddam had become one of the administration's last remaining rationalizations for going to war. All of the other trumped-up rationalizations have collapsed. Saddam was not on the verge of acquiring nuclear weapons. He had no persuasive link to al Qaeda. He had nothing to do with September 11. We have found no weapons of mass destruction.

So it is human rights that the Administration turned to in order to justify its decision to go to war. On December 24, 2003—the day Saddam was captured—President Bush said, "For the vast majority of Iraqi citizens who wish to live as free men and women, this event brings further assurance that the torture chambers and the secret police are gone forever."

—Senator Edward Kennedy, *Statement on Iraqi Prisoner Abuse Allegations*, May 10, 2004

Understanding Abu Ghraib is essential to understanding the loss of American moral authority for many Iraqis immediately after the prison scandal became global news. If these kinds of abuses, which had taken place under Saddam, also happened under the

United States, what credibility would Americans have with the Iraqi people? To those Iraqis who were on the fence, the news of Abu Ghraib, delivered by Arab media outlets with no desire to shy away from the lurid details, only created more hostility to the CPA and the interim government.

Who Did It?

Are the excesses at Abu Ghraib the result of the misdeeds of a few low-ranking officers (or undisciplined enlisted personnel), as the Bush administration initially claimed … or were these excesses the result of initiatives from people considerably higher up?

Consider that the scandal broke in the spring of 2004, but at issue are events from May 2003 onward. Well *before* those events, in March 2003, the Bush administration had drafted a legal opinion holding that President Bush was not obliged to obey *American* anti-torture laws—or, for that matter international anti-torture treaties—when acting in his capacity as commander in chief. The opinion contended that that "(i)n order to respect the president's inherent constitutional authority to manage a military campaign, (prohibitions on torture) … must be construed as inapplicable to interrogation undertaken pursuant to his commander-in-chief authority."

Consider, too, that most of the seven enlisted personnel who were charged with criminal violations related to the abuses at Abu Ghraib insisted that their actions took place with the assent or active encouragement of military intelligence officials. Indeed, some of the abuses precede the arrival of the seven accused enlisted personnel at Abu Ghraib.

The Taguba Report

It would be easiest to accept that this torture was just a case of young soldiers, left without responsible authority, going "too far" in response to the constant attacks their comrades were facing around the country. However, that theory minimizes the role of higher command in the events that took place at Abu Ghraib, and it minimizes the professionalism and conviction of the typical American soldier. The report of General Antonio M. Taguba, which was the first official inquiry into the abuses at Abu Ghraib, voiced suspicions that intelligence officers (sent in from Guantanamo) were "directly or indirectly responsible" for the abuses at Abu Ghraib. In fact, Brigadier General Janis Karpinski, an Army Reservist who ran Abu Ghraib, was stripped of her command of a Military Police Brigade as a result of what happened there. Her dismissal shows that senior officers were held accountable, but not directly blamed, for the abuses.

Still, other officers argued that the torture was ordered. On June 18, 2004, for instance, *USA TODAY* reported that Lieutenant Colonel Steven Jordan, the officer in charge of the Abu Ghraib prison's questioning of detainees, had submitted a sworn account that he had been told in September 2003 that staff at the White House were eager to "pull the intelligence out" of the questioning sessions at Abu Ghraib. Jordan also claimed that there were "incidents where I feel that there was additional pressure" from high Bush administration officials to secure information from detainees at Abu Ghraib.

Pressure on Jordan was also evident, according to the statement, from the repeated instructions he received to secure more intelligence from detainees at the prison. Jordan testified that he was reminded of the necessity of expanding the prison's intelligence yield "many, many, many times." Jordan's sworn statement offered little specific information about who authorized the brutality at Abu Ghraib, but it made clear that White House attention to the Abu Ghraib interrogations was intense during the period when the abuses took place.

Why Did It Happen?

Remember the intense pressure on the Bush administration at that time. As we saw earlier in this chapter, the Coalition victory and occupation of Iraq was degenerating into a guerilla war, and U.S. casualties were mounting. The prisoners at Abu Ghraib may have held some critical information that could have stopped future attacks.

The picture that emerges is one of a White House and a Defense Department intensely concerned with the business of securing information from prisoners … and considerably less interested in the niceties of the Geneva Convention or the obligation to make full disclosures to the Red Cross, as required under law. Again, many Americans in the post-September 11 world might accept that practice when it applies to al Qaeda terrorists in U.S. custody. Some might even accept that practice when it comes to Iraqis blowing up U.S. soldiers with crude car bombs. However, accepting this new standard of practice becomes a turning point for the American people, as much as it was for the Iraqi people in the wake of the Abu Ghraib story hitting the wires. If torture is acceptable for terrorists bent on destroying America and Americans, does it become acceptable for insurgents fighting a guerilla war? And, if it becomes acceptable for insurgent captives, how does one define an insurgent? If it is acceptable, a new kind of war has come to the American people: a war literally to the death against all enemies that do not fight in organized military units, not just terrorists and their supporters.

The Least You Need to Know

- ◆ The insurgency in Iraq has different motivations depending on whether Sunnis or Shiites are involved, even though the outcome is the same on the ground.

- ◆ Heavy-handed practices by the Coalition Provisional Authority, coupled with resentment for the Coalition military occupation, triggered a persistent insurgency in both Sunni and Shiite areas.

- ◆ The Kurds could become another problem for the peace in Iraq.

- ◆ The torture at Abu Ghraib prison fundamentally changed Iraqi perceptions of the U.S. occupation, and poses a different set of challenges to Americans in the post-September 11 environment.

Chapter 23

Rebuilding Iraq

In This Chapter

 ◆ Spin control after the invasion, when pre-invasion justifications are not proven

 ◆ The war on terror shifts to Iraq

 ◆ The Coalition splinters

 ◆ Progress on rebuilding slows

Before Operation Iraqi Freedom, the dominant message from the Bush administration was that Saddam Hussein posed an imminent threat to the United States because of evidence of weapons of mass destruction. At that point, the official line ran along the lines of a statement by the White House spokesman:

> But make no mistake—as I said earlier—we have high confidence that they have weapons of mass destruction. That is what this war was about and it is about. And we have high confidence it will be found. (Ari Fleischer, April 10, 2003)

In the weeks and months that followed the collapse of the Hussein regime the justifications that the Bush administration had offered for ousting

Hussein became considerably less clear, because no one could find any weapons of mass destruction inside Iraq.

Why Did We Do This, Again?

Not only was the media primed to find the "smoking gun," but so was the Bush administration. For example, on May 29, 2003, President Bush said in an interview with Polish television, "We found the weapons of mass destruction. We found biological laboratories ... and we'll find more weapons as time goes on. But, for those who say we haven't found the banned manufacturing devices or banned weapons, they're wrong, we found them." The administration later backed away from such statements after it was confirmed that the so-called "biological laboratories" could not be used to manufacture biological weapons. Nonetheless, the desire to prove the justification for invasion has remained intense.

On June 3, 2003, Iraqi nuclear expert Mahdi Obeidi was taken into Coalition custody and interrogated about Saddam's nuclear program. Obeidi reportedly pointed out during his interrogation that the aluminum tubes that were cited as evidence of an active nuclear weapons program have a diameter of 88 millimeters. These tubes would have been impossible to use in the centrifuge equipment in question, which required tubes of a different size. Obeidi was released from custody on June 17, 2003, and later went to live in the United States.

When pressed about the tubes in a press conference, in July 9, 2004, Acting CIA Director, John McLaughlin made the following statement:

> I must always remind people that the National Intelligence Estimate ... said he did not have nuclear weapons yet ... These tubes were detected as part of the things that could have contributed eventually to an enrichment program. In fact, there's a success story buried in this that very few people know about. That is working with our partners overseas we kept, if my memory serves, close to 100,000 of these tubes from ever getting into Iraq. I believe the tubes that were found in Iraq were not of the high tolerances as the ones going in, and all of the agencies who looked at these tubes thought they could be adapted. Even the Department of Energy, which had a very strong view on these particular things, agreed with the overall assessment in the Estimate that he was reconstituting his nuclear program.

This refrain was echoed by others in the Bush Administration, and by Tony Blair in Britain. The "clarification" to the original claims that Iraq had weapons of mass destruction was that while Saddam did not have the weapons at the time of the invasion, he was working on getting them.

It could very well be true that Saddam Hussein was indeed working on WMD programs in 2002. However, according to statements of various U.S. senators in the wake of the Select Committee on Intelligence's report on Iraq intelligence in the run up to Operation Iraqi Freedom, it is quite likely Congress would not have authorized the invasion had the senators been aware of the lack of physical evidence. Although it might be considered politically opportunistic to make such statements today, when the evidence is so clearly against the initial arguments made by the Bush administration, the lesson is telling. Will the United States be less eager to act against other nations that are developing their own programs—nations like Iran and North Korea, under the "once burned, twice shy" principle?

The War on Terror

As the WMD threat thesis began to crumble, the Bush administration turned to the other key reason originally cited for invading Iraq: Saddam Hussein's regime was aiding terrorists, including al Qaeda. Looking back, it is certainly true that Saddam aided terrorists. He offered cash to the families of Palestinian suicide bombers, for example. Still, no evidence has been uncovered that shows a clear link between Saddam Hussein and al Qaeda. On July 12, 2003, the Associated Press reported that an unidentified Bush administration official acknowledged that the contact between al Qaeda and Iraq was "episodic not continuous." A year later, in July 2004, the formal report issued by the National Commission on Terrorist Attacks Upon the United States (the 9/11 Commission) concluded that there was no operational connection between Iraq and al Qaeda relevant to the September 11 attacks.

As the likelihood that weapons of mass destruction would be found in a neat pile sitting in warehouse became more remote, the Bush administration began to emphasize the other reason cited for going to war: the dangers Saddam Hussein posed to his people and the world as a sponsor of terrorism, and the emergence of Iraq as an arena for terrorism. This argument was restated by Deputy Secretary of Defense Paul Wolfowitz, on June 25, 2004:

> Saddam Hussein led one of the most vicious regimes in the world. He not only invaded his neighbors, but he oppressed his own people with incredible brutality …

Increase Your Iraq IQ

Had this report come out in January like it should have done, we would have known these things before the war in Iraq, which would not have suited the Administration.

—Senator Max Cleland On July 24, 2003, referring to the report by the National Commission on Terrorist Attacks upon the United States (the 9-11 Commission) regarding September 11th, 2001 attacks.

Iraq is presently the central battle in the war on terrorism. The terrorists understand that their defeat in Iraq will be a major victory for us.

Terrorists Take Advantage

As Secretary Wolfowitz stated, by July 2004 Iraq had indeed become a central battleground in the war on terrorism. But Iraq became that central battleground *because* of the invasion and subsequent occupation, not the other way around. The chaos inside Iraq in late 2003 and into 2004 created an opportunity for terrorists to pursue their own agenda there. The two primary factors contributing to terrorism are as follows:

♦ The continuing chaos enables the terrorist groups to operate more aggressively, given the relative inability of the Coalition troops or the Iraqi police forces to get to them.

♦ The extended occupation, and the missteps and resentment that have resulted, are pulling in more recruits to the terrorists banner.

Recruiting Tool

These terrorists, by July 2004, were adopting new tactics aimed at ...

♦ Destabilizing the new government.

♦ Disrupting the reconstruction of Iraq.

♦ Breaking the Coalition.

> **Increase Your Iraq IQ**
>
> Let's face it, if you are a terrorist in the Middle East and you have a mission to kill Americans, Iraq is now the place you're going to want to go.
>
> —James Rubin, former U.S. Deputy Secretary State under President Clinton, in interview on CNN, August 20, 2003.

Some experts say that as many as 3,000 Saudis entered Iraq in June and July of 2003 alone, to fight against the Coalition forces. Dr. Saad al-Faqih, a Saudi expert on al Qaeda, made this claim in the wake of the UN Baghdad headquarters bombings in 2003. Dr. al-Faqih believed the Saudis were entering Iraq via Syria, Jordan, and Kuwait. To be sure, more than just Saudis were coming to Iraq to fight, but it is worth noting that the strict *Wahabism* (fundamentalist Sunni) taught throughout many Saudi *madrases* has resulted in many Saudis joining al Qaeda (including 8 of the September 11 hijackers).

With the situation so chaotic inside Iraq it is much easier for these terrorists to ply their trade there, than in their home countries. For example, under U.S. pressure, the Saudi government began to crack down on al Qaeda and other Islamic fundamentalists in the wake of a series of attacks on Saudi oil infrastructure and abductions and public murder of Western oil technicians. (In a particularly gruesome episode, the head of a murdered U.S. hostage—whose beheading was posted on the Internet—was discovered in a freezer during a raid on a suspected al Qaeda staging house in Riyadh on July 21, 2004.)

Desert Diction

Madrases are Islamic schools. **Wahabism** is a particularly conservative version of Islam that is prevalent in madrases in Saudi Arabia. The Taliban in Afghanistan, who sponsored al Qaeda, adhered to the Wahabi view of Islam.

Terror Tactic 1: Destabilize the New Government

On September 25, 2003, Aqila Al-Hashmi, one of three women named to the Iraqi governing council, died from wounds sustained during an assassination attempt. Among the Iraqi Government officialdom, Issam Jassem Qassim Al-Dijali, of the Iraqi Defense Ministry, and Hazem Ainachi, leader of the Basra Provincial Council and former deputy governor of Basra, were killed in late July 2004. Along with these three, many other Iraqi leaders have been targets for assassination. The attacks on interim government leaders, and governing council leaders before that, are a constant threat to those individuals who would serve in Iraq's new government. Although not all of the deaths are attributable to al Qaeda operatives, the operatives claim responsibility for many of the attacks. In addition to Iraqi leaders, other symbols of the new government, specifically police and the new Iraqi army, came under increasing attack by insurgents and terrorists. Some of the more violent attacks are detailed here:

October 27, 2003. Coordinated suicide bomb attacks in Baghdad kill 43 people and wound more than 200; police stations and offices of the Red Crescent are targeted.

February 10, 2004. A car bomb explodes in front of a police station in Baghdad, killing 50 and wounding 50.

February 11, 2004. A car bomb explodes outside an Iraqi Army recruiting station, killing 46.

Increase Your Iraq IQ

The Red Crescent is the Muslim equivalent of the Red Cross. In fact, the two organizations are closely tied, and call themselves the "International Order of the Red Cross and Red Crescent"

March 2, 2004. Explosions target Shia Muslims in Baghdad and Karbala on the holiest day in the Shia Muslim calendar, killing 180 people.

The attacks on police stations and army recruitment centers were a deliberate strategy to warn people that if they cooperated with the U.S.-led coalition they ran the risk of being murdered.

Terror Tactic 2: Disrupt the Recovery

Terrorists and other insurgents also attacked economic and infrastructure targets, in order to discredit the reconstruction process and weaken the power of the interim government by prolonging its inability to provide for the needs of the Iraqi people.

The terrorists and insurgents who perpetrate these attacks do damage on two levels:

♦ They damage physical plants and vital equipment.

♦ They frighten off foreign technical experts, whose skills are critical to maintaining and upgrading the aging power grid, water supply, irrigation systems, sewers and roads and bridges.

These groups launched repeated attacks on oil pipelines throughout the country, as well as on water treatment facilities, hospitals, and power lines. As noted earlier in the book, there were just not enough Coalition troops to go around, and until the Iraqi forces could be deployed (a process still in its earliest stages as of this writing) a great deal of the critical infrastructure in the country was left vulnerable to attack.

Increase Your Iraq IQ
We are ashamed because these terrorists carried out this revolting and inhumane act in the name of our religion and culture. This disgusting brutality can never be justified and has nothing to do with Islam or with our Arab values. We pray for [the Berg family] to find the courage and strength to deal with their loss." —United Arab Emirate Information Minister Sheikh Abdullah bin Zayed al-Nahayan

Western businessmen and technicians, as well as truck drivers and lawyers, became targets of the terrorists. An American entrepreneur, Nicholas Berg, was kidnapped and later beheaded. The terrorists recorded the whole event on film, and posted it on the Internet. (Berg had been warned to leave Iraq by the U.S. army, who had even detained him for a few days because he kept traveling to dangerous areas.)

The tactic worked to a great extent, as technicians from firms like Siemans and General Electric were pulled out of the country when the situation became too dangerous. With them went much needed expertise to aid the reconstruction.

Remove the UN

The terrorists also wanted to get the UN out of Iraq. A stable UN presence would lend credibility to the interim government, and hasten the reconstruction. On August 20, 2003, a truck bomb exploded at UN Headquarters in Baghdad, killing 20 people, including the chief UN envoy, Sergio Vieira de Mello, and injuring more than 100. Witnesses report that Mello was trapped in the rubble alive for hours before he died. On October 31, 2003, the UN withdrew its staff from Baghdad, citing the deterioration of security conditions. The UN would not return formally until July 2004, when new envoy Ashraf Jehangir Qazi, the former Ambassador for Pakistan to the United States, took his post.

Terror Tactic 3: Take the Fight to the Home Front

The terrorists also have been committing very violent, highly publicized, acts of terror in order to sway the citizens of the Coalition partners.

The terrorists have conducted operations of global reach, utilizing the Internet and Arab and Western media to broadcast their murderous acts across the globe. The terrorist hope that by literally terrorizing the folks at home, they can induce their governments to leave Iraq.

The public spectacle aspect of the attacks is a critical component to their effect. Terrorism works when single acts create a climate that forces a nation or people to accede to the terrorists' demands.

As of this writing, such tactics are proving surprisingly successful. Although just about every government says it will not negotiate with terrorists, or let terrorists determine their national course of action, at least two Coalition partners have bowed to the terrorists' demands and pulled their troops out of Iraq.

> **Increase Your Iraq IQ**
>
> I think that the press made him much more capable, much smarter and much more of a threat than actually he really is
>
> —Jordan's King Abdullah II, referring to Abu Musab Al-Zarqawi on July 18, 2004. Al-Zarqawi is believed to have masterminded a terror attack on the Jordanian Embassy in Iraq, which killed 10 people in 2003.

Spanish Fly

In the worst act of terror on a Western nation since September 11, 2001, al Qaeda blew up a train in Madrid on March 11, 2004, killing more than 200 people. The attack was intended to influence the upcoming Spanish national elections, and it worked. The ruling conservative Popular Party, under Prime Minister Jose Maria Aznar, had been a member of the U.S.-led Coalition, but the Spanish involvement in Iraq had not been popular with the Spanish people. Three days after the Madrid train attack, the citizens voted out the Popular Party, choosing the Socialist Party to rule in its place. The new Spanish Prime Minister, Jose Luis Rodriguez Zapatero, immediately announced that Spanish forces would be withdrawn from Iraq unless the United Nations assumed control. The UN was not in a position to act that swiftly, if at all, and so the Spanish withdrew their 1,300 troops later in April 2004.

Philippines Follow

In early July 2004, al Qaeda leader Abu Musab al-Zarqawi's followers announced that they had taken a 46-year-old truck driver, Angelo de la Cruz, hostage. They threatened to behead de la Cruz unless the Philippines government withdrew their forces by the end of July 2004. After initially refusing to do so, the Philippines government reversed its position, and acquiesced to the terrorists' demands. The 51 Filipino humanitarian troops were withdrawn on July 20, 2004, and de la Cruz was released unharmed. Not every Coalition country was so easily cowed. In June 2004, al-Zarqawi's follower kidnapped a South Korean translator, Kim Sun-il. He was beheaded after the South Korean government refused to withdraw from the Coalition.

The Terrorists Grow Bolder

Terrorism has been extended to include warning off other Arab and Muslim nations from participating in the reconstruction of Iraq. On July 20, 2004, the Unification and Jihad (the group led by al Qaeda operative al-Zarqawi) issued statements directly warning Muslim nations like Indonesia (with the largest Muslim population in the world) and Turkey, and the Arab nations, not to support Iraq's recovery, stating "… And for Arab and Muslim forces, we advise you not to obey if you are forced to be sent to Iraq and if you don't, then, the laden cars will be waiting for you and we will not stop."

Fresh on the heels of the Philippines' withdrawal of its 50 humanitarian forces from Iraq, Al-Zarqawi's Unification and Jihad terrorists then threatened Japan (who had 550 humanitarian troops in Iraq in July 2004) with the same fate:

> Do like what the Philippines did. No one will help you if you don't and we will not forgive or disregard anybody who came to Iraq. You didn't come to support the Iraqi people but to protect the Americans; your fate will be exactly the same as the Americans and others.

The end result of the terrorists' strategies in Iraq is that the United States finds itself increasingly alone as it wrestles with the problems of reconstructing Iraq of setting the fledgling new Iraqi government on its own course. Many analysts agree that the terrorism now being visited on Iraqi government officials, the Iraqi people, and the Coalition forces and civilian contractors ultimately will not stop the reconstruction process. Nevertheless, the terrorists are increasing the misery of all involved. Ironically, the Bush administration was right after all; Iraq has indeed become a hotbed of terrorism.

Rebuilding Iraq's Infrastructure

The difficulties created by the terrorist and Sunni and Shiite insurgents have certainly complicated the reconstruction of Iraq. Billions of dollars of aid, much of it from the United States, has poured in to Iraq to pay for rebuilding the nation's infrastructure. In a campaign that was designed to win the hearts and minds of the Iraqi people, the results have been uneven.

On the public relations side, even this massive reconstruction effort drew criticism from Iraqis and traditional U.S. allies. Simply put, the Coalition Provisional Authority (CPA) did not spread the wealth around enough to satisfy very many people. On December 9, 2003, Deputy Secretary of Defense Paul Wolfowitz issued an order prohibiting French, German, Canadian, Mexican, Chinese, and Russian companies from bidding on contracts for the rebuilding of Iraq. Only U.S. and Coalition country companies were going to be allowed to bid. Even Iraqi companies were not allowed to bid initially. While that policy changed in 2004, it generated even more ill will in the international community.

Why did the CPA adopt this tactic? The United States was rewarding its allies in the Coalition, and punishing those who had not supported the war. As for the Iraqi companies not being allowed to participate, that decision was based largely on the fact that those companies had been run by Ba'thist administrators. In the de-Ba'thification drive, these companies were excluded. Even with the limited number of companies involved, Iraqi reconstruction has had an immediate positive impact on hundreds of thousands of Iraqis. Over one-half million new jobs were created in Iraq, for Iraqis, by the time the CPA handed authority over to the interim government.

Every Bit Helps

Efforts to rebuild Iraq came on several levels. Foreign firms under contract, local Iraqi organizations, and even U.S. troops on their own initiative worked on reconstruction projects. In one case, the 1st Cavalry Division, based in Baghdad, set up a program to rebuild Iraqi schools. They made a grassroots appeal to the folks at home, and as of this writing, more than 235 tons of school supplies, toys, teddy bears, and sports equipment had been donated by thousands of Americans, all shipped to Iraq via Parcel Post, in over 19,000 boxes. Ironically, these same soldiers who would help rebuild Iraq elementary education one day would be called upon to battle insurgents the next.

Increase Your Iraq IQ

The program [rebuilding Iraqi schools] is going strong. As you would expect, the pace of the transition to authority to the Iraqi people and the training of a New Iraqi Army is a high priority for our unit. Your impact will be felt for years to come, as the children you help through your donations become adults in a free Iraq. The looks on the faces of the kids as they receive pencils, pens, paper, crayons, soccer balls, Frisbees, stuffed animals, toys, and other items is a motivating factor in this country for the men of the 1st Squadron, 7th U.S. Cavalry, 1st Cavalry Division. In the past three months the Officers, Non Commissioned Officers and Troopers of this Squadron, have ridden an emotional roller coaster when it comes to the execution of this mission in Iraq. What most people don't realize is that on a daily basis we are shot at, Improvised Explosive Devices (IED) are detonated or found, soldiers are wounded, and on May 15, 2004 SSG Rene Ledesma was killed as he was conducting a reconnaissance patrol in Baghdad. Even with this happening your sons and daughters continue to make an impact on the children of this country. The pain of the loss makes it all the more important to get this country back on track so that their blood was not shed in vain."

—Letter from Major Nate Hines, 1st Cavalry Division, on *www.iraqischools.com*

Even Better Is Not Good Enough

The major reconstruction programs in Iraq have made some successes, but the manner in which they have been implemented has alienated many of the Sunnis, and failed to impress many of the Shiites. A bellwether for the recovery is the availability of electric power in Iraq. Media reports show disgruntled Iraqis in Baghdad, complaining about the fact that electric power still had not been restored to pre-war levels as of mid-2004. This was true, but the details tell a different story.

The Iraqi Government website (www.iraqcoalition.org) posted the following questions and answers, to respond to criticisms that the power restoration program was failing:

QUESTION: If there is more power today, why do Iraqis only have 8–12 hours of power in their homes?

ANSWER: With more than half a million new jobs created, new industries and new factories coming on line and with the sale of thousands of home appliances such as washing machines and air conditioners, Iraq has experienced a rapid increase in electricity demand. The increase in demand is a good sign of a thriving economy emerging out from three decades of isolation. As demand continues to increase, the Ministry of Electricity will continue to work to increase the nation's available power. Nearly one billion dollars has already been allocated with several billion more coming from the US Congress to help improve the supply of electricity throughout Iraq.

QUESTION: People in Baghdad constantly speak of how things were better under Saddam. How do you counter these claims?

ANSWER: It is important to remember that under Saddam, those loyal to his regime were the benefactors of all of the nation's riches. Electricity is yet another example of how Saddam used everything in Iraq as a weapon against those opposed to his regime. Before the liberation, Saddam drained power from throughout the country to feed Baghdad, leaving more than 80% of the country to fend for themselves with private generators and the whatever power they could scrape together from the grid. Even with this unfair system of power, Saddam was only able to power Baghdad 20-22 hours a day. After the liberation, the power system was redistributed equitably throughout the nation.

Basically, sharing the electricity more equally means the Sunnis in Baghdad have less than they enjoyed under Saddam. But the Shiites have a great deal more than they ever did under Hussein. The perception, inside Iraq and in the media, is that the electricity program is failing. Although there have been significant setbacks, due to sabotage by insurgents, loss of outside expertise due to terrorism, and the problems of working with an antiquated infrastructure, the program is succeeding in bringing electricity to the Iraqi people. The same combination of losses holds true in water treatment, sewerage, roads, and irrigation. These losses combine to create the impression that the Iraqi government is ineffective, the very goal of those who oppose the Coalition occupation. Keeping the lights on, in more places, for more of the time, will be a critical indicator of the chances for success for the interim government. The public focus on electricity is one of the reasons the power system is such a terrorist target.

Thanks for Nothing

Even providing services like electricity won't necessarily win over the hearts and minds of the people. The deep resentment toward occupying troops, the frustration with the pace of recovery, and the constant violence outweigh a working air conditioner. Even in Shiite areas, where people are seeing the first decent services in decades, there is scant praise for the Coalition engineers or the progress that is being made by the new government. These people have suffered through years of deprivation and now toil under the weight of occupation and uncertainty, and it will take much to overcome the hostility created in that environment.

Not Fast Enough

Despite the massive rebuilding efforts, the slow pace of recovery, and the continued battles between insurgents and Coalition troops, and repeated of terror attacks, have taken a tremendous toll in Iraq. Noncombatant civilians are caught in the crossfire during fire-fights in the streets, and they are killed or maimed when car bombs explode. They also suffer from disease, injuries, inadequate medical facilities, and contaminated drinking water. Estimates of the number of civilian deaths in Iraq since March 2003 (just prior to the start of Operation Iraqi Freedom) to July 2004, range in the high tens of thousands.

Unexploded ordinance (UXO), most of which was dropped from Coalition aircraft during the war and failed to detonate, are a serious hazard and have caused thousands of casualties among soldiers and civilians alike.

Along with the unexploded bombs, there are literally piles of weapons and ammunition scattered around the country. Some was abandoned by retreating Iraqi Army troops, some was cached by insurgents or terrorists, and some are of unknown origin. These old weapons and shells are just as dangerous as the unexploded ordinance that are still being uncovered.

Old ammunition stashes are scattered throughout the country.

Progress Amidst the Destruction

Despite it all, progress is being made on the reconstruction of Iraqi infrastructure. This progress is critical to the establishment of a stable government and civil society in Iraq along the lines envisioned by the Bush administration. Without adequate electricity, food, water, and services, a new government can never succeed. Even with those services, as we will see in the next chapter, success for the new government is still in doubt.

The Least You Need to Know

- The Bush administration cited terrorism as one of the reasons for toppling Saddam Hussein.

- Rather than be wiped out, terrorism has taken hold in Iraq, and galvanized support from across the Muslim Middle East.

- The terrorists have succeeded in eroding the U.S.-led Coalition.

- Rebuilding is going slow, but progress is being made in the restoration of critical services.

- The plight of the Iraqi civilian is improving, but not quickly enough to suit most of the people.

Chapter 24

Independent Iraq

In This Chapter

- ◆ The Iraqi interim government and a new Constitution
- ◆ The delicate balancing act between Shiites, Sunnis, and Kurds
- ◆ The delicate balancing act between tribal leaders, clerics, and Central Authority
- ◆ The question of the clerics

In Chapter 23, we looked at the attacks perpetrated by external terrorist movements operating inside Iraq, and the effect of those attacks on shaky Coalition allies. We also saw how the reconstruction of Iraq is moving ahead slowly. We also saw how the realities of reconstruction often were obscured by incomplete media coverage and personal biases for or against the Coalition and its role in Iraq. Through all of this insurgency, terrorism, and rebuilding, the Interim Iraqi Government has begun to assert its role on the road to an independent Iraq. In this chapter, we'll take a look at the Interim Iraqi Government, and the critical elements at play in an independent Iraq.

The Interim Government's Difficult Heritage

In late June 2003, as the chaos of post-Saddam Iraq continued to grow, Coalition military officials demanded that the spontaneous local elections and self-government efforts in cities and towns across Iraq be stopped. The Coalition commanders wanted to halt the local elections for the following reasons:

◆ They were wary of a local leader calling for open resistance to the occupation troops.

◆ They wanted leaders they could work with.

◆ They wanted to ensure that the new interim government would not have to overcome a group of autonomous leaders across the provinces.

One of the many damaged portraits of Saddam Hussein in Iraq. During his regime, portraits and statues of Saddam were everywhere, even wristwatches!

Instead of allowing local elections, the Coalition appointed administrators as leaders in provincial governments to replace Ba'th officials who had been appointed under Hussein. Because many new appointees were regarded as pawns of the occupying forces, these new appointees had a difficult task. The results of this move were mixed. The Coalition got their network of cooperative administrators, but they also encountered stiffening resistance. Why? Basically, there already was a network of autonomous leaders in Iraq. The Coalition had ignored where the real local authority is in Iraq ... the tribal leaders.

The Role of Tribal Leadership

As we have seen earlier in this book, Iraq is a tribal society. The tribal leaders hold local power, and when they are allied with the central government, they can extend that government's power into remote reaches of the country. Saddam even relied on local tribal leaders to patrol remote Iraqi borders, rather than trying to do it with border guards.

The leaders of the tribes hold the real power at the local level, and they can make or break national policies at the local level. Even Saddam Hussein had to accommodate the tribal leaders in the aftermath of the first Gulf War, when his central power was weakest. The Coalition authorities neglected to incorporate local leaders' opinions into their earliest appointments, and ended up alienating these powerful and critical voices.

From Saddam to a New Government

Initially, the tribal elders were not considered in the reconstruction process. The steps originally envisioned between the fall of Hussein government and a fully independent, democratic government included a series of transitional bodies leading to a permanent Iraqi government, as follows:

- Coalition Provisional Authority (CPA) (May 2003–June 2004)

- Interim *Governing Council* (July 2003–June 2004)

- Interim Iraqi Government (July 2004–January 2005)

- Iraqi National Congress (to "advise" the interim government in the run up to national elections) (August 2004–January 2005)

- New, democratically elected Iraqi Government (January 2005–   )

Desert Diction

The **Governing Council** was a group of 25 prominent Iraqi men and women who advised the Coalition Provisional Authority (CPA) on the development of the Transitional Authority Law (also called the interim constitution). The Governing Council was disbanded on June 28, 2004, when power was handed over by the CPA to the Iraq interim government.

The CPA created the 25-member Interim Governing Council and announced the members on July 13, 2003. The members were drawn from all segments of Iraqi society and included a number of exiles who had returned after Saddam's fall. The notorious Ahmed Chalabi was appointed to the Governing Council, but was later implicated in a scheme to send information to the Iranians. U.S. troops raided his house looking for evidence, and an outraged Chalabi denounced the CPA.

Oil Spill Ahead

Dr. Ahmed Chalabi was the leader of the Iraqi National Congress (INC), an Iraqi exile group during the Saddam era. Chalabi was a controversial figure in the years prior to Operation Iraqi Freedom. The Pentagon gave great weight to Chalabi's "intelligence" regarding Saddam's weapons programs, while the State Department had a more cautious view of his claims. Chalabi, a Shiite, was already on the defensive due to the bad intel he had passed to the Bush administration, when the accusations that he was forwarding sensitive information to Iran surfaced in early 2004. Chalabi has been cut out of any role in the Interim Iraqi Government that replaced the Governing Council. As of this writing, Chalabi was facing potential extradition to Jordan, where he is wanted on suspicion of bank fraud. The U.S. government has ended the monthly payments of $335,000 it was making to the INC.

Hasty Handover

On November 15, 2003, the Coalition Provisional Authority announced its intention to hand sovereignty over to an interim Iraqi government by June 30, 2004. The transfer of sovereignty did not equate to a withdrawal of Coalition troops, who will remain in Iraq for 5 to 10 more years, according to the Coalition and interim government leaders. In addition, the nature of the "sovereignty" to be transferred to the Iraqis is vague. It is unclear, for instance, what will happen if the newly sovereign Iraqi government were to demand that Coalition forces leave Iraq.

Ambassador L. Paul Bremer reads the Iraqi Sovereignty document at a ceremony held in the Iraqi interim government building in Baghdad, Iraq, transferring full governmental authority to the Iraqi interim government, June 28, 2004. Those present at the ceremony include Iraqi Prime Minister Ayad Allawi (left, hidden), UK Special Representative David Richmond, and Iraqi President Sheikh Ghazi Ajil al-Yawar (right).

(DoD photo by Staff Sgt. D. Myles Cullen, U.S. Air Force.)

On February 19, 2004, the UN announced that it agreed with the Coalition transfer plan. Because of the threat of particularly intense violence on June 30, 2004, the CPA passed authority to the Interim Iraqi Government two days early, on June 28, 2004. The transfer went smoothly, and although there were outbreaks of violence, it was less than anticipated.

The Interim Government

Gradually, as the summer of 2004 wore on, the Iraqi government began to assert more control over its own affairs and more authority over its country. For example ...

◆ The interim government has formed a small cadre of security troops (unlike the earlier groups of reluctant police) that are taking over security patrols in sensitive areas.

◆ The government took custody of Saddam Hussein in July 2004, and is prosecuting him in Iraqi courts. The trial of Saddam is a powerful symbol of the new government's authority.

◆ The government authorized a Coalition air strike on a terrorist safe house in Fallujah in late July 2004, showing its willingness to prosecute the war on foreign terrorists in Iraq by whatever means available.

◆ In August, 2004, the government negotiated an apparent end to the fighting in Najaf, by getting Shiite insurgents to agree to stop fighting and join the political process.

Iraqi National Guard (ING) soldiers walk to the next residency to search in Mosul, Iraq on July 3, 2004. The Iraqi police and the Iraqi National Guard are conducting the search, while U.S. Army units remain outside of town in supporting positions.

(U.S.Army photo by Sgt. Jeremiah Johnson)

Prime Minister Ayad Allawi also showed his ability to incorporate the tribal leadership into the interim government. The crucial ministries of Defense, Interior, and the Intelligence head are all former tribal leaders, whose appointment shows a commitment to the importance of the tribes in the future security of Iraq. However, Allawi did not include any leaders from the Sunni tribes in the Anbar Province (the location of Fallujah and a Sunni stronghold), notably the powerful Delaimi tribe. Some experts believe that if the interim government included representative of those Anbar-based tribes, the insurgency in Fallujah would diminish. These experts also believe that if the tribal leaders did not want Syrian, Saudi and Jordanian terrorist operating on their turf, the terrorists would be gone. But, given the close ties the Anbar tribes had to Saddam Hussein, it was apparently impossible for Allawi to bring them into the interim government.

What Kind of Government?

The Interim Government is charged with laying the groundwork for a lasting democracy in Arab, Muslim Iraq. But what does Arab-Muslim democracy look like? The answer is that nobody knows, because there are no Arab, Muslim democracies. The CPA and the governing council were trying to frame a government that has no precedent. Perhaps the inclusion of a strong religious role (while contrary to Western notions of the separation of Church and State) is an essential element for this democracy. In the same way, it could be that the recognition of the traditional role of the local tribal leadership is also required for the government to last. The real challenge will come once the constitution starts to face its first tests and legal challenges. Amendments will no doubt be offered, and some accepted and some rejected in heated debates. One only has to consider the first years of the United States to get an idea of what awaits the Iraqis.

We the People?

The CPA, in consultation with the interim governing council, had designed the interim constitution for Iraq. It was formalized and adopted on March 8, 2004. This constitution attempts to accommodate the major powers in Iraq: Shiites, Kurds, clerics, and tribal leaders (making amends for the initial error of ignoring the tribal leaders). Only the Sunni are not specifically accommodated, as they were not even that involved in the creation of the document. Still, the Sunni are not explicitly denied any rights, though they are denied the relative amount of power they once held.

The interim Iraqi constitution enters uncharted waters, which could prove perilous for the new ship of state. The new constitution must deal with the following elements:

- The existence of an autonomous region (Kurdistan) inside the country's borders

- The need to accommodate two main languages (Arabic and Kurdish) as well as a range of smaller languages

- The need to explicitly acknowledge the authority of a religion (Islam) in the state

- The need to exclude specific groups (former Ba'thists) from participation in the government.

The framers of the interim Iraqi constitution can look to other examples of national parliaments with autonomous regions (the UK government and the Scottish parliament come to mind). They can look at other models for how to accommodate language and ethnicity (the Canadian parliament and the official status of French alongside English, and the relative powers granted to Quebec). Most constitutional models do *not* explicitly acknowledge the authority of a religion in the new state, but given the power of the Shiite clerics, the new Iraqi interim constitution does. In addition, the new constitution deliberately excludes individuals who were Ba'th Party members (even though many of these people could be effective members of a new government), and it also excludes individuals who perpetrated the official oppression of the Shiites and Kurds. So, while there may be some examples of constitutions that address specific issues of a society, the Iraq Constitution is rare in that it must address all of the issues in one framework.

The Iraqi Constitution

The interim Constitution defines a system of Prime Minister and Council of Ministers, a National Assembly, and independent Judiciary, and a ceremonial President. The Constitution also acknowledges a role for local tribal leaders (through regional "governates") and the clerics (by recognizing Islam as the official religion of the state). The Constitution also guarantees education for men and women, and equal rights for both sexes.

The Shiite Reaction to the Interim Constitution

Grand Ayatollah Sistani issued a fatwa (religious opinion) criticizing the new constitution, but later called upon Shiites to support the interim Iraqi government. Sistani may have been reacting to the violence being created by Moqtada al-Sadr's radical followers, whose continued resistance threatened to destroy Iraq's recovery. At any rate, Sistani's fatwa and the attention it gained from the Shiite community showed the delicate balance of power that exists between the government, the tribal leaders, and the clerics. Under Saddam, the clerics had little political influence, and generally kept a low profile. It is interesting to note that al-Sadr's father, himself an influential Shiite cleric, was murdered under the Hussein regime. As of this writing, most of the Shiite imams are following the call of Grand Ayatollah Sistani, and are cooperating with the interim government. Moqtada al-Sadr and his Mehdi army are the notable exception. Al-Sadr has refused to meet with the Interim Government. Al-Sadr's resistance aside, the new Constitution does acknowledge the role of Islam in Iraqi society.

Increase Your Iraq IQ

Article 7 of the Interim Constitution:

(a) Islam is the official religion of the State and is to be considered a source of legislation. No law that contradicts the universally agreed tenets of Islam, the principles of democracy, or the rights cited in Chapter Two of this Law may be enacted during the transitional period. This Law respects the Islamic identity of the majority of the Iraqi people and guarantees the full religious rights of all individuals to freedom of religious belief and practice.

♦ Iraq is a country of many nationalities, and the Arab people in Iraq are an inseparable part of the Arab nation.

The New Government's Delicate Dance

Article 7 of the interim constitution acknowledges the wishes of the Shiite clerics by asserting the primacy of Islam. It also acknowledges that Iraq is a part of the "Arab nation." (Despite the fact that there is a large minority of Kurds in the north).

As of this writing, the government and the Shiite clerics remain in tacit cooperation. Not only did the interim government flex its muscles regarding Sunni insurgents and al Qaeda terrorists in the Sunni Triangle, it also showed its commitment to bringing other Shiite power groups into the process. Still, the interim government is building its own authority in Iraq, and is attempting to enforce that authority (albeit with US military backing). For example, Prime Minister Allawi reopened Moqtada al-Sadr's outspoken al-Hawza newspaper in July 2004, which the CPA had ordered shut down in 2003. The move was not popular with the United States, but it showed the interim government's willingness to start on its own path of assembling a mainstream power base that includes the Shiite plurality of conservatives (like Sistani) and radicals (like al-Sadr). At the same time, Allawi's government took the lead in declaring al-Sadr and his followers who were holed up in the *Imam Ali Mosque* in Najaf to be outlaws, and committed to removing them by force if negotiations did not succeed. Eventually, al-Sadr's followers did leave the Mosque, after a deal initially brokered by Grand Ayatollah Sistani, with the support of Allawi (and heavily armored U.S. troops).

> **Desert Diction**
>
> The **Imam Ali Mosque** in Najaf is considered one of the holiest sites in Shia Islam. Ali, Mohammed's cousin and son-in-law, is buried there. Shia comes from the Arabic term "Shiat Ali" or "followers of Ali." The Shiites believe that only descendents of Ali can be the imam, or leader of the Faithful.

Certainly, al-Sadr's supporters do not speak for all the Iraqi Shiite's, even in the restive city of Najaf. According to *The Guardian* newspaper, when al-Sistani's followers finally left the Mosque area, Iraq security forces found a room filled with 20 rotting corpses (including one with a noose around its neck), a makeshift dungeon, and scared civilians who, in *The Guardian*'s words, referred to a "reign of terror" under the Mehdi Army. It would appear that Allawi is attempting to deal not only with al-Sadr, but with any other radical cleric who may emerge once al-Sadr is neutralized (or killed). By taking a firm hand on the illegality of open insurrection, while still allowing a public debate (and being careful not to damage the Mosque in combat) the interim Iraqi government is staking its claim to being the legitimate authority in Iraq. This balancing act will continue through the elections in January 2005 and beyond.

Balancing Act A: Sunni-Shiite-Kurd

As we have seen, Iraq is not a monolithic state. It is an uneasy combination of Sunni Arabs, Shiite Arabs, and Kurds, with a scattering of smaller minorities, all lumped together in a country that was assembled by a foreign power (the British combining the old Baghdad and Basra vilayets of the Ottoman Empire), and later augmented with more territory because of the oil that lay beneath it (the British adding the Mosul vilayet). The groups that inhabit these areas have mixed allegiances, often to peoples living across the borders of neighboring countries rather than to their fellow Iraqi citizens. The Shiites in the Basra area are more sympathetic in many ways to the Iranian Shiites across the border (even if those Shiites are Persian, and not Arab). The Kurds in the Mosul area have a greater affinity for the Kurds in Iran, Turkey, and Syria. In fact, many of these Kurds feel that they deserve their own nation. (Remember our discussion of Kurdistan in Chapter 2).

So if Iraq is so divisive, how has it stayed together so far? Basically, the country has been held together through the cohesive force of dictatorships. Even before the rise of the Ba'th regime, Iraq was ruled by a king, with an ineffective parliament. After the Ba'th came to power, Ahmed Hassan al Bakr and Saddam Hussein were particularly effective and brutal rulers.

In the tribal system of Iraq, that meant empowering and rewarding those closest to them, in Saddam's case the Tikriti tribe. Tribes who supported Saddam got some of the goodies. Any rivals were destroyed. As it played out, that meant the Shiites and Kurds were brutally suppressed (remember, it was Saddam who used poison gas on the Kurds, and was draining the marshes in Faw to destroy the Shiite "Marsh Arab" culture), and even rival Sunni tribes were punished. The rule was one of force, which resulted in a sort of stability inside Iraq, but by no means a calm one.

So Iraq was united by force, and held together by force, which poses a fundamental challenge to democracy. Typically, democracies require the willing consent of the governed, and the willing participation of the various interest groups involved. When that willing collaboration is not there, civil war usually results. These civil wars can either strengthen the democratic union or signal the beginning of a slide into chaos. The critical factor is whether the various factions are willing to cooperate in trying to make the new government work.

Let's take a look at what the three groups in Iraq are facing today.

Sunnis: Nothing to Lose But Their Losses

The minority Sunnis need to gain something, or else they will not participate in the new regime. If the new regime becomes a framework for Shiite revenge against the Sunnis, the Sunnis would resist the new regime with all they have. Even if the new government simply allocated resources more equitably, the Sunnis would be unhappy, because they traditionally had enjoyed the most and the best, while the rest of the country had to make do. Saddam was a Sunni, and the Sunnis generally enjoyed the best access to resources and opportunity during Saddam's regime. Think of it like a series of concentric rings: Saddam and his closest supporters in the very center, the Tikriti tribe in the next ring, supporting Sunni tribes in the next ring, all other Sunnis in the next ring, then Shiites and Kurds on the outside. While certainly not secure under Saddam, the Sunnis were at least not afraid of Shiite reprisals, because Saddam's secret police kept close watch and a tight lid on everybody.

With Saddam gone, the Sunnis are reacting to the political changes based upon which ring they occupied. Saddam's closest followers and his Tikriti clansmen have reacted with the most violence against a new regime (and the occupying troops which support it), with the rest of the Sunnis taking a less violent stance, but still looking for protection and willing to fight for it. With the exclusion of the three Sunni tribes that occupy Anbar Province, the Sunni insurgency has remained potent, and probably will remain so unless the majority of Sunnis feel they have a stake in the new order of things.

The Sunnis might also fear reprisals, through direct attacks or indirect policies and legislation, under a more representative democracy. The centuries-old pattern of Shiite repression and Sunni reward has exacerbated deep-seated religious tensions, and layered the motive of revenge on top. In the post-Saddam era, the urge to settle the score against previous tormentors who killed a son, a wife, a husband, or a child constantly threatens to reignite bloodshed. The Sunnis probably have little faith yet in the new government and are suspicious of the greater Shiite role in that government.

Shiites: Taking Power or Sharing It?

Before the majority Shiites can address the issue of how much power they will hold in the new Iraqi state, they have to resolve two other issues:

◆ Can they speak with one voice, and who will speak for them—clerics or secular leaders?

◆ Can they manage Iranian pressures and intrigues that might tear down the new state edifice?

The Shiites are not a single block, but a range of interests. (No doubt, the Sunnis include many viewpoints, too. Historically, however, the Sunnis have presented a more unified front, and are only more united under the current threat to their traditional power role.) The Shiites need to determine if they will rally behind any single point of view and whether that point of view will be religious or secular in its tone. That ordering process will be played out over several years, and may never be finalized, particularly if a truly democratic system is established. Instead, we might see a number of Shiite political parties emerge, representing the spectrum of Shiite viewpoints. The more fractured the Shiite bloc, the more power the Sunnis will be able to wield in a new democratic government.

The clerics are important players in the Shiite community. Grand Ayatollah Sistani wields a great deal of influence over a large segment of Iraqi Shiites. His statements will go a long way toward defining Shiite support for or against the Interim Iraqi Government. Also influential is the leadership of Iran. Many Shiites in Iraq see the Shiite Iranian leadership as a champion of their concerns. The Iranian government has focused on supporting Shiite clerics who are sympathetic to the Iranian view. In post-Saddam Iraq, that might mean supporting clerics who oppose the interim government if the new government does not align itself with Iranian goals. As we will see in the next chapter, Iran is applying pressure on the Iraqi Shiites through agents and aid that it sends to specific groups in Shiite Iraq.

Whither the Kurds?

The Kurds find themselves once again on the verge of being left out. Long oppressed under Saddam's regime, the Kurds enjoyed a period of relative freedom and autonomy under U.S. and UK *No-Fly Zone* protection during the last decade. The Kurds must address the following two questions:

- Are the Kurds better off trying to exist within the new Iraqi state, or falling back on their tradition of resistance to the central authority in Baghdad?

- Who will speak for the Iraqi Kurds?

The Kurds have been able to gain some representation in the new government, including the largely ceremonial post of Deputy President in the Iraqi interim government. Dr. Rowsch Shaways took that position in the new government on June 28, 2004. Prior to that, Dr. Shaways was the Prime Minister of the provisional government in Kurdish Iraq, which assumed control after the U.S.-patrolled no-fly zone prohibited Hussein's troops from operating in the area in 1991. Dr. Shaways was also a member of the Kurdistan Democratic Party. The Minister of Foreign Affairs, Hoshyar Zebari, is also a Kurd. Prior to being named to the interim government in June 2004, Mr. Zebari was a prominent leader of the Kurdistan Democratic Party. The important role of National Security chief was given to Mr. Barham Saleh, a leader in the Patriotic Union of Kurdistan. By naming these three figures to prominent position in the interim government, the United States was hoping to give the Kurds a seat at the table as the new Iraqi state is defined. Even prior to the handover of power on June 28, 2004, the Kurds had threatened to leave the new government unless Prime Minister Allawi confirmed the constitution's commitment to creating an autonomous Kurdish region.

The challenge the Kurds face, along with simply getting a piece of the action in the new government, is whether they will be able to maintain a unified voice in that national government. Right now, the January 2005 election deadline calls for a National parliament to be elected, but it also recognizes a Kurdish regional assembly. The idea of the regional assembly is to give the Kurds more direct control over their local affairs, plus it acknowledges the fact that the Kurdistan National Assembly has existed for over a decade, and the Kurds are not willing to give it up. The interim constitution guarantees the Kurds autonomy, but it remains to be seen how this autonomy will be exercised once the national elections take place.

Article 54 of the interim constitution states:

> (a) The Kurdistan Regional Government shall continue to perform its current functions throughout the transitional period, except with regard to those issues which fall within the exclusive competence of the federal government as specified in this Law. Financing for these functions shall come from the federal government, consistent with current practice and in accordance with Article 25(e) of this Law. The Kurdistan Regional Government shall retain regional control over police forces and internal security, and it will have the right to impose taxes and fees within the Kurdistan region.

> (b) With regard to the application of federal laws in the Kurdistan region, the Kurdistan National Assembly shall be permitted to amend the application of any such law within the Kurdistan region, but only to the extent that this relates to matters that are not within the provisions of Articles 25 and 43(d) of this Law and that fall within the exclusive competence of the federal government.

Desert Diction

The Kurdistan Democratic Party (KDP) and the Patriotic Union of Kurdistan (PUK) are the two main organizations that represent Kurds in Iraq. These two groups have jockeyed for power, sometimes violently, over the years.

The Kurds will have their regional control, but exerting power on the national level will be a different story. Only time will tell if the Kurds are able to maintain autonomy at the national level, particularly if they do not vote as a single bloc in the new National Assembly that will be elected in January 2005. Given their relatively smaller numbers, if the voice for the Kurds in the new national parliament is split along the traditional rivalry of the *Patriotic Union of Kurdistan (PUK)* and the Kurdistan Democratic Party (PDK) the Sunnis and Shiites would be able to legislate the Kurds into a secondary role.

Balancing Act B: Tribal Leader-Cleric-Central Authority

The interim government is also faced with the fact that two traditional power bases exist in Iraq, and that these existed long before Saddam Hussein or the Hashemite monarchs ever ruled. These two constants in Iraqi society are the tribal leaders and the clerics.

A Nod to the Inevitable: Power Granted to the Local Leader

As we have seen, the CPA made the initial mistake of appointing their own people provincial leadership roles, and not consulting with the local tribal elders. Having learned its lesson, the Iraqi interim government was set up with these tribal leaders in mind. The powerful position of Defense Minister was given to Hazem Shalan al-Khuzaei, a tribal leader from Diwaniyah province (and former exile from the Hussein era). Prime Minister Allawi has also been careful to acknowledge the role played by the local leadership, hoping to shore up the government's authority and capabilities.

The interim constitution also recognized the role of the local authorities in the daily life of most Iraqis. Article 55 spells out the local authority granted to the 18 provincial "governates" of Iraq:

> *(a) Each governorate shall have the right to form a Governorate Council, name a Governor, and form municipal and local councils. No member of any regional government, governor, or member of any governorate, municipal, or local council may be dismissed by the federal government or any official thereof, except upon conviction of a crime by a court of competent jurisdiction as provided by law. No regional government may dismiss a Governor or member or members of any governorate, municipal, or local council. No Governor or member of any Governorate, municipal, or local council shall be subject to the control of the federal government except to the extent that the matter relates to the competences set forth in Article 25 and 43(D), above.*

Bringing the tribal leaders into the new government is crucial. Local enforcement of governmental laws requires the cooperation of the mukhtars (local tribal elders). The societal structure of Iraq gives these individuals enormous influence over daily life on the local level. Even Saddam Hussein, with all of his secret police and enormous army, needed to enlist the support of the mukhtars to help guard Iraqi boarders in the farthest-flung regions of the country.

The Clerics: Give Them an Inch ...

The challenge for Allawi will be to figure out a way to accommodate the Shiite clerics while keeping the Sunnis and Kurds happy. Both of those groups are extremely wary of Shiite dominance of the new government. The Kurds almost bolted from the government in May 2004, and the Sunni have engaged in a steady insurgency against the occupying forces and the new security forces of the interimgovernment. Any perceived signs of Shiite dominance could result in a Kurd withdrawal from the political process and an increased level of Sunni resistance.

If the Shiite clerics wish, they can create considerable havoc in the Shiite areas by calling for jihad against the interim government (and by extension the U.S. occupying forces). The resulting turmoil would effectively destroy the democratic state building process, and probably would result in years of civil war inside Iraq. The stakes for the interim government, and its U.S. supporters, could not be greater.

The Least You Need to Know

- The interim government is beginning to assert its own authority in Iraq, with Coalition military support.

- The delicate balancing act between the three main groups (Sunni, Shiite, and Kurd) is a constant challenge for the fledging government.

- The same delicacy is needed to balance the three powers of tribal leaders, clerics, and central authority as the new government defines is place in the Iraqi state.

- The Shiite clerics are a critical component in the new Iraqi state. They could make or break any democratic process in its earliest stages.

Chapter 25

Iraq's Place in the World

In This Chapter

- ◆ Iraq's fledgling democracy must deal with several factors outside its immediate control

- ◆ Iran is a constant force to be reckoned with

- ◆ U.S. voters' attitudes will significantly impact the new government's chances for success

- ◆ Global oil markets hold the key to a successful recovery

- ◆ The outcome for Iraq is not certain, even with a massive U.S. troop presence

In the previous chapter, we looked at the delicate balancing acts that the interim Iraqi government is forced to perform, if it is to survive and fulfill its constitutional vision. In the chapter, we'll run through the various external factors confronting the new state.

External Factors Play a Major Role

Iraq must continually deal with changes in three main external forces:

- ◆ Iran and its desires to create a pliable state on its border

- U.S. domestic attitudes toward the U.S. role in Iraq

- Global demand for oil, whose revenues finance the state and its recovery

Iranian Intrigue

Iran cannot be ignored. The Iraqis have long defined themselves as the bulwark of the Arab world against the Persians in Iran. However, the common bond of Shia Islam pulls the two countries together. The Iranians exert powerful influence over some groups of Iraqi Shiites, and indirectly the Iranians may even have some sway in the interim government.

One of the traditional opposition groups to Saddam Hussein is the *Supreme Council for Islamic Revolution in Iraq* (SCIRI). Composed of Iraqi Shiite exiles, SCIRI was based in Tehran, and operated against the Hussein regime. SCIRI operatives were present at the end of Operation Iraqi Freedom, and were channeling Iranian resources to various Shiite groups that were sympathetic to the concept of an Islamic Republic in Iraq. SCIRI even created a military wing, known as the Badr Brigade. These fighters were present in Iraq during the closing days of Operation Iraqi Freedom. Adil Abdel-Mahdi, the interim Finance Minister, is a SCIRI member. He was included in the interim Council of Ministers in order to accommodate the more fundamentalist Shiites. SCIRI also owes much to Tehran, and so the Finance Minister in the interim government may feel some sense of affinity toward Iran, or at least sympathy to Iranian objectives.

> **Iraq Fact**
>
> The **Supreme Council for Islamic Revolution in Iraq** (SCIRI) is based in Tehran, but dedicated to the creation of an Islamic state in Iraq. SCIRI has recruited the paramilitary Badr Brigades made up of Iraqi Shiite exiles and deserters during the Saddam era. Coalition troops confronted the Badr Brigade during Operation Iraqi Freedom and expelled them from Iraq.

What Iran Wants

Iran wants to increase its own security. Right now, Iran finds itself facing a U.S.-backed government and U.S. troops in Afghanistan on one side, and a U.S.-backed government and significant U.S. troop presence in Iraq on the other side. Saddam may be gone, the Great Satan (America) is there, with an even more powerful military capability. Iran sees its security in a destabilized Iraq, where U.S. military resources are focused on maintaining stability, and not on threatening Iran. Remember, too, that Iran is pursuing a nuclear weapons development program. The Iranians deny that they are developing weapons, and insist the program is for peaceful purposes, even though the International Atomic Energy Agency of the UN thinks that the Iranians are developing weapons.

How Iran Will Do It

The Iranian leaders (Shiite clerics, mainly) can keep the pressure on Iraq by pushing a radical Shiite agenda in Iraq. The Iranians can assert that pressure by aiding radical Shiite clerics who oppose the new government. This aid can consist of funding, arms, and people. The Iranians can step up this aid any time they choose. It is a constant element that the Iraqi government will have to contend with as they strive to create a stable democracy.

Uncle Sam's Will

The Iraqi government also has to contend with the varying attitudes toward the Iraq occupation in the United States. American voters, and the presidents they elect, may demand a change in the U.S. stance in Iraq. This change could include a more rapid withdrawal from Iraq than the new government would want. At the same time, Iranian intrigues could prolong a larger U.S. military presence in Iraq, which could also be something the interim government does not want.

It is important that the new Iraqi government is not seen as a puppet of the United States, while at the same time, the new Iraqi government needs the U.S. military to help it survive. The Iraqi government cannot influence U.S. voters, but will be heavily dependent upon U.S. voter's desires. If the U.S. electorate demands that U.S. troops come home, the Iraqi government will be left to its own devices. Internal unrest could increase and destroy the fragile democracy.

U.S. interest in Iraq will also be influenced by Iraqi oil. If the Iraqi government can set and maintain a high level of oil exports, global prices should moderate, improving the U.S. economy. If the new government cannot keep the oil flowing (meaning it cannot keep the oil product infrastructure safe from sabotage), higher oil prices will further exasperate the U.S. voter.

Black Gold

The oil is the key. The interim government needs stability to survive. Stability at the end of an American tank muzzle is not sustainable. Stability due to the lack of domestic unrest is sustainable. That kind of stability can only come if the interim

government can sell enough oil to generate the money it needs to finance the reconstruction of the country and its infrastructure. Keeping the lights on, the factories
running, and water flowing will do more to stabilize the country than an extra division of troops. The anger that the insurgents rely on to generate recruits will only
subside when the standard of living improves for the vast majority of Iraqis.

The enemies of the new government also realize this, and so have persistently
attacked the Iraqi oil production, transmission, and export infrastructure. During
August of 2004, saboteurs succeeding more than halving the volume of oil exports
from Iraq. They blew up the main export pipeline from the Kirkuk fields in the
north, and heavily damaged the key pipelines to the Gulf in the south. The new government has to be able to repair and secure the oil infrastructure in order to optimize
oil receipts.

Even if the oil deliveries can be increased, the global demand for oil is outside of the
Iraqis' control. If the global economy contracts, oil demand will drop, and Iraqi oil
receipts will drop. Smaller oil revenues will mean fewer investments in infrastructure,
and potentially more instability. On the other hand, a continued global economic
expansion, with China and India claiming ever larger shares of oil, will keep oil prices
high. Higher prices mean higher oil receipt, and more money for domestic improvements.

An Uncertain Future

Iraq is faced with external factors it cannot control, but must adjust to constantly. Add
in the current domestic unrest, the agendas of the terrorists, insurgents, and radical
Shiites, and the future of the Iraqi state is murky indeed.

Some possible outcomes for the new Iraq include …

- A democracy (tumultuous and vibrant, rather than quiet)
- An Islamic republic
- The new Beirut
- TCFKAI (The Country Formerly Known As Iraq)
- An acceptable dictatorship

Let's consider each of the possible scenarios.

Democratic Beacon?

One pillar of the Bush Doctrine is the creation and strengthening of democracy worldwide. The idea is that with U.S. military, economic, and technical backing, truly democratic institutions can take hold in countries around the world, even Iraq. The theory is that a democratic Iraq would become a stable, democratic friend of the United States, and a challenge to the monarchies and dictatorships in the region. U.S. interests would be further secured in the Middle East with a democratic Iraq sitting in the middle of it.

This is a tempting vision, but a fragile reality. Iraq has never been a democratic state. The country is really a grouping of three peoples who historically have battled one another for supremacy. The likelihood of a stable democracy emerging in such a divided place is remote unless several elements align in perfect order. Expert states-manship must be combined with artful compromise and the mutual goal of demo-cratic future for the Iraqi people, on the part of all players. Oil deliveries must increase and be sustained, and the United States must stay the course for as long as it takes. The interim government is attempting to perform that delicate balancing act, but it is not going to be easy.

Islamic Republic?

The much-feared specter of an Iranian-style Islamic republic taking hold in Iraq lurks in the background. When we consider Iran, it's not an "Islamic Republic," it's a *Shia* Islamic Republic. The difference is that where Iran is almost entirely Shiite Muslims, Iraq is only 65 percent Shiite Muslims. The Sunni Arabs and Kurds (who are also Sunni) would not join with the Iraqi Shiites to create an Islamic Republic under Shiite religious rule. The chance for a Shiite Islamic Republic would be more likely if Iraq were to break up.

The Clerics Are the Key

The key is the Shiite clerics. If they do not wish to compromise with the new Iraqi gov-ernment, then the likelihood that the interim Iraqi government will establish a representa-tive democracy is decreased. If the clerics call for a jihad against the new government, the resultant *intifada* in Shiite Iraq would probably turn into a protracted civil war that would

Desert Diction

An **intifada** (from the Arabic "to shake off") is the term for an uprising against a govern-ing authority.

ultimately result in the dissolution of the Iraqi state, or the establishment of another dictatorship. The clerics, themselves, range from fringe radicals (like Moqtada al-Sadr) to conservative (like Grand Ayatollah Sistani). So far, the radicals have not overwhelmed the conservatives. But if Sistani wants more of a role for Shia Islam in the new Iraqi state, the interim government may not be able to keep it all together, and the feared civil war could erupt.

TCFKAI: "The Country Formerly Known as Iraq?"

Iraq could break into two or three pieces if …

◆ The Shiite clerics push a more religious agenda on the new government.

◆ The Sunni and Shiites push a heavily Arab-centric agenda.

If either of these events were to happen, the other groups would resist the changes, or simply opt to dissolve the current union. If the Shiite clerics called for jihad, or if the Allawi government pushed the SCIRI agenda, the Sunni insurgency could gain even more momentum, and civil war could erupt.

Kurds Take Advantage?

If conflict broke out between the Sunni and the Shiites, the Kurds might opt to press their case in the north. With the Sunni preoccupied with the Shiites, the Kurds could push for their own break away state. The Iranians, who oppose the creation of an independent Kurdish state, might even help the Kurds in order to open a second front and increase the Shiites' chances of winning the Sunni-Shiite conflict. Again, the United States might find itself in the difficult position of having to support the Sunni against the Kurds, or brokering an agreement that gives the Kurds autonomy. This outcome would be further complicated by Turkey, which could find itself compelled to support the Sunnis in Iraq in order to keep the Kurds from winning in the north. The United States would then find itself in the position of having to accommodate the demands of its Turkish NATO ally and risk an escalation of a regional war.

If Iraq did break up, it's conceivable that the United States would work for a two-state solution, in which the Shiites would have their own state, and the Sunnis would have their own state, but also incorporate an autonomous Kurdish region within its borders. The Shiite state would be closely allied to Iran, and the United States would try to maintain constructive relations with that state, to retain access to the oil there, and to keep an open channel to Iran.

Increase Your Iraq IQ

We are willing to be part of a federal, democratic Iraq, but should you, my Arab compatriot, contemplate turning Iraq into a fundamentalist state or an Arab nationalist dictatorship, again, I am sorry ... but we are not willing to be part of such a country ....
We understand our geopolitical predicament. We also understand that a federal, democratic Iraq, a prosperous, stable Iraq, can be good for the Kurdish people ... We are willing to work with our Iraqi compatriots to turn the tide and make sure that Iraq will have a future, but we cannot do it on our own ... Should it fail, there is nothing I can do to convince my people of being committed to this, and I will not do anything in my position, or any other position that I'll be in, to try.

—Barham Salih, a Kurd, and Deputy Prime Minister of the interim Iraqi government in an interview in May 2004.

These break-up scenarios should help explain why the United States and the UN repeatedly state that their goal is to maintain the territorial integrity of Iraq. The devil you know is better than the devil you don't.

The New Beirut?

In the absence of a strong central leader, Iraq could become a country whose government is powerless to enforce order in its own country. In such a scenario, while the borders might remain the same, localized power blocks would run their portions of the country. The central government might have nominal backing of the United States and regional Arab powers, but it would not effectively govern more than a small portion of the current state. Instead, there would probably be an Iranian dominated Shiite area in the south, a restive Kurdish area in the north, and a Sunni area in the center. The U.S. military would patrol the borders, keeping the Iranians in check and the Turks out.

It's All About the Oil

Oil would play a critical role in funding the regional power bases, and as long as that oil kept flowing, the United States and its allies would give their tacit acceptance of the situation by not militarily supporting the position of the central government, beyond ensuring its survival. Rather than promote a central government, the U.S. troops would be there to maintain the balance of power, and to wage war against terrorist groups, and defend the borders from open incursions by Iran or Turkey.

Acceptable Dictatorship

If a democracy doesn't take hold (in whatever form it ends up taking in Iraq), there is always the possibility that Iraq will evolve into a stable regional power, under the control of a U.S. backed, Sunni strongman. In this scenario, the United States would basically anoint a new Saddam to run the show, keep a lid on the internal chaos, crack down on foreign terror groups, and keep the oil flowing. This would be the "SOB" principle, from the old saying about why the U.S. sponsored certain dictators: "He may be an SOB, but at least he's our SOB." (Remember that in the early 1980s, Saddam was our SOB).

In this scenario, the chaos would be the justification for the interim government to issue a declaration of marshal law and postponement of open, popular elections. It also might be the basis for an adjustment to the government structure to concentrate more power in the hands of the government leader, and weaken other institutions (court and parliament) that otherwise would be checks on the executive power.

What Can the United States Do?

The key question is whether the United States can determine what will happen, or if it can only try to influence what will happen. Given the domestic U.S. pressures, Iranian intrigues, and local Iraqi realities, U.S. presidential administrations will find themselves limited in what they can hope to achieve in Iraq.

Ruins of an Iraqi Air Force training jet, with a note for the kids back home.

Lessons from History

When we think about what will happen in Iraq, we can draw powerful lessons from history. Americans have a tendency to think about the situation from a U.S. perspective, but it's subject to forces that are unique to Iraq. In addition, U.S. policy shifts with each new presidential administration, and so we can expect many twists and turns in the U.S.-Iraq relationship over the coming years. Still, the United States and the rest of the world that would influence the outcomes in Iraq would do well to keep a few key lessons in mind.

Have an End Strategy, and Stick to It

The United States runs the classic risk that superpowers incur in operations in foreign lands, be it the British in the American colonies, the Soviets in Afghanistan, or the United States on the French heels in Vietnam. Historians debate the factors that led to the superpowers' defeats in these conflicts, but one factor that was common to them all is the lack of clear goals for the superpower involved. U.S. policy makers will be faced with the challenge of staying on target, across different presidential administrations, changing domestic attitudes, as well as shifting patterns of violence and external intervention inside Iraq. These factors will occur in times and places that the United States will not be able to choose, but will need to react to.

> **Increase Your Iraq IQ**
>
> When you appeal to force, there's one thing you must never do—lose.
>
> —Former President Dwight D. Eisenhower

Beware of Thinking the United States Can Guarantee the Outcome

As the sole superpower in the world today, the United States and its policy makers tend to carry an element of inevitability in its worldview. U.S. policy makers tend to think that the United States can do what it pleases, or at least make decisions about when and where it will make its moves. The reality is that U.S. global preeminence does not translate to complete ability to achieve the desired outcome.

Two things that are out of U.S. control need to happen for relative calm to take hold. First, the Iraqi people need to trust that their government—whether democratically elected or not—can provide security; and second, the Iraqis need to take a stand themselves against the insurgents, who are killing Iraqi civilians as well as troops and security forces.

Coalition forces secure the scene of a car bombing that killed both occupants, approximately 500 meters from the entrance to the Coalition Provisional Authority Headquarters in Baghdad, Iraq, May 24, 2004.

(DoD photo by Tech. Sgt Roy Santana, U.S Air Force)

Backing a Tyrant Has Its Risks

The United States and its allies will be focused on their own strategic needs, and that focus may allow them to tolerate, or even support, a despotic regime taking root in Iraq. The would-be despot could suspend civil liberties and upcoming elections in the name of preserving stability and security.

Take the example of, Mohammed Reza Pahlevi, the Shah of Iran, who was the U.S. strongman in Iran in the 1970s. U.S. strategy called for a stable and U.S.-friendly Iran and Pahlevi delivered both for years. Of course, under the cover of his regime, the Iranian people suffered under the Shah's heavy-handed policies, and finally resorted to Islamic fundamentalism to throw off the Shah's abusive regime. I do not think the average Iranian in the 1970s was a frustrated fundamentalist yearning for an Islamic republic, but as time went on, only the fundamentalist religious leaders provided a sustained opportunity for resistance to the government. The same situation could occur in Iraq, particularly in the Shiite areas. If the United States props up a despotic and unpopular regime in Iraq, it could open the door for Islamic fundamentalists to create a revolution in streets, resulting in the dissolution of Iraq and creating an Iran-style Islamic Republic in the Shiite areas.

The Last Word

The critical component for the success of Iraqi democracy is compromise. If the various parties are not willing to compromise in the name of a greater good, then democracy will fail in Iraq, and a strong man will emerge, or chaos will reign. Compromise, in turn, requires the parties committing to the compromise to trust in one another. There has been little trust among the Kurds, Sunnis, and Shiites in the past, and there are many threats to creating that trust in the future. Trust ... compromise ... new constitutional model ... much has to go right for democracy to work in Iraq, because so much can go wrong.

The future of Iraq seems uncertain. The Interim Government is taking the reins of power, but a massive U.S. military force remains in place, shoring up the government and absorbing continued attacks from insurgents and terrorists that show no signs of diminishing. The recovery progresses, but at an excruciatingly slow pace, and oil, deliveries seem doomed to never fully be restored. Whether Iraq emerges as the first Arab Muslim democracy, devolves into a dictatorship, or splits into two pieces—one a dictatorship, the other an Islamic theocracy—comes down to whether the collective group of Iraqi peoples feels that they have a stake in the new state. That is, if the Iraqi people feel that there is hope. Prime Minister Allawi offered this sentiment, at the transition ceremony on June 28, 2004: "We have our resources, our oil and our agriculture. Great changes in societies take years, not months. Have patience and faith in the future of democracy."

The Least You Need to Know

- Iraq is faced with many challenges to establishing a democracy, even with massive U.S. support.

- Iraq could conceivably break up, become a chaotic shell state, or devolve into a dictatorship.

- The United States will have some say in what happens in Iraq, but it can't guarantee any outcome.

- Oil prices will play a major role in any economic recovery in Iraq.

- Iraq's neighbors, most notably Iran, will also have a lot to say about the future of Iraq.

A 10,000-Year Timeline for Iraq: 8000 B.C.E. to 2004 C.E.

8000 B.C.E.   First human settlements in evidence in Jericho.

5000 B.C.E.   First settlements in evidence in Mesopotamia near modern Jarmo.

3000–2000 B.C.E.   Sumerians emerge, settle cities of Ur and Uruk in lower Mesopotamian region.

1900–1600 B.C.E.   Amorite Empire.

1600–1100 B.C.E.   Hittite Empire.

1500–1200 B.C.E.   Kassite Empire (in central Mesopotamia).

1200–612 B.C.E.   Assyrian Empire in Mesopotamia.

612–539 B.C.E.   Chaldean Empire (also known as New Babylonian Period).

539–331 B.C.E.   Persian Empire encompasses Mesopotamia.

331–170 B.C.E.   Greek/Macedonian Empire (led by Alexander the Great) encompasses Mesopotamia.

170 B.C.E. –224 C.E.   Parthian Empire in Mesopotamia.

224–637 C.E.   Sassanid Empire includes Mesopotamia.

638–1100   Arab Empire and Golden Age of Baghdad.

661   The Shiite Schism. When Ali ibn Abi Talib, Mohammad's cousin, son-in-law, and last of a group known as the Rightly Guided Caliphs, was assassinated, and a nonfamily member was made caliph. Debates regarding succession lead to the development of Shiism, a sect of Islam that recognizes Mohammad's descendants through Ali as the only legitimate heads of the Islamic community.

770–945   Abassid Empire.

945–1045   Buwhayid Empire.

1045–1258   Seljuk Empire.

1155–1258   Local strongmen rule various territories in Mesopotamia.

1258–1355   Period of Mongol invasions. Baghdad plundered.

1355–1400   The Jalayirids rule Mesopotamia.

1401–1405   Tamerlane invades Mesopotamia. Baghdad plundered again.

1500–1722   Savafid Empire in Mesopotamia.

1534–1918   Ottoman Empire. Three vilayets: Mosul, Baghdad, and Basra are formed, which will later become modern Iraq, are established during this period.

1900   British become interested in Mesopotamia, first as land-link to India, and later as source of oil.

1912   Turkish Petroleum Company (TPC) formed.

1914   Anglo-Persian Oil Company (British owned) takes 50 percent stake in TPC; World War I begins. British invade Mesopotamia to safeguard their Turkish Petroleum Company holdings.

1918   World War I ends. Iraq established as a "Class A" Mandate, under British protection.

1921   Faisal I is set up as King of Iraq, though British influence remains strong.

1928   Gulf Oil Company joins TPC, the first U.S. oil company to enter Iraqi oil fields.

1929   TPC changes name to Iraqi Petroleum Company (IPC).

1932   Mosul Oil Company formed to manage northern IPC concessions.

1932 (October 13)   Iraq admitted into League of Nations as an independent nation.

1938   Basra Oil Company formed to manage southern IPC concessions.

1941   Britain again invades Iraq, establishes pro-British government in Baghdad.

1948–49   Israel War of Independence; Iraq participates in attacks on Israel and is one of the most belligerent adversaries in the Arab coalition confronting Israel.

1954   The Eisenhower administration agrees to provide military aid to Iraq, to help defend their oil interests in Iraq. Marks the transfer of influence from the British to the Americans.

1955   Baghdad Pact formed, as bulwark against Soviet expansionism. Iraq is a founding member.

1958 (May 12)   Arab Union formed between Iraq and Jordan.

1958 (July 14)   Iraqi General Abdul Karim Kassem leads a coup d'état that overthrows the Hashemite monarchy.

1960 (July)   Iraq threatens to invade Kuwait. British respond by sending troops. Invasion never happens.

1963 (February 8)   Ba'th coup overthrows Republican government, but is overthrown itself within six months.

1963 (November 18)   Abdul Salam Arif leads officer coup that overthrows brief, bloody Ba'th regime.

1966   Republican government repeals 99.5 percent of original IPC concession, Mosul Oil nationalized.

1967   Six-Day War. The economic chaos in Iraq as a result of reduced oil exports during the fighting contributes to Ba'th coup in July 1968.

1968 (July 17)   Ba'th Revolution that finally establishes Ba'th control over Iraq.

1972   Ba'th government repeals remaining IPC concessions.

1973   Ba'th government nationalizes Basra Petroleum Company.

1973 (October 6–October 23)   Yom Kippur War. War eventually leads to Egyptian-Israeli détente and re-assertion of Iraq leadership in pan-Arab affairs.

1979 (July 16)   Saddam Hussein becomes President of Iraq, taking over for Hassan al-Bakr. He stages a public purge of Bakr supporters, to consolidate his own grip on power.

1980 (September 23)   Iran-Iraq War begins.

1981 (June 8)   Israel bombs Iraqi nuclear reactor at Osirek.

1982 (June 10)   War-weary Iraq announces a cease-fire, but Iran ignores the offer.

1982 (July 13)   Iranian troops make first push into Iraqi territory.

1983 (July 20)   Iranian troops attack northern Iraq.

1984 (February)   Iraq uses mustard gas on Iranian troops in central Iraq around the Majnoon Islands.

1984 (March)   "Tanker War" (Iran and Iraq attack each other's Gulf oil shipments) starts.

1985 (May)   "Battle of the Cities" phase of Iran-Iraq War begins. Both sides launch bombing and missile raids on each other's cities.

1986 (August 2)   Saddam Hussein proposes peace in open letter to the Ayatollah. The offer is rejected.

1987 (May 17)   Iraq mistakenly hits the USS *Stark* with a missile. Thirty-seven U.S. sailors die. Saddam Hussein apologizes for the attack.

1988 (March 16)   Saddam Hussein attacks Kurds around Halabja with chemical weapons. More than 5,000 Kurds are killed.

1988 (April)   Iraq begins to make progress in the war, Iran slowly retreats from Iraqi territory.

1988 (August 20)   Iran-Iraq War ends in cease fire, as a standoff.

1990 (July 18)   Iraq accuses Kuwait of "stealing" Iraqi oil. Saddam threatens dire consequences. Kuwait denies the charges.

1990 (August 2)   Iraq invades Kuwait.

1990 (August 6)   Operation Desert Shield, the military build up in Saudi Arabia by an Arab-Western Coalition, begins.

1990 (November 29)   The UN Security Council passes Resolution 678, authorizing use of force to "expel" Iraq from Kuwait.

1991 (January 17)   Operation Desert Storm begins with Coalition bombing that continues for the next five weeks.

1991 (January 22)   Iraq launches SCUD missiles on Israel and Saudi Arabia in attempt to draw Israel into the war and split the U.S.-Arab Coalition.

1991 (February 24)   Ground phase of Desert Storm begins.

1991 (February 26)   Ground phase of Desert Storm ends.

1991–1992   Iraqi army attacks Kurds, 1.5 million Kurds flee to Turkey.

1991 (July 25)   Northern no-fly zone established.

1992 (April 2)   Southern no-fly zone established.

1993 (April 14)   Saddam Hussein attempts to assassinate former President Bush while Bush is visiting Kuwait. Clinton administration responds by launching cruise missile attack on Iraqi intelligence center in Baghdad.

1994 (October)   Iraq moves troops toward Kuwait. U.S. and UK bombing forces bomb the Iraqis to stop them short of invading again.

1995 (August 8)   Two of Saddam Hussein's sons-in-law and their families flee Iraq and end up in Jordan. They are Lieutenant General Hussein Kamel Hassan al-Majid, who was in charge of Iraq's weapons programs, and his brother, Lieutenant Colonel Saddam Kamel Hassan al-Majid, who was in charge of presidential security. The information they disclose prompts Iraq to offer more details on its mass-destruction weapons programs. The brothers return to Iraq in February 1996, under Saddam Hussein's guarantees that he will not harm them. They are shot three days after they return.

1998 (August 5)   Saddam Hussein unilaterally evicts UNSCOM weapons inspectors.

1998 (December 18)   In response to Saddam Hussein's unilateral refusal to comply with UNSCOM weapons inspections, the United States and United Kingdom launch Operation Desert Fox. The campaign is a coordinated bombing attack on Iraqi weapons targets by U.S. and UK aircraft and missiles.

2001 (September 11)   Terrorist attacks on the World Trade Center and the Pentagon. Saddam Hussein is the only Arab head of state not to express condolences for the attack.

2002 (January 29)   President George W. Bush lists Iraq as a member of the "Axis of Evil" that includes Iraq, Iran, and North Korea. The inference is that these countries foster state terrorism.

2002 (April 23)   Iraq suspends oil deliveries in protest of escalated violence between Palestinians and Israelis. Suspension lifted one month later.

2002 (July)   Saddam Hussein refuses to allow UN weapons inspectors into Iraq, again. This refusal is in direct defiance of UN Security Council resolutions.

2002 (September 12)   President George W. Bush, in a speech to the UN General Assembly, challenges the UN to act on the potential threat Iraq poses (and back up their own Resolutions) or else the United States will deal with Iraq.

2002 (October 11)   Military action on Iraq is authorized by United States Congress.

2002 (November)   UN weapons inspectors return to Iraq after a four-year absence.

2003 (March)   Rejecting a massive aid package, NATO member Turkey refuses to let the United States stage troops there, in preparation to attack Iraq from the north.

2003 (March 17)   President George W. Bush announces that Saddam Hussein and his regime have 48 hours to leave Iraq or face war with the United States and its allies. Weapons inspectors evacuate Iraq.

2003 (March 20)   Operation Iraqi Freedom begins.

2003 (March 23)   U.S. Marines overcome stiff Iraqi resistance at Nasiriya. Turkey agrees to allow U.S. planes to transit Turkish airspace.

2003 (March 26)   A massive paratroop landing by the U.S. 173rd Airborne Brigade takes place in northern Iraq, opening a second front.

2003 (April 9)   Baghdad falls; U.S. forces gain control of the city.

2003 (April 14)   U.S. forces take Tikrit; the Pentagon states that major combat is now over.

2003 (April 23)   Shiite pilgrims are able to march into Karbala on the final day of Ashura (a 40-day period honoring Imam Hussein bin Ali). The event marks the first time in decades the Shiites are allowed to do this, as Saddam Hussein's security forces would not permit it. As an indicator of things to come, the Shiite crowd mixes shouts of gratitude to U.S. troops with calls for them to leave Iraq.

2003 (May)   Coalition Provisional Authority removes the Ba'th party from power, and disbands the Iraqi Army. Thousands of now-unemployed men return home to a chaotic situation. Many of these will join the Sunni insurgency in the so-called Sunni Triangle.

2003 (July 22)   Saddam Hussein's sons Uday and Qusay are killed in Mosul.

2003 (August)   U.S. troops face increasingly pervasive guerilla warfare in the Sunni Triangle, and around the Shiite holy cities of Karbala and Najaf.

2003 (August 20)   A car bomb kills the UN envoy to Iraq, Sergio Vieira de Mello, and 19 others. Over 100 are wounded.

2003 (August 29)   Shia leader Ayatollah Mohammed Baqr al-Hakim and 124 others are killed by a car bomb in Najaf.

2003 (September 25)   Aqila Al-Hashmi, one of three women named to the Iraqi governing council, dies from wounds sustained during an assassination attempt.

2003 (October 27)   Coordinated suicide bomb attacks in Baghdad kill 43 people and wound over 200; police stations and Red Crescent offices are targeted.

2003 (October 31)   The UN pulls out of Iraq citing security concerns.

2003 (December 14)   Saddam Hussein is captured in a hole in a farmyard near Tikrit.

2004 (February)   Suicide attack in Irbil kills more than 100.

2004 (February 10)   A car bomb explodes in front of a police station in Baghdad, killing 50 and wounding 50.

2004 (February 11)   A car bomb in front of an Army recruiting facility explodes; 46 fatalities.

2004 (March 2)   Car bombs target Shia Muslims in Baghdad and Karbala on the holiest day in the Shia Muslim calendar, killing 180 people.

2004 (March 8)   An interim constitution is finally agreed upon and signed by Iraqi governing council. The Shiite and Kurds are heavily represented in the constitutional deliberations, but the Sunnis are not.

2004 (March 11)   Al Qaeda terrorists blow up a commuter train in Madrid, killing 200. The terrorists hope to influence the upcoming national elections in Spain, where Spanish participation in the Coalition is widely criticized.

2004 (March 14)   In Spain, the Socialist Party wins the national elections, ousting the conservative Popular Party. The new Prime Minister Jose Luis Rodriguez Zapatero, announces he will pull Spain's troops out of Iraq.

2004 (March 31)   Four U.S. civilian contractors are killed when their vehicle is hit by rocket-propelled grenades, and their burned and mutilated bodies hung from a bridge by cheering mobs in Fallujah, in the heart of the Sunni Triangle. U.S. troops retaliate and the fighting continues throughout the remainder of 2004.

2004 (April 11)   With U.S. troops encircling the city, Sunni insurgents agree to a cease-fire in Fallujah. The cease-fire is viewed as a U.S. retreat by many Sunnis there, as former insurgents now become members of the Iraqi security forces who patrol the city.

2004 (April 30)   Evidence of Iraqi prisoner abuse by U.S. troops at Abu Ghraib prison is made public. President George W. Bush later condemns the actions, and several low-ranking personnel are held accountable. An investigation is launched to determine if the abuse was encouraged by higher-ranking officials in an effort to extract information.

2004 (May 11)   Al Qaeda operative Abu Musab Al-Zarqawi's Unification and Jihad terrorist group beheads captured 26-year-old American civilian Nicholas Berg. The group cites the abuse of Iraqi detainees at Abu Ghraib prison. Graphic footage of Berg's decapitation is posted on the Internet.

2004 (May 21)   The last of 1,300 Spanish troops in the Coalition leave Iraq.

2004 (May 28)   An interim government is set up, headed by Prime Minister Iyad Allawi. They will govern alongside the Coalition Provisional Authority until the formal transfer of power.

2004 (June 1)   Ghazi Al-Yawer is selected as the President of Iraq. Like most Parliamentary governments, the position is largely ceremonial, but holds important symbolic value.

2004 (June 16)   The Commission on Terror Attacks on the United States (9/11 Commission) reports that there is "no credible evidence that Iraq and al Qaeda cooperated on attacks against the United States."

2004 (June 22) Abu Musab Al-Zarqawi's Unification and Jihad terrorist group beheads captured 33-year-old South Korean translator, Kim Sun-il, after South Korean government refuses to leave Iraq as demanded by the terrorists. Graphic footage of Kim's murder is posted on the Internet.

2004 (June 26) Two car bombs explode at a mosque in the Shiite city of Hillah, killing 40 and wounding 22.

2004 (June 28) The United States formally hands sovereignty over to the Iraqi interim government two days ahead of the stated June 30 deadline. The handover takes place early in an effort to avoid anticipated attacks by insurgents on June 30.

2004 (June 30) Custody rights over Saddam Hussein are transferred to the Iraqi Interim Government. His trial begins, with an Iraqi judge hearing the case.

2004 (July 6) Abu Musab Al-Zarqawi's Unification and Jihad announces it has taken 46-year-old Filipino truck driver Angelo de la Cruz hostage. They demand that the Philippines government withdraw its 51 humanitarian troops from Iraq by the end of July, or they will kill Cruz.

2004 (July 13) Abu Musab Al-Zarqawi's Unification and Jihad terrorist group beheads a captured Bulgarian truck driver, Georgi Lazov. His body is later found floating in the Tigris River.

2004 (July 15) The Senate Select Committee on Intelligence releases a report on U.S. intelligence performance in the run-up to Operation Iraqi Freedom. The report blames the U.S. intelligence community for faulty intelligence regarding weapons of mass destruction in Iraq. The commission delays releasing its findings on whether the Bush administration deliberately misused the intelligence as a pretext for invasion.

2004 (July 19) The Philippines withdraws its 51 humanitarian troops from Iraq, meeting the demands of Unification and Jihad. Truck driver Angelo de la Cruz is released unharmed the next day.

2004 (July 20) At the request of President George W. Bush, the United States Congress authorizes the resumption of arms sales to Iraq. On the same day, Unification and Jihad posts Internet messages warning Islamic and Arab nations not to participate in Iraq reconstruction. Japan is specifically warned to leave Iraq.

2004 (July 21) The UN announces a new envoy to Iraq, and that it will return to Baghdad in the coming weeks.

2004 (July 22) Iraqi police forces, supported by U.S. Marines, round up 270 suspected Iraqi insurgents and non-Iraqi Arabs. A firefight ensues, and 25 insurgents are killed, while 14 Marines are wounded. The raid is one of the first steps by the interim Iraqi government to take control of the violence inside Iraq.

2004 (August 1)   U.S. deaths in Iraq (both combat and noncombat related) since the start of Operation Iraqi Freedom in March 2003, exceed 900. Iraqi civilian deaths (due to combat operations, car bombs, being caught in the crossfire between Coalition troops and insurgents, stumbling onto unexploded ordinance, etc.) are estimated in the tens of thousands.

2004 (September 7)   The number of U.S. Soldiers killed in Iraq tops 1,000.

Glossary

Abbasids   Named for Abu Abbas, the early leader of the group that founded an empire in 770 C.E. that included Mesopotamia.

Abu Ghraib   Site of prison where U.S. troops tortured Iraqi detainees in 2003. The prison had long been a feared place of torture under Saddam Hussein's regime.

Akkadians   Invaders of Mesopotamia around 2340 B.C.E. The Akkadians were a Semitic people and spoke a language that is related to Hebrew and Arabic. They founded a capital city at Akkad, later called Babylon.

Iyad Allawi   Prime Minister of the interim Iraqi governing authority, which took over from the Coalition Provisional Authority on June 28, 2004.

Amorites   Invaders of Mesopotamia around 1900 to 1600 B.C.E. The Amorite capital is known as Old Babylon, and the Amorite Empire is known as the Old Babylon period.

Arab   A linguistic group of 256 million that many experts believe originated in the Hijaz region in what is now Saudi Arabia. The Arabs have spread across northern Africa and the Middle East. The Iraqis (except the Kurds) are Arabs.

Arab League   Formally called the League of Arab States, includes Egypt, Jordan, Lebanon, Saudi Arabia, Syria, Yemen, and Iraq. The Arab League was formed with British encouragement, as a bulwark against Soviet expansion into the Middle East. The League exists to this day, but its mission now focuses more on issues that affect the collective Arab states.

Arab Union   Short-lived combination of Iraq and Jordan, founded in 1958. Established as a counter to the Nasser-dominated UAR.

Assyrians   Invaders who established an empire in Mesopotamia from 1200 to 612 B.C.E. The Assyrian capital was a new city, called Nineveh. The last great Assyrian king, Ashurbanipal, assembled a huge library of Sumerian writings at Nineveh. The Assyrians were a highly militaristic society. They developed a number of innovative weapons, and their technological advancements include the development of latitude and longitude, 360-degree partition of the circle, medical science, iron swords, body armor, and the battering ram. Modern Assyrians remain a sizable minority in northwestern Iraq.

Ayatollah Ruhollah Khomeini (1900–1989)   A supreme religious leader of the Twelver Shiite, and leader of Iran from 1979 to his death in 1989. The last decade of his life was filled with turmoil, notably the hostage crisis at the former U.S. embassy in Tehran and the Iran-Iraq War.

Babylon   Ancient city that emerged from the ancient Akkadian capital of Akkad. Babylon was the central city for the Chaldeans during the "New Babylonian Period."

Baghdad   Capital city of Iraq. As heart of the Arab Empire, it was second only to Constantinople in terms of size and grandeur in 1000 C.E.

Hassan al-Bakr (1914–1982)   President of Iraq from 1968 to 1979. Relative of Saddam Hussein.

Basra   City in southern Iraq, heart of Shiite territory. Chief city of Ottoman vilayet of the same name.

Ba'th   The Arab Ba'th Socialist Resurrection Party. Formed by two Syrian university students, Michel Aflaq and Salah ad-Din al-Bitar, and formally founded on April 7, 1947. The Ba'th (also "Baath") Party tenets include adherence to socialism (including state ownership of the key segments of the economy), political freedom (an inclusive process), and pan-Arab unity. Ba'th parties are in power in Syria and Iraq.

Lakhdar Brahimi   Special Advisor to the Secretary General of the United Nations, on Iraq (January 1, 2004–   ). A veteran UN official, Algerian-born Mr. Brahimi has been heavily involved in UN-related decisions regarding Iraq.

L. Paul Bremer   Administrator of the Coalition Provisional Authority from May 2003 to its formal hand-off of authority to the Iraqi governing authority on June 2004. Bremer was a highly visible, and often outspoken, symbol of the U.S. occupation during that time.

Buwayhids   A powerful military clan that originated in Shiite Iran, they ruled Mesopotamia from 945 to 1045 C.E.

Caliph   Spiritual leader of Islam.

Chaldeans Ruled Mesopotamia after the Assyrians, from 612 to 539 B.C.E. Their period of rule is dominated by Nebuchadnezzar II.

Coalition Provisional Authority (CPA) Governing body in Iraq from the fall of the Hussein government from April 2003 to June 28, 2004. The CPA was run by Paul Bremer, a U.S. State Department veteran, and was responsible for overseeing all aspects of Iraqi government, from services to security, and for overseeing the massive rebuilding program.

cuneiform Wedge style writing, originally created by pressing a reed end into wet clay. "Cuneiform" is the Latin word for "wedge-writing." The writing form first emerged around 3600 B.C.E. Cuneiform was at first a pictographic language (like Chinese), where the symbols represented things, but it gradually evolved into an alphabet style language, with syllabic "letters" that formed "words." Because the cuneiform was written on clay, lots of tablets have survived and they are invaluable to showing us daily life in Mesopotamia.

Epic of Gilgamesh A collection of legends of the ancient Sumerian king, Gilgamesh. Around 2600 B.C.E., Gilgamesh was king of Uruk (known as Erech in the Hebrew Scriptures). *The Epic of Gilgamesh* offers a number of stories recounting his exploits as king, his friendship with Enkidu, a wild man, and their adventures together. They are in actuality both elements of the same humanity, and their stories reflect not just man's struggles against outside evils, but also man's struggle to master himself.

Euphrates One of two main rivers in ancient Mesopotamia (now modern Iraq, eastern Turkey and northern Syria).

Fallujah City in the Sunni region, stronghold of Sunni resistance to U.S.-led occupation forces in Iraq. Also stronghold of al Qaeda leader, Abu Musab Al Zarqawi

al-Faw A peninsula on the Iraqi Persian Gulf coast, where the offshore oil terminals are located. Scene of heavy fighting during Iran-Iraq War.

Fedayeen Saddam "Saddam's Men of Sacrifice," a paramilitary group, founded in 1995 by Uday Hussein, of men ultra-loyal to Saddam Hussein. The Fedayeen carried out military operations against Coalition forces during Operation Iraqi Freedom.

Sheik Ghazi Ajil al-Yawar President of the interim Iraqi governing authority.

Golden Age of Baghdad The period from 638 to 1100 C.E., when Baghdad flourished as a center of learning, commerce, and philosophy, at the heart of the Arab world.

Hammurabi Code Early compilation of law based on *lex talonica*, a principle that establishes the role of state as agent of revenge for wrong-doing, instead of individuals.

Hashemites The Hashemite kings came from a prominent Saudi Arabian family. Iraq was ruled by a member of the Hashemite family of Husayn ibn Ali, sharif of Mecca, who claimed descent from the family of the Prophet Muhammad. The British placed Faisal, who was a member of this family, as the King of Iraq.

Hittites   Invaders who ruled Mesopotamia from 1900 to 1100 B.C.E. The Hittites were responsible for spreading Sumerian culture through trade and hegemony.

interim Iraqi government   Provisional governing authority in Iraq from June 28, 2004, to the creation of a new Iraqi government via national elections (scheduled for early 2005). According to the CPA, the interim government was assembled in consultation with Iraqi political, religious, and tribal leaders. The IIG is lead by President Sheik Ghazi Ajil al-Yawar and Prime Minister Iyad Allawi.

Iran   Now the Islamic Republic of Iran, it borders Iraq to the east. Iran's population is mostly Persian, with Kurd and Arab minorities. The majority of Iranians are Shiite Muslims (the only Shiite-dominated Muslim country in the world). Persian Iran is the ancient enemy of Arab Iraq.

Iraq   Republic of Iraq *(Al Jumhuriyah al Iraqiyah)*. Country created in 1923, by a European convention, from the Ottoman vilayets of Mosul, Baghdad, and Basra. The Iraqi people are mostly Arabs, with a Kurd minority.

Iraqi governing council   Provisional governing body of Iraqi leaders that nominally shared power with the Coalition Provisional Authority in 2004.

Iraqi Intervention Force   New, anti-insurgency units of the post-Saddam Iraqi army. These highly trained and well-armed units were created to transition security operations from U.S. to Iraqi troops in the summer or 2004.

Islam   Religion founded by the Prophet Muhammad. "Islam" translates as "submission." "Muslim" translates as "one who submits." The emphasis in Islam is on submission to the will of a single God. The "five pillars" of this great and enduring religious tradition are: (1) Confession of faith in God and in his prophet Muhammad ("There is no God but God; Muhammad is the Prophet of God"); (2) Ritual worship; (3) Almsgiving; (4) Fasting; (5) Pilgrimage.

Israel War of Independence   (1948–1949). Egypt, Transjordan, Iraq, Palestine, and Syria waged war against the new state of Israel; the Arab states eventually negotiated separate armistices after military attacks failed. Iraq was particularly aggressive in this war.

Jalayirids   The Jalayirids ruled Mesopotamia from 1355 until about 1400 C.E.

Jarmo   The area where the first indications of human settlement are found in Iraq, including pottery and domesticated animals.

Jericho   The city located in modern Israel where the first indications of urban life are found, dating back to 8000 B.C.E.

Karbala   Holy site for Shia Islam, located in southern Iraq. Karbala is burial place of Imam Hussein, the son of Ali Ibn Abu Talib, the Prophet Mohammed's cousin and son-in-law. Hussein was killed during a battle with the Sunni army of Ummayad Caliph Yazid in 680. The city has been the scene of fighting between Shiite Iraqi insurgents and US-led Coalition troops in 2003 and 2004.

Kassites   Invaders who established a competing empire with the Hittites, in central Mesopotamia, from 1500 to 1200 B.C.E.

Al-Khawarizmi   Abu Ja'far Muhammed ibn Musa al-Khawarizmi was the leading Arab mathematician of the Golden Age who lived in Baghdad. Al-Khawarizmi developed some of the key concepts of what would eventually be known as algebra, and he presented the new concept of the zero to the West.

Khuzestan   Region in Iran, bordering Iraq, that has Arab population instead of Persian (that dominates elsewhere in Iran).

Kirkuk   City in northern Iraq, in Kurd region

Kurds   Nationality of 25 million people. The Kurds are not Arab, Turkic, or Persian, yet their traditional homelands are located in Iraq, Turkey, and Iran. The Kurds have waged an ongoing rebellion for autonomy in these three countries, with limited success. Saddam Hussein has waged extensive military campaigns against the Kurds in Iraq, including gas attacks in 1988. After the Persian Gulf War, under the protection of a U.S.- and UK-maintained no-fly zone, the Kurds enjoy relative autonomy and prosperity in northern Iraq. The prospects for an independent Kurdistan are minimal, given the adamant refusal of Turkey and Iran (and Iraq) to grant independence to their Kurdish minorities.

Kuwait   Kingdom on southern border of Iraq. Invaded and occupied by Iraq in 1990, and liberated in Operation Desert Storm in 1991. Kuwait was founded on June 19, 1961. There are less than one million ethnic Kuwaitis living in Kuwait. Kuwait is one of the richest oil producing nations in the world. The country is ruled by Shaykh Jabir al Ahmad.

Lawrence of Arabia   Thomas Edward Lawrence (1888–1935), a British Military Intelligence Service officer stationed in Cairo at the start of World War I. Lawrence cultivated a strong bond with Prince Faisal (later King Faisal of Iraq). During the war, Lawrence organized and fought alongside these Arab allies against the Ottoman armies in the region. He died in a motorcycle accident in England in 1935.

Mamluks   Slave-warriors and palace guards. Under the Buwayhids, they were officers and even administrators in the Baghdad bureaucracy.

Mandate   League of Nations term for status of Iraq immediately following World War I. Mandates were "administered" by a Western power. Iraq was a "Class A" Mandate (meaning it was intended to gain independence) under British protection from 1918 to 1923.

Mesopotamia The Greek term meaning "the land between the rivers" includes the area between the Tigris and Euphrates Rivers. This region stretches from the Persian Gulf through modern Iraq, into the northwest portion of modern Syria. With abundant water, fertile land, and an agreeable climate, early civilizations emerged here.

Mohammed The founder of Islam. Mohammed (also "Muhammad") was born in Mecca (in present-day Saudi Arabia) around the year 570. He is believed to have experienced the first of a series of intense religious visions around the year 610 in a cave near Mecca. The Qur'an, Islam's central religious text, is held to record that encounter and the later revelations of Mohammed, and is regarded as the final and authoritative word of Allah (God). After over a decade of preaching, Mohammed had been unsuccessful in converting Mecca to the new faith; in 622 he and his followers moved to Yathrib (later known as Medina, the "City of the Prophet"). Mohammed continued to encounter resistance in spreading the new doctrine, but his followers eventually mounted a military and religious campaign that succeeded in unifying Arabia behind a single faith. Mohammed is regarded by Muslims as Allah's final prophet, and Islam is seen as the fulfillment of all previous human religious experiences. Mohammed's birthplace, Mecca, is now regarded as the great Holy City of Islam, and is the destination of annual pilgrimages by millions of Muslims.

Mongols Invaders from the Asian steppes, originated from the area that is now Mongolia. Led by Hulegu Khan, the grandson of Ghengis Khan, the Mongol horde took Baghdad in 1258 and plundered the riches of the city.

Mosul City in northern Iraq, oil processing center, and central city of Mosul vilayet during Ottoman times.

Mother of All Battles Saddam Hussein's name for the 100-hour ground war during Operation Desert Storm. Saddam portrayed the battle as an Iraqi victory.

Mukhtar Hereditary leader of an Iraqi village. Cooperation of the mukhtars is critical for any local programs to succeed.

Muslim An adherent of the global religion known as Islam, which traces its origin to the prophet Mohammed (570? –632).

An-Najaf The most revered Shia Muslim holy site, located in southern Iraq. It is the burial place of Ali Ibn Abu Talib, the Prophet Mohammed's cousin and son-in-law. The Shiites believe that Ali and his descendants, through their blood kinship with Mohammad, are the rightful leaders of the Muslim faith. The name means "High Place" in Arabic, and Shia Muslims hope to be buried there. The Ayatollah Ruhollah Khomeini was exiled here in the 1960s and 1970s. Najaf was the site of major fighting between Shiite insurgents and U.S.-led Coalition forces in 2003 and 2004.

Gamal abdel Nasser First independent Arab leader of Egypt, he competed with Iraqi leaders for leadership of Arab world during the 1950s.

National Assembly   The 275-member parliament in the post-Saddam Iraq.

John Negroponte   U.S. Ambassador to Iraq (2004–   ). Ambassador Negroponte took over the newly opened U.S. embassy in Iraq on June 29, 2004, the day after the Coalition Provisional Authority formally transferred power to the Iraqi governing authority. The U.S. embassy staff (over 1,000) in Iraq is one of the largest for the United States in any country.

no-fly zones   The United States, Britain, and France unilaterally established two no-fly zones in Iraq. The northern no-fly zone, called Operation Provide Comfort, was established in April 1991 to protect the Kurds. The no-fly zone area is bounded by the thirty-sixth parallel. The southern no-fly zone was established in August 1992 to protect the Shiite rebels. Called Operation Southern Watch, the southern zone was first bounded at the thirty-second parallel (to protect the Shiites in the marsh regions) and later extended to the thirty-third parallel.

oil–for–food   Program set up the UN on April 14, 1995, as a vehicle to generate revenues for the purchase of nonmilitary materials to Iraq. At that time, UN sanctions (maintained primarily by the United States and United Kingdom) had denied the Saddam Hussein regime the ability to sell its oil on the world markets, in order to keep Hussein from procuring arms or weapons of mass destruction. In response to the suffering of the Iraqi people, the UN set up this program to allow Iraq to generate revenues to procure nonmilitary items. The program was fraught with controversy: The Hussein regime was allowed to distribute the materials it purchased, giving Saddam a powerful tool to punish his enemies and reward his followers inside Iraq. On November 21, 2003, the Coalition Provisional Authority took over control of the program. Control of the program was passed to the interim governing authority on July 1, 2004. Generating over $46 billion during its existence, suspicions of a massive fraud and kickback schemes involving UN officials charged with overseeing the program are under investigation at the time of this writing.

OPEC   Organization of Petroleum Exporting Countries. These oil-rich countries control a significant portion of the world's oil. Iraq is a member of OPEC.

Operation Desert Shield   Military build-up of Arab-Western coalition troops in Saudi Arabia in 1990 and early 1991.

Operation Desert Storm   Military operations that started on January 16, 1991, with a bombing campaign, followed by a ground invasion on February 23 and 24, 1991. The ground war lasted 100 hours and resulted in a spectacularly one-sided military victory for the Coalition.

Ottomans   Turkic people who established an empire that first emerged in Anatolia in 1301, conquered Constantinople (now Istanbul) in 1453, and the Arab lands (including what is now Iraq) from 1516 to 1517. The empire became known as the "Sick Man of

Europe" in the decades leading up to World War I. The Ottoman Empire formally ceased to exist in 1918.

Pan-Arabism   The international Arab movement, dedicated to the creation of a unified Arab state and promoting Arab interests.

Parthians   Invaders from Persia, who consolidated their grip on Mesopotamia from to 170 B.C.E. to 224 C.E.

Persians   Ethnic group that settled in what is now Iran. The Persians were rivals for control of Mesopotamia with the Greeks, and later the Arabs.

Portsmouth Treaty   Signed in 1948, the treaty defined the relationship between Iraq and Britain in a way that was completely in Britain's favor. The agreement required Iraq and Britain to reach agreement on all matters pertaining to Iraqi defense. The treaty severely compromised Iraqi sovereignty, and outraged Iraqi nationalists.

Republican Guard   Iraqi troops, recruited from the Sunni ruling elites who are personally loyal to Saddam Hussein. The Republican Guard—comprised of armored, mechanized, and infantry divisions, as well as special operations brigades—is considered the elite fighting force in the Iraqi army.

Revolutionary Command Council   Otherwise called the RCC, the council is the real decision making authority in Iraq. The RCC consists of 8 to 10 members, and is directed by a chairman, currently Saddam Hussein. The chairman of the RCC is also the president of Iraq, the supreme commander of the military, and general secretary of the Ba'th Party, and the prime minister. The Revolutionary Command Council was formed after the July 30, 1968, coup, when the Ba'th Party finally assumed complete control over the country.

Saddam Hussein (1937–   )   Ba'thist leader of Iraq from 1979 to present. Saddam is President of Iraq, Chairman of the Revolutionary Command Council, Commander in Chief of the Army, and (apparently) a descendent of Mohammed.

Muqtada al-Sadr   Radical Shiite cleric, whose supporters are called the Mehdi Army, who has opposed U.S.-led occupation forces in the aftermath of Saddam Hussein's fall. The son of revered Shiite cleric Mohammed Sadiq Sadr, who had been killed by the Saddam Hussein's regime, Sadr and his followers represent the more militant elements of Shiite Muslims in Iraq.

Safavids   Turkman and Kurd invaders of Mesopotamia who took control around 1508 C.E.

sanctions   UN-imposed set of restrictions on imports into Iraq. The sanctions were intended to limit Iraq's ability to re-arm, and develop weapons of mass destruction. The shortages of food and medicine caused by the sanctions has resulted in the deaths of thousands of Iraqi civilians, and become a PR nightmare of the United States. The United

States is pushing to redefine the broad sanctions to a more narrow, more strictly enforced "smart sanctions" that will focus only on military items, but allow unlimited imports of foods, medicine and humanitarian supplies.

Sassanids   Invaders who ruled Mesopotamia from 224 to 637 C.E. The Sassanians resisted Roman and later Byzantine attacks on their territories.

Saudi Arabia   Oil-rich kingdom bordering Iraq to the south. The Saudi ruling family is considered the protector and custodian of Medina and Mecca, the holiest sites in Islam. The formal title of the current Saudi King is: "Fahd bin Abd al-Aziz Al Saud, Custodian of the Two Holy Mosques, King of the Kingdom of Saudi Arabia."

SCUD   Soviet-made, medium-range ballistic missiles that Saddam Hussein launched at Israel and Saudi Arabia during the Persian Gulf War.

Seljuks   Turkman invaders who ruled Mesopotamia from 1045 to 1258 C.E. At its height, the area that was to become Iraq experienced a minor renaissance. Infrastructure was rebuilt, and science and cultural institutions were refounded in the major Arab cities.

Shatt-al-Arab   Waterway created by the confluence of the rivers Tigris and Euphrates, it flows to the Persian Gulf.

Shiite (also called Shia)   Only significant surviving Muslim sect other than the Sunni. Less than 5 percent of all Muslims worldwide, the Shiite make up 65 percent of Iraq's population and almost all of Iran's population.

Grand Ayatollah Ali Sistani   The most senior Shiite cleric in Iraq, and one of five living grand ayatollahs, Sistani is considered the prime marja, or spiritual leader of the Shiites. After maintaining a relatively low profile during the Saddam Hussein regime, Sistani has emerged as a powerful figure in post-Saddam Iraq. Followers of Sistani have clashed with more militant followers of al-Sadr in 2004. Sistani has been critical of the U.S. led occupation of Iraq, but has called for Shiites to support the interim Iraqi government. Sistani, as prime marja, plays a critical role in molding Shiite attitudes toward the new Iraqi government.

Sultan   A ruler in the Ottoman Empire. The Sultans assumed political authority over their territories, unlike the Abassid caliphs who claimed both religious and secular authority.

Sumerians   Founders of urban centers in the lower Mesopotamia area around 3000 B.C.E.

Sunni   The vast majority (97 percent) of Muslims worldwide. In Iraq, the Sunni are the minority (32 percent) compared to Shiite.

Supreme Council for Islamic Revolution in Iraq   Known as SCIRI, made up of Iraqi exiles from the Saddam Hussein regime, this Iranian-backed group desires the establishment of an Islamic state in Iraq.

Tamerlane   Timur "the Lame" Central Asian atabeg, whose army plundered Baghdad in 1400 C.E.

terrorism   The practice of waging war on civilian populations by military or nonmilitary forces.

Tigris   One of two main rivers in Mesopotamia (now modern Iraq).

Tikriti   Saddam Hussein's Sunni tribal group, centered around the town of Tikrit, in central Iraq.

Transitional Authority Law (TAL)   The body of law governing Iraq during the transitional period leading up to elections and formation of a new Iraqi government.

Turkey   A Muslim country, bordering Iraq on the north. A member of NATO, Turkey is a critical U.S. ally in the region. The people of Turkey are Muslim, but they are not Arab (they are Turkic). Like Iraq and Iran, the Turks also have a Kurd minority within their borders. Turkey emerged at the end of World War I from the ruins of the Ottoman Empire.

UAR   The United Arab Republic, established by Egypt and Syria in 1958.

Unification and Jihad   The name of the al Qaeda–linked terrorist organization lead by Abu Musab al-Zarqawi.

UNMOVIC   The United Nations Monitoring, Verification, and Inspection Commission that was created as replacement to UNSCOM. The Iraqis have refused to allow UNMOVIC inspectors into the country.

UNSCOM   The United Nations Special Commission on Inspections, created at the end of the Persian Gulf War, to identify and destroy Iraqi weapons of mass destruction.

Ur   Ancient city in Mesopotamia, and center of early empire in the region.

Uruk   Also called Erech, an ancient city in Mesopotamia, and home to Gilgamesh.

vilayet   Province in the Ottoman Empire. Modern-day Iraq was pieced together from three Ottoman vilayets (Mosul, Baghdad, and Basra).

weapons of mass destruction   Chemical, biological, and nuclear weapons. These weapons are capable of destroying enormous numbers of people and vast areas, hence the name. Saddam Hussein has used weapons of mass destruction on the Iranian army during the Iran-Iraq War, and on the Kurds in 1988.

Yom Kippur War   On October 6, 1973, the Jewish holy day of Yom Kippur, the Arab states around Israel attacked. Initial Arab gains were reversed by Israeli counterattacks. U.S. and Soviet diplomacy, along with a rapidly deteriorating military situation for the Arabs, forced a cease-fire on October 23, 1973. Egypt and Israel signed a peace treaty in November, but Syria and Iraq kept fighting until 1974.

Abu Musab al-Zarqawi   Jordanian-born al Qaeda leader, currently based in the Iraqi city of Fallujah. Al-Zarqawi is considered to be the mastermind behind many of the attacks in 2003 and 2004 on U.S. troops and Iraqi security forces and government figures.

Ziggurats   Temples that the Sumerians and their successors built throughout Mesopotamian city-states, to honor various deities. The ziggurat temple was a tower. Like Medieval cathedrals, ziggurats were as much a symbol of the power and prestige of the city that built it, as they were an affirmation of faith.

Zoroastrianism   Religion that originated in Persia. Zoroastrians see the world as an epic struggle between the forces of good and evil.

Magazines, Websites, and Books

Magazines

Several popular magazines regularly feature articles on Iraq, and the Middle East in general, and are excellent sources for keeping up with ongoing developments. These periodicals range from conservative to liberal, but together can show the various interpretations of what is happening.

American Heritage	*The New Yorker*
The Atlantic Monthly	*New Republic*
Business Week	*Time*
The Financial Times	*U.S. News & World Report*
Forbes	*Utne Reader*
The Guardian	*Vanity Fair*
National Review	*The Wall Street Journal*
Newsweek	*The Washington Post*
The New York Times	

Websites

Many websites offer information and opinions on Iraq. I encourage you to review all web resources, but please be mindful of the source and political motivations of the website creators. The following sites provide a variety of views of Iraq:

Encyclopedia Reference to Iraq

encarta.msn.com/Microsoft's Encarta encyclopedia website

Governmental Sites on Iraq

www.iraqcoalition.org
The official website of the Coalition Provisional Authority. No longer updated, but an excellent source of official information on the CPA and its programs.

http://iraq.usembassy.gov
Website of the U.S. embassy in Iraq, and a great source of information on interim Iraqi government.

www.un.org
United Nations' website, with specific sections on UNSCOM and the sanctions applied to Iraq.

www.loc.gov
The Library of Congress website, with links to Congressional Research Service reports.

www.state.gov/www/global/terrorism/index.html
Website of the State Department Office of the Coordinator for Counter-Terrorism.

www.energy.gov
Website of the U.S. Department of Energy, with information on OPEC, Iraqi oil and U.S.-Iraq oil trade.

Other Websites on Iraq

www.cnn.com
Major U.S. news service.

http://english.aljazeera.com
English version of the Arab news service.

www.iacenter.org
Website of the International Action Center. Generally critical of U.S. policy toward Iraq.

www.countrywatch.com
CountryWatch monitors geopolitical developments around the world.

www.hrw.org
Website for Human Rights Watch. This group monitors human rights around the world.

www.iraqwatch.org
Website maintained by the Wisconsin Project that monitors Iraq's weapons of mass destruction programs and their current status in post-Saddam Iraq.

www.iraqischools.com
Website created by supporters of the U.S. 1st Cavalry Division's grassroots effort to rebuild Iraqi elementary schools.

www.foreignpolicy2000.org/home/home.cfm
Website of the Council on Foreign Relations, a think-tank that focuses on a variety of issues affecting U.S. foreign policy.

www.kurdistan.org
Website of the American-Kurdish Information Network, promoting Kurdish causes in the United States.

Books and U.S. Government Reports

Arendt, Hannah. *The Origins of Totalitarianism*. New York: Harcourt Brace Javanovich, 1973.

Bush, George. *All the Best, George Bush*. New York: Scribner, 1999.

Economist Intelligence Unit. *Iraq: Country Report*. London: The Economist Newspaper, 1998.

Encyclopedia Britannica. Chicago: Britannica, 1996.

The Epic of Gilgamesh: An English Translation. N. K. Sanders, translator. New York: Penguin, 1987.

Ghareeb, Edmund. *The Kurdish Question in Iraq*. Syracuse: Syracuse University Press, 1981.

Helms, Christine Moss. *Iraq: Eastern Flank of the Arab World*. Washington, D.C.: Brookings Institution, 1991.

Hodgson, Marshall. *The Venture of Islam*. Chicago: University of Chicago Press, 1974.

The Holy Bible. King James Version. Camden, NJ: Thomas Nelson, 1972.

Kramer, Samuel Noah. *History Begins at Sumer*. New York: Doubleday & Company, 1969.

Lukitz, Liora. *Iraq: The Search for National Identity*. London: Frank Cass & Co, 1995.

Mallowan, M.E.L. *Early Mesopotamia and Iran*. New York: McGraw-Hill, 1985.

Marr, Phoebe. *The Modern History of Iraq*. Boulder, Colorado: Westview Press, 1985.

National Committee on Terrorist Attacks Upon the United States, *The 9/11 Commission Report*. WW Norton: New York, 2004.

Orwell, George. *Animal Farm*. New York: Harcourt Brace Jovanovich, 1949.

U.S. Central Intelligence Agency. *World Fact Book*. Washington, D.C.: USGPO, 2002.

U.S. Senate Select Committee on Intelligence, Report on U.S. Intelligence Community's Prewar Intelligence Assessments on Iraq. Washington, D.C.: USGPO, 2004.

Reference Databases

These online databases provide excellent, up-to-date articles on Iraq, from thousands of magazine, journals, and newspapers. These databases may be accessed via most public libraries and universities in North America, and around the world.

MasterFile Premier
Designed for Public Library users, provided by EBSCO Publishing (www.epnet.com)

Academic Search Premier
Designed for Academic Library users, provided by EBSCO Publishing (www.epnet.com)

Index